BLACK FEMINIST THOUGHT

PERSPECTIVES ON GENDER

Volume 1: *Pleasure, Power, and Technology: Some Tales of Gender, Engineering, and the Cooperative Workplace*

Sally Hacker

Volume 2: *Black Feminist Thought: Knowledge, Consciousness, and the Politics of Empowerment*

Patricia Hill Collins

Volume 3: *Understanding Sexual Violence: A Study of Convicted Rapists*

Diana Scully

Additional titles in preparation

BLACK FEMINIST THOUGHT

Knowledge, Consciousness, and the Politics of Empowerment

Perspectives on Gender, Volume 2

Patricia Hill Collins

Boston
UNWIN HYMAN
London   Sydney   Wellington

Unwin Hyman, Inc.
955 Massachusetts Avenue, Cambridge, MA 02139, USA

Published by the Academic Division of
Unwin Hyman Ltd
15/17 Broadwick Street, London W1V 1FP, UK

Allen & Unwin (Australia) Ltd,
8 Napier Street, North Sydney, NSW 2060, Australia

Allen & Unwin (New Zealand) Ltd in association with the
Port Nicholson Press Ltd,
Compusales Building, 75 Ghuznee Street, Wellington 1, New Zealand

First published in 1990.

Library of Congress Cataloging-in-Publication Data

Collins, Patricia Hill, 1948–
      Black feminist thought: knowledge, consciousness, and the
      politics of empowerment/Patricia Hill Collins.
         p. cm. — (Perspectives on gender; v. 2)
      Includes bibliographical references.
      ISBN 0–04–445137–7. – 0–04–445138–5 (pbk.)
       1. Feminism—United States. 2. Afro-American women.
    3. United States—Race relations. I. Title. II. Series.
    HQ1426.C633 1990
    305.42'08996073—dc20   90–31998
                                                         CIP

British Library Cataloguing in Publication Data

Collins, Patricia Hill, _1948–_
      Black feminist thought: Knowledge, consciousness, and the
    politics of empowerment. – (Perspectives on gender : 2)
    1.United States. Black Women feminism
    I. Title II. Series
    305.4208996073

    ISBN 0–04–445137–7

Typeset in Times and Gill Sans
Printed in Great Britain by The University Press, Cambridge.

CONTENTS

Part Two

CORE THEMES IN BLACK FEMINIST THOUGHT

Part Three

BLACK FEMINISM AND EPISTEMOLOGY

PREFACE

When I was five years old, I was chosen to play Spring in my preschool pageant. Sitting on my throne, I proudly presided over a court of children portraying birds, flowers, and the other, "lesser" seasons. Being surrounded by children like myself—the daughters and sons of laborers, domestic workers, secretaries, and factory workers—affirmed who I was. When my turn came to speak, I delivered my few lines masterfully, with great enthusiasm and energy. I loved my part because I was Spring, the season of new life and hope. All of the grown-ups told me how vital my part was and congratulated me on how well I had done. Their words and hugs made me feel that I was important and that what I thought, and felt, and accomplished mattered.

As my world expanded, I learned that not everyone agreed with them. Beginning in adolescence, I was increasingly the "first," or "one of the few," or the "only" African-American and/or woman and/or working-class person in my schools, communities, and work settings. I saw nothing wrong with being who I was, but apparently many others did. My world grew larger, but I felt I was growing smaller. I tried to disappear into myself in order to deflect the painful, daily assaults designed to teach me that being an African-American, working-class woman made me lesser than those who were not. And as I felt smaller, I became quieter and eventually was virtually silenced.

This book reflects one stage in my ongoing struggle to regain my voice. Over the years I have tried to replace the external definitions of my life forwarded by dominant groups with my own self-defined standpoint. But while my personal odyssey forms the catalyst for this volume, I now know that my experiences are far from unique. Like African-American women, many others who occupy societally denigrated categories have been similarly silenced. So the voice that I now seek is both individual and collective, personal and political, one reflecting the intersection of my unique biography with the larger meaning of my historical times.

I share this part of the context that stimulated this book because that context influenced my choices concerning the volume itself. First, I was committed to making this book intellectually rigorous, well researched, and accessible to more than the select few fortunate enough to receive elite educations. I could not write a book about Black women's ideas that the vast majority of African-American women could not read and understand. Theory of all types is often presented as being so abstract that it can be appreciated only by a select few. Though often highly satisfying to academics, this definition excludes those who do not speak the language of elites and thus reinforces social relations of domination. Educated elites typically claim that only they are qualified to produce theory and believe that only they can interpret not only their own but everyone else's experiences. Moreover, educated elites often use this belief to uphold their own privilege.

I felt that it was important to examine the complexity of ideas that exist in both scholarly and everyday life and present those ideas in a way that made them not less powerful or rigorous but accessible. Approaching theory in this way challenges both the ideas of educated elites and the role of theory in sustaining hierarchies of privilege. The resulting volume is theoretical in that it reflects diverse theoretical traditions such as Afrocentric philosophy, feminist theory, Marxist social thought, the sociology of knowledge, critical theory, and postmodernism; and yet the standard vocabulary of these traditions, citations of their major works and key proponents, and these terms themselves rarely appear in the text. To me the ideas themselves are important, not the labels we attach to them.

Second, I place Black women's experiences and ideas at the center of analysis. For those accustomed to having subordinate groups such as African–American women frame our ideas in ways that are convenient for the more powerful, this centrality can be unsettling. For example, white, middle-class, feminist readers will find few references to so-called white feminist thought. I have deliberately chosen not to begin with feminist tenets developed from the experiences of white, middle-class, Western women and then insert the ideas and experiences of African-American women. While I am quite familiar with a range of historical and contemporary white feminist theorists and certainly value their contributions to our understanding of gender, this is not a book about what Black women think of white feminist ideas or how Black women's ideas compare with those of prominent white feminist theorists. I take a similar stance regarding Marxist social theory and Afrocentric thought. In order to capture the interconnections of race, gender, and social class in Black women's lives and their effect on Black feminist thought, I explicitly rejected grounding my analysis in any single theoretical tradition.

Oppressed groups are frequently placed in the situation of being listened to only if we frame our ideas in the language that is familiar to and comfortable for a dominant group. This requirement often changes the meaning of our ideas and works to elevate the ideas of dominant groups. In this volume, by placing African-American women's ideas in the center of analysis, I not only privilege those ideas but encourage white feminists, African-American men, and all others to investigate the similarities and differences among their own standpoints and those of African-American women.

Third, I deliberately include numerous quotations from a range of African–American women thinkers, some well known and others rarely heard from. Explicitly grounding my analysis in multiple voices highlights the diversity, richness, and power of Black women's ideas as part of a long-standing African–American women's intellectual community. Moreover, this approach counteracts the tendency of mainstream scholarship to canonize a few Black women as spokespersons for the group and then refuse to listen to any but these select few. While it is certainly appealing to receive recognition for one's accomplishments, my experiences as the "first," "one of the few," and the "only" have shown me how effective selecting a few and using them to control the many can be in stifling subordinate groups. Assuming that only a few exceptional Black women have been able to do theory homogenizes African-American women and silences the majority. In contrast, I maintain that theory and intellectual creativity are not the province of a select few but instead emanate from a range of people.

Fourth, I used a distinctive methodology in preparing this manuscript which illustrates how thought and action can work together in generating theory. Much of my formal academic training has been designed to show me that I must alienate myself from my communities, my family, and even my own self in order to produce credible intellectual work. Instead of viewing the everyday as a negative influence on my theorizing, I tried to see how the everyday actions and ideas of the Black women in my life reflected the theoretical issues I claimed were so important to them. Lacking grants, fellowships, release time, or other benefits that allow scholars to remove themselves from everyday life and contemplate its contours and meaning, I wrote this book while fully immersed in ordinary activities that brought me into contact with a variety of African-American women. Through caring for my daughter, mentoring Black women undergraduates, assisting a Brownie troop, and engaging in other "unscholarly" activities, I reassessed my relationships with a range of African-American women and their relationships with one another. Theory allowed me to see all of these associations with fresh eyes, while concrete experiences challenged the worldviews offered by theory. During this period of self-reflection, work on this manuscript inched along and I produced little "theory." But without this involvement in the everyday, the theory in this volume would have been greatly impoverished.

Fifth, in order to demonstrate the existence and authenticity of Black feminist thought, I present it as being coherent and basically complete. This portrayal is in contrast to my actual view that theory is rarely this smoothly constructed. Most theories are characterized by internal instability, are contested, and are divided by competing emphases and interests. When I considered that Black feminist thought is currently embedded in a larger political and intellectual context that challenges its very right to exist, I decided not to stress the contradictions, frictions, and inconsistencies of Black feminist thought. Instead I present Black feminist thought as overly coherent, but I do so because I suspect that this approach is most appropriate for this historical moment. I hope to see other volumes emerge which will be more willing to present Black feminist thought as a shifting mosaic of competing ideas and interests. I have focused on the pieces of the mosaic—perhaps others will emphasize the disjunctures distinguishing the pieces of the mosaic from one another.

Finally, writing this book has convinced me of the need to reconcile subjectivity and objectivity in producing scholarship. Initially I found the movement between my training as an "objective" social scientist and my daily experiences as an African-American woman jarring. But reconciling what we have been trained to see as opposites, a reconciliation signaled by my inserting myself in the text by using "I," "we," and "our" instead of the more distancing terms "they" and "one," was freeing for me. I discovered that the both/and conceptual stance of Black feminist thought allowed me to be both objective and subjective, to possess both an Afrocentric and a feminist consciousness, and to be both a respectable scholar and an acceptable mother.

When I began this book, I had to overcome my reluctance concerning committing my ideas to paper. "How can I as one person speak for such a large and complex group as African-American women?" I asked myself. The answer is that I cannot and should not because each of us must learn to speak for herself. In the course of writing the book I came to see my work as being part of a larger process, as one voice in a dialogue among people who had been silenced. I know that I will never again possess the curious coexistence of naiveté and unshakable confidence that I had when I portrayed Spring. But I hope to recapture those elements of the voice of Spring that were honest, genuine, and empowering. More important, my hope is that others who were formerly and are currently silenced will find their voices. I, for one, certainly want to hear what they have to say.

ACKNOWLEDGMENTS

Writing this book was a collaborative effort, and I would like to thank those most essential to its completion. For three years my husband, Roger L. Collins, and daughter, Valerie L. Collins, lived with my uncertainty and struggles while I wrote this volume. During that time we all ate far too much fast food and certainly did not reside in a spotless house. But despite this book—or perhaps because of it—we are a stronger family.

I also wish to thank those individuals who could not be with me while I produced this volume but whose contributions are reflected on every page. I drew much of my inspiration from the many Black women who have touched my life. They include my aunts, Mildred Walker, Marjorie Edwards, and Bertha Henry; teachers, friends, and othermothers who helped me along the way, Pauli Murray, Consuelo, Eloise "Muff" Smith, and Deborah Lewis; and countless Black women ancestors, both famous and anonymous, whose struggles created the foundation that nurtured me. I especially acknowledge the spirit of my mother, Eunice Randolph Hill. Often when I became discouraged, I thought of her and told myself that if she could persist despite the obstacles that she faced, then so could I. One great regret of my life is that my mother and my daughter will never meet. I hope these pages will bring them closer together.

Many of my colleagues listened to partially articulated ideas, read earlier drafts of chapters, and generally offered the encouragement and intellectual stimulation that enabled me to remain critical of my own work yet persevere. Special thanks to Margaret L. Andersen, Elsa Barkley Brown, Lynn Weber Cannon, Bonnie Thornton Dill, Cheryl Townsend Gilkes, Evelyn Nakano Glenn, Sandra Harding, Deborah K. King, and Maxine Baca Zinn for their enthusiastic support. I am especially indebted to the Center for Research on Women at Memphis State University for providing resources, ideas, and overall assistance. Also, I am deeply grateful to Elizabeth Higginbotham and Rosemarie Tong for reading this manuscript in its entirety and offering helpful suggestions.

I would like to thank the following for permission to reproduce these copyright materials: Earlier versions of Chapters 2 and 10 appeared in *Signs* 14 (4), Summer, 1989, pp. 745–73, and *Social Problems* 33 (6), Oct./Dec., 1986, pp. S14–S32; June Jordan and South End Press for *On Call*, 1985; Marilyn Richardson and Indiana University Press for *Maria W. Stewart, America's First Black Woman Political Writer*, edited by Marilyn Richardson, 1987; from *Drylongso, A Self-Portrait of Black America* by John Langston Gwaltney, copyright 1980 by John Langston Gwaltney, reprinted by permission of Random House, Inc.; "Strange Fruit" by Lewis Allan, copyright 1939, Edward B. Marks Music Company, copyright renewed, used by permission, all rights reserved; "Tain't Nobody's Biz-ness if I Do" words and music by Porter Grainger and Everett Robbins, copyright 1922 by MCA Music Publishing, copyright renewed 1949 and assigned to MCA Music Publishing, copyright 1960, 1963 by MCA Music Publishing, a division of MCA Inc., New York, NY 10019, used by permission, all rights reserved; and "Respect" lyrics and music by Otis Redding, copyright 1965 and 1967 by Irving Music, Inc. (BMI), international copyright secured, all rights reserved.

Finally, one special person participated in virtually every phase of this project. As a research assistant for this volume, she prepared literature reviews, read and commented on chapter drafts, and skillfully located even the most obscure materials. Her contributions often surpassed the scholarly—she provided child care so I could work and even fed my family's cats. During our many long conversations, she patiently listened to my ideas, bravely shared parts of her life that profoundly influenced my thinking, and in many unspoken ways told me on a daily basis how important it was that I keep going. Special thanks therefore go out to Patrice L. Dickerson, an emerging Black feminist intellectual, a future colleague, and always a solid sister-friend.

Part One

THE SOCIAL CONSTRUCTION OF BLACK FEMINIST THOUGHT

Chapter 1

THE POLITICS OF BLACK FEMINIST THOUGHT

In 1831 Maria W. Stewart asked, "How long shall the fair daughters of Africa be compelled to bury their minds and talents beneath a load of iron pots and kettles?" Orphaned at age five, bound out to a clergyman's family as a domestic servant, Stewart struggled to gather isolated fragments of an education when and where she could. As the first American woman to lecture in public on political issues and to leave copies of her texts, this early Black woman intellectual foreshadowed a variety of themes taken up by her Black feminist successors (Richardson 1987).

Maria Stewart challenged African-American women to reject the negative images of Black womanhood so prominent in her times, pointing out that racial and sexual oppression were the fundamental causes of Black women's poverty. In an 1833 speech she proclaimed, "like King Solomon, who put neither nail nor hammer to the temple, yet received the praise; so also have the white Americans gained themselves a name . . . while in reality we have been their principal foundation and support." Stewart objected to the injustice of this situation: "We have pursued the shadow, they have obtained the substance: we have performed the labor, they have received the profits; we have planted the vines, they have eaten the fruits of them" (Richardson 1987, 59).

Maria Stewart was not content to point out the source of Black women's oppression. She urged Black women to forge self-definitions of self-reliance and independence. "It is useless for us any longer to sit with

3

our hands folded, reproaching the whites; for that will never elevate us," she exhorted. "Possess the spirit of independence. . . . Possess the spirit of men, bold and enterprising, fearless and undaunted" (p. 53). To Stewart, the power of self-definition was essential, for Black women's survival was at stake. "Sue for your rights and privileges. Know the reason you cannot attain them. Weary them with your importunities. You can but die if you make the attempt; and we shall certainly die if you do not" (p. 38).

Stewart also challenged Black women to use their special roles as mothers to forge powerful mechanisms of political action. "O, ye mothers, what a responsibility rests on you!" Stewart preached. "You have souls committed to your charge. . . . It is you that must create in the minds of your little girls and boys a thirst for knowledge, the love of virtue, . . . and the cultivation of a pure heart." Stewart recognized the magnitude of the task at hand. "Do not say you cannot make any thing of your children; but say . . . we will try" (p. 35).

Maria Stewart was one of the first Black feminists to champion the utility of Black women's relationships with one another in providing a community for Black women's activism and self-determination. "Shall it any longer be said of the daughters of Africa, they have no ambition, they have no force?" she questioned. "By no means. Let every female heart become united, and let us raise a fund ourselves; and at the end of one year and a half, we might be able to lay the corner stone for the building of a High School, that the higher branches of knowledge might be enjoyed by us" (p. 37). Stewart saw the potential for Black women's activism as educators. She advised, "turn your attention to knowledge and improvement; for knowledge is power" (p. 41).

Though she said little in her speeches about the sexual politics of her time, her advice to African-American women suggests that she was painfully aware of the sexual abuse visited upon Black women. She continued to "plead the cause of virtue and the pure principles of morality" (p. 31) for Black women. And to those whites who thought that Black women were inherently inferior, Stewart offered a biting response: "Our souls are fired with the same love of liberty and independence with which your souls are fired . . . too much of your blood flows in our veins, too much of your color in our skins, for us not to possess your spirits" (p. 40).

Despite Maria Stewart's intellectual prowess, the ideas of this extraordinary woman come to us only in scattered fragments that not only suggest her brilliance but speak tellingly of the fate of countless Black women intellectuals. Recent scholarship has uncovered many Maria Stewarts, African-American women whose minds and talents have been suppressed by the pots and kettles symbolic of Black women's subordination (Guy-Sheftall 1986).[1] Far too many African-American women intellectuals have labored in isolation and obscurity and, like Zora Neale Hurston, lie buried in unmarked graves.

Some have been more fortunate, for they have become known to us, largely through the efforts of contemporary Black women scholars (Higginbotham and Watts 1988). Like Alice Walker, these scholars sense that "a people do not throw their geniuses away" and that, "if they are thrown away, it is our duty as artists, scholars, and witnesses for the future to collect them again for the sake of our children, . . . if necessary, bone by bone" (Walker 1983, 92).

This painstaking process of collecting the ideas and actions of "thrown away" Black women like Maria Stewart has revealed one important discovery. Black women intellectuals have laid a vital analytical foundation for a distinctive standpoint on self, community, and society and, in doing so, created a Black women's intellectual tradition. While clear discontinuities in this tradition exist—times when Black women's voices were strong and others when assuming a more muted tone was essential—one striking dimension of the ideas of Maria W. Stewart and her successors is the thematic consistency of their work.

If such a rich intellectual tradition exists, why has it remained virtually invisible until now? In 1905 Fannie Barrier Williams lamented, "the colored girl . . . is not known and hence not believed in; she belongs to a race that is best designated by the term 'problem,' and she lives beneath the shadow of that problem which envelops and obscures her" (Williams 1987, 150). Why are African-American women and our ideas not known and not believed in?

The shadow obscuring the Black women's intellectual tradition is neither accidental nor benign. Suppressing the knowledge produced by any oppressed group makes it easier for dominant groups to rule because the seeming absence of an independent consciousness in the oppressed can be taken to mean that subordinate groups willingly collaborate in their own victimization (Fanon 1963; Friere 1970; Scott 1985). Maintaining the invisibility of Black women and our ideas is critical in structuring patterned relations of race, gender, and class inequality that pervade the entire social structure.

In spite of this suppression, African-American women have managed to do intellectual work, to have our ideas matter. Anna Julia Cooper, Sojourner Truth, Mary McLeod Behune, Toni Morrison, Barbara Smith, Ida B. Wells, and countless others have consistently struggled to make themselves heard and have used their voices to raise essential issues affecting Black women. Like the work of Maria W. Stewart, Black women's intellectual work has fostered Black women's resistance and activism.

This dialectic of oppression and activism, the tension between the

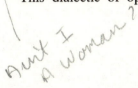

Aint I
A Woman?

suppression of Black women's ideas and our intellectual activism in the face of that suppression, comprises the politics of Black feminist thought. More important, understanding this dialectical relationship is critical in assessing how Black feminist thought—its definitions, core themes, and epistemological significance—is fundamentally embedded in a political context that has challenged its very right to exist.

THE SUPPRESSION OF BLACK FEMINIST THOUGHT

The vast majority of African-American women were brought to the United States to work as slaves. This initial condition shaped all subsequent relationships that Black women had within African-American families and communities, with employers, and among each other, and created the political context for Black women's intellectual work.

Black women's oppression has been structured along three interdependent dimensions. First, the exploitation of Black women's labor—the "iron pots and kettles" symbolizing Black women's long-standing ghettoization in service occupations—represents the economic dimension of oppression (Davis 1981; Marable 1983; Jones 1985). Survival for most African-American women has been such an all-consuming activity that most have had few opportunities to do intellectual work as it has been traditionally defined. The drudgery of enslaved African-American women's work and the grinding poverty of "free" wage labor in the rural South tellingly illustrate the high costs Black women have paid for survival. The millions of impoverished African-American women currently ghettoized in inner cities demonstrate the continuation of these earlier forms of Black women's economic exploitation.

Second, the political dimension of oppression has denied African-American women the rights and privileges routinely extended to white male citizens (Prestage 1980; Burnham 1987; Scarborough 1989). Forbidding Black women to vote, excluding African-Americans and women from public office, and withholding equitable treatment in the criminal justice system all substantiate the political subordination of Black women. Educational institutions have also fostered this pattern of disenfranchisement. Past practices such as denying literacy to slaves and relegating Black women to underfunded, segregated Southern schools worked to ensure that a quality education for Black women remained the exception rather than the rule (Perkins 1983; Mullings 1986b). The large numbers of young Black women in inner cities and impoverished rural areas who continue to leave school before attaining full literacy represent the continued efficacy of the political dimension of Black women's oppression.

Finally, the controlling images of Black women that originated during the slave era attest to the ideological dimension of Black women's oppression (King 1973; D. White 1985; Carby 1987). Ideology represents the process by which certain assumed qualities are attached to Black women and how those qualities are used to justify oppression. From the mammies, Jezebels, and breeder women of slavery to the smiling Aunt Jemimas on pancake mix boxes, ubiquitous Black prostitutes, and ever-present welfare mothers of contemporary popular culture, the nexus of negative stereotypical images applied to African-American women has been fundamental to Black women's oppression.

Taken together, the seamless web of economy, polity, and ideology function as a highly effective system of social control designed to keep African-American women in an assigned, subordinate place. This larger system of oppression works to suppress the ideas of Black women intellectuals and to protect elite white male interests and worldviews. Denying African-American women the credentials to become literate certainly excluded most African-American women from positions as scholars, teachers, authors, poets, and critics. Moreover, while Black women historians, writers, and social scientists have long existed, until recently these women have not held leadership positions in universities, professional associations, publishing concerns, broadcast media, and other social institutions of knowledge validation. Black women's exclusion from positions of power within mainstream institutions has led to the elevation of elite white male ideas and interests and the corresponding suppression of Black women's ideas and interests in traditional scholarship and popular culture (Scott 1982a; Higginbotham 1989).

Women's studies has offered one major challenge to the allegedly hegemonic ideas of elite white men. Ironically, feminist theory has also suppressed Black women's ideas. Even though Black women intellectuals have long expressed a unique feminist consciousness about the intersection of race and class in structuring gender, historically we have not been full participants in white feminist organizations (Hooks 1981; Giddings 1984; Andolsen 1986; Zinn et al. 1986). Even today African-American, Hispanic, Native American, and Asian-American women criticize the feminist movement and its scholarship for being racist and overly concerned with white, middle-class women's issues (Hooks 1981; Moraga and Anzaldua 1981; Cross et al. 1982; Smith 1982a; Dill 1983; Andolsen 1986; Davis 1989).

This historical suppression of Black women's ideas has had a pronounced influence on feminist theory. Theories advanced as being universally applicable to women as a group on closer examination appear greatly limited by the white, middle-class origins of their proponents. For example,

Nancy Chodorow's (1974, 1978) work on sex role socialization and Carol Gilligan's (1982) study of the moral development of women both rely heavily on white, middle-class samples. While these two classics make key contributions to feminist theory, they simultaneously promote the notion of a generic woman who is white and middle class. The absence of Black feminist ideas from these and other studies places them in a much more tenuous position to challenge the hegemony of mainstream scholarship on behalf of all women.

Black social and political thought has also challenged mainstream scholarship. In this case the patterns of suppressing Black women's ideas have been quite different. Unlike the history of excluding Black women from both dominant academic discourse and white feminist arenas, African-American women have long been included in Black social and political organizations. But with the exception of Black women's organizations, male-run organizations have not stressed Black women's issues (Beale 1970; Hooks 1981; Marable 1983). Even though Black women intellectuals have asserted their right to speak both as African-Americans and as women, historically these women have not held top leadership positions in Black organizations (Giddings 1984).

Civil rights activist Ella Baker's experiences in the Southern Christian Leadership Conference illustrate one form that suppressing Black women's ideas and talents can take. Ms. Baker virtually ran the entire organization, yet had to defer to the decision-making authority of the exclusively male leadership group (Cantarow 1980). Civil rights activist Septima Clark describes similar experiences: "I found all over the South that whatever the man said had to be right. They had the whole say. The woman couldn't say a thing" (C. Brown 1986, 79).[2]

Black social and political thought has been limited by both the reformist postures toward change assumed by many Black intellectuals (Cruse 1967; West 1977–78; Childs 1984) and the secondary status afforded the ideas and experiences of African-American women. Adhering to a male-defined ethos that far too often equates racial progress with the acquisition of an ill-defined manhood has left Black thought with a prominent masculinist bias. Calvin Hernton points out that the "masculine perspective itself, concerning the manhood of the black race, has always occupied center stage in the drama of Afro-American literature" (1985, 7). Black feminist activist Pauli Murray (1970) found that from its founding in 1916 to 1970, the *Journal of Negro History* published only five articles devoted exclusively to Black women.

Much of contemporary Black feminist thought stems from Black women's increasing willingness to strive for gender equality within African-American organizations. Septima Clark describes this transformation:

> I used to feel that women couldn't speak up, because when district meetings were being held at my home . . . I didn't feel as if I could tell them what I had in mind. . . . But later on, I found out that women had a lot to say, and what they had to say was really worthwhile. . . . So we started talking, and have been talking quite a bit since that time. (C. Brown 1986, 82)

African-American women intellectuals have been "talking quite a bit" since 1970 and have insisted that both the masculinist bias in Black social and political thought and the racist bias in feminist theory be corrected (see, e.g., Bambara 1970; Hooks 1981; Jordan 1981). Recent works in both African-American and feminist scholarship indicate that Black women's voices are being heard. For example, Manning Marable (1983) devotes an entire chapter in *How Capitalism Underdeveloped Black America* to how sexism has been a primary deterrent to Black community development. Similarly, works by prominent white feminist theorists (see, e.g., Spelman 1982; Harding 1986; Andersen 1987) reflect similar efforts to incorporate Black women's ideas.

While these signs are promising, the recent resurgence of Black women's ideas has not gone unopposed. The virulent reaction to earlier Black women's writings by some Black men, such as Robert Staples's (1979) analysis of Ntozake Shange's (1975) choreopoem, *For Colored Girls Who Have Considered Suicide*, and Michele Wallace's (1978) admittedly flawed volume, *Black Macho and the Myth of the Superwoman*, illustrates the difficulty of challenging the masculinist bias in Black social and political thought. In describing the response of Black men to the outpouring of publications by Black women writers in the 1970s and 1980s, Calvin Hernton offers an incisive criticism of the seeming tenacity of a masculinist bias:

> The telling thing about the hostile attitude of black men toward black women writers is that they interpret the new thrust of the women as being "counter-productive" to the historical goal of the Black struggle. Revealingly, while black men have achieved outstanding recognition throughout the history of black writing, black women have not accused the men of collaborating with the enemy and setting back the progress of the race. (1985, 5)

Though less overtly hostile, the resistance to Black women's ideas in the white feminist scholarly community has been similarly entrenched. Alice Walker (1983) writes of her stint sharing an office with a prominent white feminist who expressed superficial interest in Black women's ideas yet compiled an anthology of women writers from which women of color were noticeably absent. Similarly, white women who possess great competence in researching a range of issues omit women of color from their work claiming that they are unqualified to understand the "Black woman's experience." Both examples reflect a basic unwillingness by many white feminists to alter the paradigms that guide their work.

THE SHAPE OF ACTIVISM

Even if they appear to be otherwise, oppressive situations such as the suppression of Black women's ideas within traditional scholarship and the struggles within the critiques of that established knowledge are inherently unstable. Conditions in the wider political economy simultaneously shape Black women's subordination and foster activism. People who are oppressed usually know it. For African-American women, the knowledge gained at the intersection of race, gender, and class oppression provides the stimulus for crafting and passing on the subjugated knowledge[3] of a Black women's culture of resistance[4] (Caulfield 1974; Foucault 1980; Scott 1985).

Prior to World War II, self-contained Black communities created under slavery and maintained by de jure and de facto segregation served as one contradictory location stimulating an African-American women's culture of resistance. Even though the overriding purpose of Black ghettoization was political control and economic exploitation (Fusfeld and Bates 1984), all-Black communities simultaneously provided a separate space where African-Americans could articulate an independent Afrocentric worldview.

Every culture has a worldview that it uses to order and evaluate its own experiences (Sobel 1979). For African-Americans this worldview originates in the Afrocentric ideas of classical African civilizations, ideas sustained by the cultures and institutions of diverse West African ethnic groups (Diop 1974). By retaining significant elements of West African culture, communities of enslaved Africans offered their members alternative explanations for slavery than those advanced by slaveowners (Herskovits 1941; Gutman 1976; Webber 1978; Sobel 1979). Confining African-Americans to all-Black areas in the rural South and northern urban ghettos fostered the continuation of certain dimensions of this Afrocentric worldview (Smitherman 1977; Sobel 1979; Sudarkasa 1981b; Asante 1987). While essential to the survival of African-Americans, the knowledge produced in Black communities was hidden from and suppressed by the dominant group and thus remained extant but subjugated.

As mothers, othermothers, teachers and sisters, Black women were central to the retention and transformation of this Afrocentric worldview.

Within African-American extended families and communities, Black women fashioned an independent standpoint about the meaning of Black womanhood. These self-definitions enabled Black women to use African-derived conceptions of self and community to resist negative evaluations of Black womanhood advanced by dominant groups. In all, Black women's grounding in traditional African-American culture fostered the development of a distinctive Afrocentric women's culture.

Black women's position in the political economy, particularly ghetto-ization in domestic work, comprised another contradictory location where economic and political subordination created the conditions for Black women's resistance. Domestic work allowed African-American women to see white elites, both actual and aspiring, from perspectives largely obscured from Black men and from these groups themselves. In their white "families," Black women not only performed domestic duties but frequently formed strong ties with the children they nurtured, and with the employers themselves. On one level this insider relationship was satisfying to all concerned. Accounts of Black domestic workers stress the sense of self-affirmation the women experienced at seeing white power demystified. But on another level these Black women knew that they could never belong to their white "families," that they were economically exploited workers and thus would remain outsiders. The result was a curious outsider-within stance, a peculiar marginality that stimulated a special Black women's perspective (Collins 1986b).

Taken together, the outsider-within perspective generated by Black women's location in the labor market and this grounding in traditional African-American culture provide the material backdrop for a unique Black women's standpoint on self and society. As outsiders within, Black women have a distinct view of the contradictions between the dominant group's actions and ideologies. Nancy White, a Black inner-city resident, explores the connection between experience and beliefs:

> Now, I understand all these things from living. But you can't lay up on these flowery beds of ease and think that you are running your life, too. Some women, white women, can run their husband's lives for a while, but most of them have to . . . see what he tells them there is to see. If he tells them that they ain't seeing what they know they *are* seeing, then they have to just go on like it wasn't there! (in Gwaltney 1980, 148)

Not only does this passage speak to the power of the dominant group to suppress the knowledge produced by subordinate groups, but it illustrates how an outsider-within stance functions to create a new angle of vision on the process of suppression. Ms. White's Blackness makes her a perpetual outsider. She can never be a white middle-class woman lying on a "flowery bed of ease." But her work of caring for white women allows her an insider's view of some of the contradictions between white women thinking that they are running their lives and the actual source of power and authority in white patriarchal households.

African-American women question the contradictions between ideologies of womanhood and Black women's devalued status. If women are allegedly passive and fragile, then why are Black women treated as "mules" and assigned heavy cleaning chores? With no compelling explanations offered by a viable culture of resistance, the angle of vision created by being a devalued worker could easily be turned inward, leading to internalized oppression. But the presence of a legacy of struggle suggests that African-American culture generally and Black women's culture in particular provide potent alternative interpretations.

African-American women intellectuals are nurtured in this larger Black women's community. While the economic, political, and ideological dimensions of Black women's oppression lead directly to the suppression of the Black feminist intellectual tradition, these same conditions simultaneously foster the continuation of Afrocentric culture and the creation of an outsider-within stance essential to Black women's activism. Black women intellectuals' critical posture toward mainstream, feminist, and Black scholarly inquiry has been similarly shaped by Afrocentric culture and the outsider-within stance characterizing a more generalized Black women's culture of resistance. Out of the dialectic of oppression and activism come the experiences of African-American women generally that stimulate the ideas of Black women intellectuals.

The exclusion of Black women's ideas from mainstream academic discourse and the curious placement of African-American women intellectuals in both feminist and Black social and political thought has meant that Black women intellectuals have remained outsiders within in all three communities (Hull et al. 1982; Christian 1989). The assumptions on which full group membership are based—whiteness for feminist thought, maleness for Black social and political thought, and the combination for mainstream scholarship—all negate a Black female reality. Prevented from becoming full insiders in any of these areas of inquiry, Black women remain outsiders within, individuals whose marginality provides a distinctive angle of vision on the theories put forth by such intellectual communities.

Alice Walker's work exemplifies both of these fundamental influences on the Black women's intellectual tradition. Walker describes the impact that an outsider-within stance had on her own thinking: "I believe . . . that it was from this period—from my solitary, lonely position, the position of an outcast—that I began really to see people and things, really to notice relationships" (Walker 1983, 244). Walker realizes that "the gift of loneliness is sometimes a radical vision of society or one's people that has not previously been taken into account" (p. 264). And yet marginality is not the only influence on her work. By reclaiming the works of Zora Neale Hurston and in other ways placing Black women's experiences and culture at the center of her work, she draws on the alternative Afrocentric feminist worldview extant in Black women's culture.

RECLAIMING THE BLACK FEMINIST INTELLECTUAL TRADITION

Starting from the assumption that African-American women have created an independent, viable, yet subjugated knowledge concerning our own subordination, contemporary Black women intellectuals are engaged in the struggle to reconceptualize all dimensions of the dialectic of oppression and activism as it applies to African-American women. Central to this enterprise is reclaiming the Black feminist intellectual tradition.

Black women academicians' positions as outsiders within fosters this reclamation process. Stimulated by the knowledge that the minds and talents of our grandmothers, mothers, and sisters have been suppressed, the task of reclaiming Black women's subjugated knowledge takes on special meaning for Black women intellectuals. Alice Walker describes how this sense of purpose affects her work: "In my own work I write not only what I want to read—understanding fully and indelibly that if I don't do it no one else is so vitally interested, or capable of doing it to my satisfaction—I write all the things *I should have been able to read*" (Walker 1983, 13).

Reclaiming this tradition involves discovering, reinterpreting, and, in many cases, analyzing for the first time the works of Black women intellectuals who were so extraordinary that they did manage to have their ideas preserved through the mechanisms of mainstream scholarly discourse. In some cases this process involves locating unrecognized and unheralded works, scattered and long out of print. Marilyn Richardson's (1987) painstaking editing of the writings and speeches of Maria Stewart, Gloria Hull's (1984) careful compilation of the journals of Black feminist intellectual Alice Dunbar-Nelson, and Mary Helen Washington's (1975, 1980, 1987) collections of Black women's writings typify this process. Similarly, Alice Walker's (1979) efforts to have Zora Neale Hurston's unmarked grave recognized parallel her intellectual quest to honor Hurston's important contributions to the Black feminist literary tradition.

Reinterpreting existing works through new theoretical frameworks is another component of this process of reclaiming the Black feminist intellectual tradition. Mary Helen Washington's (1987) reassessment of anger and voice in *Maud Martha*, a much-neglected work by novelist and poet Gwendolyn Brooks, Hazel Carby's (1987) use of the lens of race, class, and gender to reinterpret the works of nineteenth-century Black women novelists, and Evelyn Brooks Higginbotham's (1989) analysis of the emerging concepts and paradigms in Black women's history all exemplify this process of reinterpreting the works of African-American women intellectuals through new theoretical frameworks.

Reclaiming the Black feminist intellectual tradition also involves searching for its expression in alternative institutional locations and among women who are not commonly perceived as intellectuals. Denied formal education, nineteenth-century Black feminist activist Sojourner Truth is not typically seen as an intellectual.[5] Yet her 1851 speech at an Akron, Ohio, women's rights convention provides an incisive analysis of the definitions of the term *woman* forwarded in the mid-1800s:

> That man over there says women need to be helped into carriages, and lifted over ditches, and to have the best place everywhere. Nobody ever helps me into carriages, or over mud-puddles, or gives me any best place! And ain't I a woman? Look at me! Look at my arm! I have ploughed, and planted, and gathered into barns, and no man could head me! And ain't I a woman? I could work as much and eat as much as a man—when I could get it—and bear the lash as well! And ain't I a woman? I have borne thirteen children, and seen them most all sold off to slavery, and when I cried out with my mother's grief, none but Jesus heard me! And ain't I a woman? (Loewenberg and Bogin 1976, 235)

Sojourner Truth exposes the concept of woman as being culturally constructed by using the contradictions between her life as an African-American woman and the qualities ascribed to women. Her life as a second-class citizen has been filled with hard physical labor, with no assistance from men. Her question, "and ain't I a woman?" points to the contradictions inherent in blanket use of the term *woman*. For those who question Truth's femininity, she invokes her status as a mother of thirteen children, all sold off into slavery, and asks again, "and ain't I a woman?" Rather than accepting the existing assumptions about what a woman was and then trying to prove that she fit the standards, Truth challenged the very standards themselves. Her actions demonstrate the process of deconstruction—namely, exposing a concept as ideological or culturally constructed rather than as natural or a simple reflection of reality (Alcoff 1988). By deconstructing the concept *woman*, Truth proved herself to be a formidable intellectual. And yet Truth was a former slave who never learned to read or write.

Examining the contributions of women like Sojourner Truth suggests that a similar process of deconstruction must be applied to the concept of *intellectual*. Just as theories, epistemologies, and facts produced by any group of individuals represent the standpoints and interests of their creators, the very definition of who is legitimated to do intellectual work is also politically contested (Mannheim 1936; Gramsci 1971). Reclaiming the Black feminist intellectual tradition involves much more than developing Black feminist analyses using standard epistemological criteria. It also involves challenging the very definitions of intellectual discourse.

Assuming new angles of vision on the definitions of who can be a Black woman intellectual and on what constitutes Black feminist thought suggests that much of the Black women's intellectual tradition has been embedded in institutional locations other than the academy. At the core of Black feminist thought lie theories created by African-American women which clarify a Black women's standpoint—in essence, an interpretation of Black women's experiences and ideas by those who participate in them. African-American women not commonly certified as intellectuals by academic institutions have long functioned as intellectuals by representing the interests of Black women as a group and fostering Black feminist thought. Without tapping these so-called nontraditional sources, much of the Black women's intellectual tradition would remain "not known and hence not believed in" (Williams 1987, 150).

Reclaiming the Black women's intellectual tradition involves examining the everyday ideas of Black women not previously considered intellectuals. The ideas we share with one another as mothers in extended families, as othermothers in Black communities, as members of Black churches, and as teachers to the Black community's children have formed one pivotal area where African-American women have hammered out a Black women's standpoint. Musicians, vocalists, poets, writers, and other artists constitute another group of Black women intellectuals who have aimed to interpret Black women's experiences. Building on the Afrocentric oral tradition, musicians in particular have enjoyed close association with the larger community of African-American women comprising their audience. Through their words and actions, political activists have also contributed to the Black women's intellectual tradition. Producing intellectual work is generally not attributed to Black women artists and political activists. Such women are typically thought of as nonintellectual and nonscholarly, classifications that create a false dichotomy between scholarship and activism, between thinking and doing. Examining the ideas and actions of these excluded groups reveals a world in which behavior is a statement

of philosophy and in which a vibrant, both/and, scholar/activist tradition
remains intact.

OBJECTIVES OF THE VOLUME

African-American women's position in the economic, political, and
ideological terrain bounding intellectual discourse has fostered a distinctive Black feminist intellectual tradition. Two basic components of
Black feminist thought—its thematic content and its epistemological
approach—have been shaped by Black women's outsider-within stance
and by our embeddedness in traditional African-American culture.

My overall goal in this book is to describe, analyze, explain the significance of, and generally further the development of Black feminist
thought. In addressing this general goal, I have several specific objec-
tives. First, I summarize some of the essential themes in Black feminist
thought by surveying their historical and contemporary expression. Drawing primarily on the works of African-American women scholars, and
on the thought produced by Black women intellectuals in everyday and
alternative locations for knowledge production, I explore several core
themes that comprise a Black women's standpoint. The vast majority
of thinkers discussed in the text are, to the best of my knowledge,
Black women. I cite a range of Black women thinkers not because I
think Black women have a monopoly on the ideas presented; instead
I aim to demonstrate the range and depth of thinkers who exist in my
community. Placing the ideas of ordinary African-American women as
well as those of better-known Black women intellectuals at the center
of analysis produces a new angle of vision on feminist and African-
American concerns, one infused with an Afrocentric feminist sensibility.

While Black women intellectuals have consistently investigated a series
of core questions, namely the simultaneity of race, class, and gender
oppression, the importance of self-definition in resisting oppression, and
analyses of specific topics such as motherhood and political activism, not all
issues have received equal theoretical attention. My second objective is to
explore selected neglected themes currently lacking a comprehensive Black
feminist analysis. For example, even though Black women have written
about topics such as rape, sterilization abuse, and sexual harassment,
comprehensive Black feminist analyses of sexual politics that incorporate
the interlocking nature of race, gender, and class oppression remain scarce.
While the ideas of African-American women intellectuals lie at the core
of all arguments forwarded in this volume, I use Black women's ideas as
a point of departure in exploring neglected topics. By synthesizing the

ideas of thinkers from diverse race and gender groups, I develop my own independent analyses of themes important to Black women.

My third objective is to develop an epistemological framework that can be used both to assess existing Black feminist thought and to clarify some of the underlying assumptions that impede the development of Black feminist thought. This issue of epistemology raises some difficult questions. I see the need to define the boundaries that delineate Black feminist thought from other arenas of intellectual inquiry. What criteria can be applied to ideas to determine whether they are in fact Black and feminist? What essential features does Black feminist thought share with other bodies of intellectual criticism, particularly feminist theory, Afrocentric theory, Marxist analyses, and postmodernism? Do African-American women implicitly rely on alternative standards for determining whether ideas are true? Traditional epistemological assumptions concerning how we arrive at "truth" simply are not sufficient to the task of furthering Black feminist thought. In the same way that concepts such as woman and intellectual must be deconstructed, the process by which we arrive at truth merits comparable scrutiny.

Finally, I aim to use this same epistemological framework in preparing the book itself. Alice Walker describes this process as one whereby "to write the books one wants to read is both to point the direction of vision and, at the same time, to follow it" (1983, 8). This was a very difficult process for me, one requiring that I not only develop standards and guidelines for assessing Black feminist thought but that I then apply those same standards and guidelines to my own work while I was creating it. For example, one dimension of Black feminist thought that I explore in Chapters 2 and 9 is that Black women intellectuals create Black feminist thought by using their own concrete experiences as situated knowers in order to express a Black women's standpoint. To adhere to this epistemological tenet required that I reject the pronouns "they" and "their" when describing Black women and our ideas and replace these terms with the terms "we," "us," and "our." Using the distancing terms "they" and "their" when describing my own group and our experiences might enhance both my credentials as a scholar and the credibility of my arguments in some academic settings. But by taking this epistemological stance that reflects my disciplinary training as a sociologist, I invoke standards of certifying truth about which I remain ambivalent.

In contrast, by identifying my position as a participant in and observer of my own community, I run the risk of being discredited as being too subjective and hence less scholarly. But by being an advocate for my material, I validate the epistemological stance that I claim is fundamental for Black feminist thought. To me, the suppression of the Black women's intellectual tradition has made this process of feeling one's way an unavoidable epistemological stance for Black women intellectuals. As Walker points out, "she must be her own model as well as the artist attending, creating, learning from, realizing the model, which is to say, herself" (1983, 8).

NOTES

1. Numerous Black women intellectuals have explored the core themes first articulated by Maria W. Stewart (see Hull et al. 1982 and Higginbotham and Watts 1988). Sharon Harley and Rosalyn Terborg-Penn's (1978) ground-breaking collection of essays on Black women's history foreshadowed volumes on Black women's history such as those by Noble (1978), Giddings (1984), and D. White (1985). A similar explosion in Black women's literary criticism has occurred, as evidenced by the publication of book-length studies of Black women writers such as those by Barbara Christian (1985) and Hazel Carby (1987).

2. Black women's acceptance of subordinate roles in Black organizations does not mean that we wield little authority or that we experience patriarchy in the same way as do white women in white organizations. See, for example, Evans (1979), Gilkes (1985), and Chapter 7, this volume.

3. My use of the term *subjugated knowledge* differs somewhat from Michel Foucault's (1980) definition. According to Foucault, subjugated knowledges are "those blocs of historical knowledge which were present but disguised," namely, "a whole set of knowledges that have been disqualified as inadequate to their task or insufficiently elaborated: naive knowledges, located low down on the hierarchy, beneath the required level of cognition or scientificity" (p. 82). I suggest that Black feminist thought is not a "naive knowledge" but has been made to appear so by those controlling knowledge validation procedures. Moreover, Foucault argues that subjugated knowledge is "a particular, local, regional knowledge, a differential knowledge incapable of unanimity and which owes its force only to the harshness with which it is opposed by everything surrounding it" (p. 82). The component of Black feminist thought that analyzes Black women's oppression certainly fits this definition, but the long-standing, independent Afrocentric foundation of Black women's thought is omitted from Foucault's analysis.

4. My use of the term *culture of resistance* should not imply that a monolithic culture of resistance exists. Instead I suggest that such cultures contain contradictory elements that foster both compliance with and resistance to oppression. Key African-American social institutions, such as the institution of Black motherhood discussed in Chapter 6 and Black women's political activism discussed in Chapter 7, illustrate these contradictions.

5. Sojourner Truth's actions exemplify Antonio Gramsci's (1971) contention that every social group creates one or more "strata of intellectuals which give it homogeneity and an awareness of its own function not only in the economic but also in the social and political fields" (p. 5). Academicians are the intellectuals trained to represent the interests of groups in power. In contrast, "organic" intellectuals depend on common sense and represent the interests of their own group. Sojourner Truth typifies an "organic" or everyday intellectual, but she may not be certified as such by the dominant group because her intellectual activity threatens the prevailing social order. The outsider-within position of Black women academicians encourages us to draw on the traditions of both our discipline of training and our experiences as Black women but to participate fully in neither (Collins 1986b).

Chapter 2

DEFINING BLACK FEMINIST THOUGHT

Widely used yet rarely defined, Black feminist thought encompasses diverse and contradictory meanings. Two interrelated tensions highlight issues in defining Black feminist thought. The first concerns the thorny question of who can be a Black feminist. One current response, explicit in Patricia Bell Scott's (1982b) "Selected Bibliography on Black Feminism," classifies all African-American women, regardless of the content of our ideas, as Black feminists. From this perspective, living as Black women provides experiences to stimulate a Black feminist consciousness. Yet indiscriminately labeling all Black women in this way simultaneously conflates the terms *woman* and *feminist* and identifies being of African descent—a questionable biological category—as being the sole determinant of a Black feminist consciousness. As Cheryl Clarke points out, "I criticized Scott. Some of the women she cited as 'black feminists' were clearly not feminist at the time they wrote their books and still are not to this day" (1983, 94).

The term *Black feminist* has also been used to apply to selected African-Americans—primarily women—who possess some version of a feminist consciousness. Beverly Guy-Sheftall (1986) contends that both men and women can be "Black feminists" and names Frederick Douglass and William E. B. DuBois as prominent examples of Black male feminists. Guy-Sheftall also identifies some distinguishing features of Black feminist ideas: namely, that Black women's experiences with both racial and gender

oppression that result in needs and problems distinct from white women and
Black men, and that Black women must struggle for equality both as women
and as African-Americans. Guy-Sheftall's definition is helpful in that its
use of ideological criteria fosters a definition of Black feminist thought that
ecompasses both experiences and ideas. In other words, she suggests that
experiences gained from living as African-American women stimulate a
Black feminist sensibility. But her definition is simultaneously troublesome
because it makes the biological category of Blackness the prerequisite
for possessing such thought. Furthermore, it does not explain why these
particular ideological criteria and not others are the distinguishing ones.

The term Black feminist has also been used to describe selected African-
American women who possess some version of a feminist consciousness
(Beale 1970; Hooks 1981; Barbara Smith 1983; White 1984). This usage
of the term yields the most restrictive notion of who can be a Black feminist. The ground-breaking Combahee River Collective (1982) document,
"A Black Feminist Statement," implicity relies on this definition. The
Collective claims that "as Black women we find any type of biological
determinism a particularly dangerous and reactionary basis upon which
to build a politic" (p.17). But in spite of this statement, by implying
that only African-American women can be Black feminists, they require
a biological prerequisite for race and gender consciousness. The Collective
also offers its own ideological criteria for identifying Black feminist ideas. In
contrast to Beverly Guy-Sheftall, the Collective places a stronger emphasis
on capitalism as a source of Black women's oppression and on political
activism as a distinguishing feature of Black feminism.

Biologically deterministic criteria for the term *black* and the accompanying assumption that being of African desccent somehow produces a certain
consciousness or perspective are inherent in these definitions. By presenting race as being fixed and immutable—something rooted in nature—these
approaches mask the historical construction of racial categories, the shifting
meaning of race, and the crucial role of politics and ideology in shaping
conceptions of race (Gould 11981; Omi and Winant 1986). In contrast, much
greater variation is afforded the term feminist. Feminists are seen as ranging
from biologically determined—as is the case in radical feminist thought,
which argues that only women can be feminists—to notions of feminists
as individuals who have undergone some type of political transformation
theoretically achievable by anyone.

Though the term Black feminist could also be used to describe any individual who embraces Black feminist ideas, the separation of biology from
ideology required for this usage is rarely seen in the works of Black women
intellectuals. Sometimes the contradictions among these competing definitions can be so great that Black women writers use all simultaneously.

Consider the following passage from Deborah McDowell's essay "New Directions for Black Feminist Criticism":

> I use the term here simply to refer to Black female critics who analyze the works of Black female writers from a feminist political perspective. But the term can also apply to any criticism written by a Black woman regardless of her subject or perspective—a book written by a male from a feminist or political perspective, a book written by a Black woman or about Black women authors in general, or any writings by women. (1985, 191)

While McDowell implies that elite white men could be "black feminists," she is clearly unwilling to state so categorically. From McDowell's perspective, whites and Black men who embrace a specific political perspective, and Black women regardless of political perspective, could all potentially be deemed Black feminist critics.

The ambiguity surrounding current perspectives on who can be a Black feminist is directly tied to a second definitional tension in Black feminist thought: the question of what constitutes Black feminism. The range of assumptions concerning the relationship between ideas and their advocates as illustrated in the works of Patricia Bell Scott, Beverly Guy-Sheftall, the Combahee River Collective, and Deborah McDowell leads to problems in defining Black feminist theory itself. Once a person is labeled a "Black feminist," then ideas forwarded by that individual often become defined as Black feminist thought. This practice accounts for neither changes in the thinking of an individual nor differences among Black feminist theorists.

A definition of Black feminist thought is needed that avoids the materialist position that being Black and/or female generates certain experiences that automatically determine variants of a Black and/or feminist consciousness. Claims that Black feminist thought is the exclusive province of African-American women, regardless of the experiences and worldview of such women, typify this position. But a definition of Black feminist thought must also avoid the idealist position that ideas can be evaluated in isolation from the groups that create them. Definitions claiming that anyone can produce and develop Black feminist thought risk obscuring the special angle of vision that Black women bring to the knowledge production process.

THE DIMENSIONS OF A BLACK WOMEN'S STANDPOINT

Developing adequate definitions of Black feminist thought involves facing this complex nexus of relationships among biological classification, the social construction of race and gender as categories of analysis, the material conditions accompanying these changing social constructions, and Black women's consciousness about these themes. One way of addressing the definitional tensions in Black feminist thought is to specify the relationship between a Black women's standpoint—those experiences and ideas shared by African-American women that provide a unique angle of vision on self, community, and society—and theories that interpret these experiences.[1] I suggest that Black feminist thought consists of specialized knowledge created by African-American women which clarifies a standpoint of and for Black women. In other words, Black feminist thought encompasses theoretical interpretations of Black women's reality by those who live it.

This definition does not mean that all African-American women generate such thought or that other groups do not play a critical role in its production. Before exploring the contours and implications of this working definition, understanding five key dimension of a Black women's standpoint is essential.

The Core Themes of a Black Women's Standpoint

All African-American women share the common experience of being Black women in a society that denigrates women of African descent. This commonality of experience suggests that certain characteristic themes will be prominent in a Black women's standpoint. For example, one core theme is a legacy of struggle. Katie Cannon observes, "throughout the history of the United States, the interrelationship of white supremacy and male superiority has characterized the Black woman's reality as a situation of struggle—a struggle to survive in two contradictory worlds simultaneously, one white, privileged, and oppressive, the other black, exploited, and oppressed" (1985, 30). Black women's vulnerability to assaults in the workplace, on the street, and at home has stimulated Black women's independence and self-reliance.

In spite of differences created by historical era, age, social class, sexual orientation, or ethnicity, the legacy of struggle against racism and sexism is a common thread binding African-American women. Anna Julia Cooper, a nineteenth-century Black woman intellectual, describes Black women's vulnerability to sexual violence:

> I would beg . . . to add my plea for the *Colored Girls* of the South:—that large, bright, promising fatally beautiful class . . . so full of promise and possibilities, yet so sure of destruction; often without a father to whom they dare apply the loving term, often without a stronger brother to espouse their cause and defend their honor with his life's blood; in the midst of pitfalls

and snares, waylaid by the lower classes of white men, with no shelter, no
protection. (Cooper 1892, 240)

Yet during this period Black women struggled and built a powerful club
movement and numerous community organizations (Giddings 1984, 1988;
Gilkes 1985).

Age offers little protection from this legacy of struggle. Far too many
young Black girls inhabit hazardous and hostile environments. In 1975 I
received an essay entitled "My World" from Sandra, a sixth-grade student
who was a resident of one of the most dangerous public housing projects
in Boston. Sandra wrote, "My world is full of people getting rape. People
shooting on another. Kids and grownups fighting over girlsfriends. And
people without jobs who can't afford to get a education so they can get
a job . . . winos on the streets raping and killing little girls." Her words
poignantly express a growing Black feminist sensibility that she may be
victimized by racism and poverty. They also reveal her awareness that she
is vulnerable to rape as a gender-specific form of sexual violence. In spite
of her feelings about her community, Sandra not only walked the streets
daily but managed safely to deliver three younger siblings to school. In
doing so she participated in a Black women's legacy of struggle.

This legacy of struggle constitutes one of several core themes of a Black
women's standpoint. Efforts to reclaim the Black feminist intellectual
tradition are revealing Black women's longstanding attention to a series
of core themes first recorded by Maria W. Stewart (Richardson 1987).
Stewart's treatment of the interlocking nature of race, gender, and class
oppression, her call for replacing denigrated images of Black womanhood with self-defined images, her belief in Black women's activism as
mothers, teachers, and Black community leaders, and her sensitivity to
sexual politics are all core themes advanced by a variety of Black feminist
intellectuals.

Variation of Responses to Core Themes

The existence of core themes does not mean that African-American women
respond to these themes in the same way. Diversity among Black women
produces different concrete experiences that in turn shape various reactions
to the core themes. For example, when faced with stereotypical, controlling
images of Black women, some women—such as Sojourner Truth—demand,
"ain't I a woman?" By deconstructing the conceptual apparatus of the
dominant group, they invoke a Black women's legacy of struggle. In
contrast, other women internalize the controlling images and come to
believe that they are the stereotypes (Brown-Collins and Sussewell 1986).

A variety of factors explain the diversity of responses. For example, although all African-American women encounter racism, social class differences among African-American women influence how racism is experienced. A young manager who graduated with honors from the University of Maryland describes the specific form racism can take for middle-class Blacks. Before flying to Cleveland to explain a marketing plan for her company, her manager made her go over it three or four times in front of him so that she would not forget *her* marketing plan. Then he explained how to check luggage at an airport and how to reclaim it. "I just sat at lunch listening to this man talking to me like I was a monkey who could remember but couldn't think," the Black female manager recalled. When she had had enough, she responded, "I asked him if he wanted to tie my money up in a handkerchief and put a note on me saying that I was an employee of this company. In case I got lost I would be picked up by Traveler's Aid, and Traveler's Aid would send me back" (Davis and Watson 1985, 86). Most middle-class Black women do not encounter such blatant incidents, but many working-class Blacks do. For both groups the racist belief that African-Americans are less intelligent than whites remains strong.

Sexual orientation provides another key factor. Black lesbians have identified homophobia in general and the issues they face living as Black lesbians in homophobic communities as being a major influence on their angle of vision on everyday events (Shockley 1974; Lorde 1982, 1984; Clarke et al. 1983; Barbara Smith 1983). Beverly Smith describes how being a lesbian affected her perceptions of the wedding of one of her closest friends: "God, I wish I had one friend here. Someone who knew me and would understand how I feel. I am masquerading as a nice, straight, middle-class Black 'girl'" (1983, 172). While the majority of those attending the wedding saw only a festive event, Beverly Smith felt that her friend was being sent into a form of bondage.

Other factors such as ethnicity, region of the country, urbanization, and age combine to produce a web of experiences shaping diversity among African-American women. As a result, it is more accurate to discuss a Black *women's* standpoint than a Black *woman's* standpoint.

The Interdependence of Experience and Consciousness

Black women's work and family experiences and grounding in traditional African-American culture suggest that African-American women as a group experience a world different from that of those who are not Black and female. Moreover, these concrete experiences can stimulate a distinctive Black feminist consciousness concerning that material reality.[2] Being Black and female may expose African-American women to certain common experiences, which in turn may predispose us to a distinctive group consciousness, but it in no way guarantees that such a consciousness will develop among all women or that it will be articulated as such by the group.

Many African-American women have grasped this connection between what one does and how one thinks. Hannah Nelson, an elderly Black domestic worker, discusses how work shapes the perspectives of African-American and white women: "Since I have to work, I don't really have to worry about most of the things that most of the white women I have worked for are worrying about. And if these women did their own work, they would think just like I do—about this, anyway" (Gwaltney 1980, 4). Ruth Shays, a Black inner-city resident, points out how variations in men's and women's experiences lead to differences in perspective. "The mind of the man and the mind of the woman is the same" she notes, "but this business of living makes women use their minds in ways that men don' even have to think about" (Gwaltney 1980, 33).

This connection between experience and consciousness that shapes the everyday lives of all African-American women pervades the works of Black women activists and scholars. In her autobiography, Ida B. Wells describes how the lynching of her friends had such an impact on her worldview that she subsequently devoted much of her life to the antilynching cause (Duster 1970). Sociologist Joyce Ladner's (1972) *Tomorrow's Tomorrow*, a groundbreaking study of Black female adolescence, emerged from her discomfort with the disparity between the teachings of mainstream scholarship and her experiences as a young Black woman in the South. Similarly, the transformed consciousness experienced by Janie, the light-skinned heroine of Zora Neale Hurston's (1937) classic *Their Eyes Were Watching God*, from obedient granddaughter and wife to a self-defined African-American woman, can be directly traced to her experiences with each of her three husbands. In one scene Janie's second husband, angry because she served him a dinner of scorched rice, underdone fish, and soggy bread, hits her. That incident stimulates Janie to stand "where he left her for unmeasured time" and think. Her thinking leads to the recognition that "her image of Jody tumbled down and shattered . . . she had an inside and an outside now and suddenly she knew how not to mix them" (p.63).

Consciousness and the Struggle for a Self-Defined Standpoint

African-American women as a group may have experiences that provide us with a unique angle of vision. But expressing a collective, self-defined Black feminist consciousness is problematic precisely because dominant groups have a vested interest in suppressing such thought.[3] As Hannah

Nelson notes, "I have grown to womanhood in a world where the saner you are, the madder you are made to appear" (Gwaltney 1980, 7). Ms. Nelson realizes that those who control the schools, media, and other cultural institutions of society prevail in establishing their viewpoint as superior to others.

An oppressed group's experiences may put its members in a position to see things differently, but their lack of control over the ideological apparatuses of society makes expressing a self-defined standpoint more difficult. Elderly domestic worker Rosa Wakefield assesses how the standpoints of the powerful and those who serve them diverge:

> If you eats these dinners and don't cook 'em, if you wears these clothes and don't buy or iron them, then you might start thinking that the good fairy or some spirit did all that. . . . Black folks don't have no time to be thinking like that. . . . But when you don't have anything else to do, you can think like that. It's bad for your mind, though. (Gwaltney 1980, 88)

Ms. Wakefield has a self-defined perspective growing from her experiences that enables her to reject the standpoint of more powerful groups. And yet ideas like hers are typically suppressed by dominant groups. Groups unequal in power are correspondingly unequal in their ability to make their standpoint known to themselves and others.

Individual African-American women have long displayed varying types of consciousness regarding our shared angle of vision. By aggregating and articulating these individual expressions of consciousness, a collective, focused group consciousness becomes possible. Black women's ability to forge these individual, unarticulated, yet potentially powerful expressions of everyday consciousness into an articulated, self-defined, collective standpoint is key to Black women's survival. As Audre Lorde points out, "it is axiomatic that if we do not define ourselves for ourselves, we will be defined by others—for their use and to our detriment" (1984, 45).

One fundamental feature of this struggle for a self-defined standpoint involves tapping sources of everyday, unarticulated consciousness that have traditionally been denigrated in white, male-controlled institutions. For Black women, the struggle involves embracing a consciousness that is simultaneously Afrocentric and feminist. What does this mean?

Research in African-American Studies suggests that an Afrocentric worldview exists which is distinct from and in many ways opposed to a Eurocentric worldview (Okanlawon 1972; Asante 1987; Myers 1988). Standard scholarly social constructions of blackness and race define these concepts as being either reflections of quantifiable, biological differences among humans or residual categories that emerged in response to institutionalized racism (Lyman 1972; Bash 1979; Gould 1981; Omi and Winant 1986). In contrast, even though it often relies on biological notions of the "race," Afrocentric scholarship suggests that "blackness" and Afrocentricity reflect longstanding belief systems among African peoples (Diop 1974; Richards 1980; Asante 1987). While Black people were forced to adapt these Afrocentric belief systems in the face of different institutional arrangements of white domination, the continuation of an Afrocentric worldview has been fundamental to African-Americans' resistance to racial oppression (Smitherman 1977; Webber 1978; Sobel 1979; Thompson 1983). In other words, being Black encompasses *both* experiencing white domination *and* individual and group valuation of an independent, long-standing Afrocentric consciousness.

African-American women draw on this Afrocentric worldview to cope with racial oppression. But far too often Black women's Afrocentric consciousness remains unarticulated and not fully developed into a self-defined standpoint. In societies that denigrate African ideas and peoples, the process of valuing an Afrocentric worldview is the result of self-conscious struggle.

Similar concerns can be raised about the issue of what constitutes feminist ideas (Eisenstein 1983; Jaggar 1983). Being a biological female does not mean that one's ideas are automatically feminist. Self-conscious struggle is needed in order to reject patriarchal perceptions of women and to value women's ideas and actions. The fact that more women than men identify themselves as feminists reflects women's greater experience with the negative consequences of gender oppression. Becoming a feminist is routinely described by women (and men) as a process of transformation, of struggling to develop new interpretations of familiar realities.

The struggles of women from different racial/ethnic groups and those of women and men within African-American communities to articulate self-defined standpoints represent similar yet distinct processes. While race and gender are both socially constructed categories, constructions of gender rest on clearer biological criteria than do constructions of race. Classifying African-Americans into specious racial categories is considerably more difficult than noting the clear biological differences distinguishing females from males (Patterson 1982). But though united by biological sex, women do not form the same type of group as do African-Americans, Jews, native Americans, Vietnamese, or other groups with distinct histories, geographic origins, cultures, and social institutions. The absence of an identifiable tradition uniting women does not mean that women are characterized more by differences than by similarities. Women do share common experiences, but the experiences are not generally the same type as those affecting racial and ethnic groups (King 1988). Thus while expressions of race and gender are both socially constructed, they are not constructed in the same way. The struggle for an Afrocentric feminist consciousness requires embracing both an Afrocentric worldview and a feminist sensibility and using both to forge a self-defined standpoint.[4]

The Interdependence of Thought and Action

One key reason that standpoints of oppressed groups are suppressed is that self-defined standpoints can stimulate resistance. Annie Adams, a Southern Black woman, describes how she became involved in civil rights activities:

> When I first went into the mill we had segregated water fountains. . . Same thing about the toilets. I had to clean the toilets for the inspection room and then, when I got ready to go to the bathroom, I had to go all the way to the bottom of the stairs to the cellar. So I asked my boss man, "what's the difference? If I can go in there and clean them toilets, why can't I use them?" Finally, I started to use that toilet. I decided I wasn't going to walk a mile to go to the bathroom. (Byerly 1986, 134).

In this case Ms. Adams found the standpoint of the "boss man" inadequate, developed one of her own, and acted on it. Her actions illustrate the connections among concrete experiences with oppression, developing a self-defined standpoint concerning those experiences, and the acts of resistance that can follow.

This interdependence of thought and action suggests that changes in thinking may be accompanied by changed actions and that altered experiences may in turn stimulate a changed consciousness. The significance of this connection is succinctly expressed by Patrice L. Dickerson, an astute Black feminist college student, who writes, "it is a fundamental contention of mine that in a social context which denies and deforms a person's capacity to realize herself, the problem of self-consciousness is not simply a problem of thought, but also a problem of practice, . . . the demand to end a deficient consciousness must be joined to a demand to eliminate the conditions which causd it" (personal communication, 1988). The struggle for a self-defined Afrocentric feminist consciousness occurs through a merger of thought and action.

This dimension of a Black women's standpoint rejects either/or dichotomous thinking that claims that *either* thought *or* concrete action is desirable and that merging the two limits the efficacy of both. Such approaches generate deep divisions among theorists and activists which are more often fabricated than real. Instead, by espousing a both/and orientation that views thought and action as part of the same process, possibilities for new relationships between thought and action emerge. That Black women should embrace a both/and conceptual orientation grows from Black women's experiences living as both African-Americans and women and, in many cases, in poverty.

Very different kinds of "thought" and "theories" emerge when abstract thought is joined with concrete action. Denied positions as scholars and writers which allow us to emphasize purely theoretical concerns, the work of most Black women intellectuals is influenced by the merger of action and theory. The activities of nineteenth-century Black women intellectuals such as Anna J. Cooper, Frances Ellen Watkins Harper, Ida B. Wells, and Mary Church Terrell exemplify this tradition of merging intellectual work and activism. These women both produced analyses of Black women's oppression and worked to eliminate that oppression. The Black women's club movement they created was both an activist and an intellectual endeavor.

Contemporary Black women intellectuals continue to draw on this tradition of using everyday actions and experiences in our theoretical work.[5] Bell Hooks describes the impact working as an operator at the telephone company had on her efforts to write *Ain't I a Woman: Black Women and Feminism* (1981). The women she worked with wanted her to "write a book that would make our lives better, one that would make other people understand the hardships of being black and female" (1989, 152). To Hooks, "it was different to be writing in a context where my ideas were not seen as separate from real people and real lives" (p. 152). Similarly, Black feminist historian Elsa Barkley Brown describes the importance her mother's ideas played in the scholarship she eventually produced on African-American washerwomen. Initially Brown used the lens provided by her training as a historian and assessed her sample group as devalued service workers. But over time she came to understand washerwomen as entrepreneurs. By taking the laundry to whoever had the largest kitchen, they created a community and a culture among themselves. In explaining the shift of vision that enabled her to reassess this portion of Black women's history, Brown notes, "it was my mother who taught me how to ask the right questions—and all of us who try to do this thing called scholarship on a regular basis are fully aware that asking the right questions is the most important part of the process" (1986, 14).

REARTICULATING A BLACK WOMEN'S STANDPOINT

The existence of a Black women's standpoint does not mean that African-American women appreciate its content, see its significance, or recognize the potential that a fully articulated Afrocentric feminist standpoint has as a catalyst for social change. One key role for Black women intellectuals is to ask the right questions and investigate all dimensions of a Black women's standpoint with and for African-American women.[6] Black women intellectuals thus stand in a special relationship to the community of African-American women of which we are a part, and this special relationship frames the contours of Black feminist thought.

This special relationship of Black women intellectuals to the community of African-American women parallels the existence of two interrelated levels of knowledge (Berger and Luckmann 1966). The commonplace, taken-for-granted knowledge shared by African-American women growing from our everyday thoughts and actions constitutes a first and most fundamental level of knowledge. The ideas that Black women share with one another on an informal, daily basis about topics such as how to style our hair, characteristics of "good" Black men, strategies for dealing with white folks, and skills of how to "get over" provide the foundations for this taken-for-granted knowledge.

Experts or specialists who participate in and emerge from a group produce a second, more specialized type of knowledge. The range of Black women intellectuals discussed in Chapter 1 are these specialists, and their theories clarifying a Black women's standpoint form the specialized knowledge of Black feminist thought. The two types of knowledge are interdependent. While Black feminist thought articulates the taken-for-granted knowledge shared by African-American women as a group, the consciousness of Black women may be transformed by such thought. The actions of educated Black women within the Black women's club movement typify this special relationship between Black women intellectuals and the wider community of African-American women:

> It is important to recognize that black women like Frances Harper, Anna Julia Cooper, and Ida B. Wells were not isolated figures of intellectual genius; they were shaped by and helped to shape a wider movement of Afro-American women. This is not to claim that they were representative of all black women; they and their counterparts formed an educated, intellectual elite, but an elite that tried to develop a cultural and historical perspective that was organic to the wider condition of black womanhood. (Carby 1987, 115).

The work of these women is important because it illustrates a tradition of joining scholarship and activism, and thus it taps the both/and conceptual orientation of a Black women's standpoint.

The suppression of Black feminist thought in mainstream scholarship and within its Afrocentric and feminist critiques has meant that Black women intellectuals have traditionally relied on alternative institutional locations to produce specialized knowledge about a Black women's standpoint. Many Black women scholars, writers, and artists have worked either alone, as was the case with Maria W. Stewart, or within African-American community organizations, the case for Black women in the club movement. The emergence of Black women's studies in colleges and universities during the 1980s, and the creation of a community of African-American women writers such as Toni Morrison, Alice Walker, and Gloria Naylor, have created new institutional locations where Black women intellectuals can produce specialized thought. Black women's history and Black feminist literary criticism constitute two focal points of this renaissance in Black women's intellectual work (Carby 1987). These are parallel movements: the former aimed at documenting social structural influences on Black women's consciousness; the latter, at exploring Black women's consciousness (self-definitions) through the freedom that art provides.

One danger facing African-American women intellectuals working in these new locations concerns the potential isolation from the types of experiences that stimulate an Afrocentric feminist consciousness—lack of access to other Black women and to a Black women's community. Another is the pressure to separate thought from action—particularly political activism—that typically accompanies training in standard academic disciplines. In spite of these hazards, contemporary Afrocentric feminist thought represents the creative energy flowing between these two focal points of history and literature, an unresolved tension that both emerges from and informs the experiences of African-American women.

The potential significance of Black feminist thought as specialized thought goes far beyond demonstrating that African-American women can be theorists. Like the Black women's activist tradition from which it grows and which it seeks to foster, Black feminist thought can create collective identity among African-American women about the dimensions of a Black women's standpoint. Through the process of rearticulation, Black women intellectuals offer African-American women a different view of themselves and their world from that forwarded by the dominant group (Omi and Winant 1986, 93). By taking the core themes of a Black women's standpoint and infusing them with new meaning, Black women intellectuals can stimulate a new consciousness that utilizes Black women's everyday, taken-for-granted knowledge. Rather than raising consciousness, Black feminist thought affirms and rearticulates a consciousness that already exists. More important, this rearticulated consciousness empowers African-American women and stimulates resistance.

Sheila Radford-Hill stresses the importance of rearticulation as an essential ingredient of an empowering Black feminist theory in her essay "Considering Feminism as a Model for Social Change." In evaluating whether Black women should espouse feminist programs, Radford-Hill suggests, "the essential issue that black women must confront when assessing a feminist position is as follows: If I, as a black woman, 'become a feminist,' what basic tools will I gain to resist my individual and group oppression" (1986, 160)? For Radford-Hill, the relevance of feminism as a vehicle for social change must be assessed in terms of its "ability to factor black women and other women of color into alternative conceptions of power and the consequences of its use" (p. 160). Thus Black feminist thought aims to develop a theory that is emancipatory and reflective and which can aid African-American women's struggles against oppression.

The earlier definition of Black feminist thought can now be reformulated to encompass the expanded definition of standpoint, the relationship between everyday and specialized thought, and the importance of rearticulation as one key dimension of Black feminist thought. Restated, Black feminist thought consists of theories or specialized thought produced by African-American women intellectuals designed to express a Black women's standpoint. The dimensions of this standpoint include the presence of characteristic core themes, the diversity of Black women's experiences in encountering these core themes, the varying expressions of Black women's Afrocentric feminist consciousness regarding the core themes and their experiences with them, and the interdependence of Black women's experiences, consciousness, and actions. This specialized thought should aim to infuse Black women's experiences and everyday thought with new meaning by rearticulating the interdependence of Black women's experiences and consciousness. Black feminist thought is *of* African-American women in that it taps the multiple relationships among Black women needed to produce a self-defined Black women's standpoint. Black feminist thought is *for* Black women in that it empowers Black women for political activism.

At first glance, this expanded definition could be read to mean that only African-American women can participate in the production of Black feminist thought and that only Black women's experiences can form the content of that thought. But this model of Black feminism is undermined as a critical perspective by being dependent on those who are biologically Black and female. Given that I reject exclusionary definitions of Black feminism which confine "black feminist criticism to black women critics of black women artists depicting black women" (Carby 1987, 9), how does the expanded definition of Black feminist thought address the two original definitional tensions?

WHO CAN BE A BLACK FEMINIST? : THE CENTRALITY OF BLACK WOMEN INTELLECTUALS TO THE PRODUCTION OF BLACK FEMINIST THOUGHT

I aim to develop a definition of Black feminist thought that relies exclusively neither on a materialist analysis—one whereby all African-American women by virtue of biology become automatically registered as "authentic Black feminists"—nor on an idealist analysis whereby the background, worldview, and interests of the thinker are deemed irrelevant in assessing his or her ideas. Resolving the tension between these two extremes involves reassessing the centrality Black women intellectuals assume in producing Black feminist thought. It also requires examining the importance of coalitions with Black men, white women, people of color, and other groups with distinctive standpoints. Such coalitions are essential in order to foster other groups' contributions as critics, teachers, advocates, and disseminators of a self-defined Afrocentric feminist standpoint.

Black women's concrete experiences as members of specific race, class, and gender groups as well as our concrete historical situations necessarily play significant roles in our perspectives on the world. No standpoint is neutral because no individual or group exists unembedded in the world. Knowledge is gained not by solitary individuals but by Black women as socially constituted members of a group (Narayan 1989). These factors all frame the definitional tensions in Black feminist thought.

Black women intellectuals are central to Black feminist thought for several reasons. First, our experiences as African-American women provide us with a unique standpoint on Black womanhood unavailable to other groups. It is more likely for Black women as members of an oppressed group to have critical insights into the condition of our own oppression than it is for those who live outside those structures. One of the characters in Frances Ellen Watkins Harper's 1892 novel, *Iola Leroy*, expresses this belief in the special vision of those who have experienced oppression:

> Miss Leroy, out of the race must come its own thinkers and writers. Authors belonging to the white race have written good books, for which I am deeply grateful, but it seems to be almost impossible for a white man to put himself completely in our place. No man can feel the iron which enters another man's soul. (Carby 1987, 62)

Only African-American women occupy this center and can "feel the iron" that enters Black women's souls, because we are the only group that has experienced race, gender, and class oppression as Black women experience them. The importance of Black women's leadership in producing Black feminist thought does not mean that others cannot participate. It does mean that the primary responsibility for defining one's own reality lies with the people who live that reality, who actually have those experiences.

Second, Black women intellectuals provide unique leadership for Black women's empowerment and resistance. In discussing Black women's involvement in the feminist movement, Sheila Radford-Hill points out the connections among self-definition, empowerment, and taking actions in one's own behalf:

> Black women now realize that part of the problem within the movement was our insistence that white women do for/with us what we must do for/with ourselves: namely, frame our own social action around our own agenda for change. . . . Critical to this discussion is the right to organize on one's own behalf. . . . Criticism by black feminists must reaffirm this principle. (1986, 162)

Black feminist thought cannot challenge race, gender, and class oppression without empowering African-American women. "Oppressed people resist by identifying themselves as subjects, by defining their reality, shaping their new identity, naming their history, telling their story," notes Bell Hooks (1989, 43). Because self-definition is key to individual and group empowerment, using an epistemology that cedes the power of self-definition to other groups, no matter how well-meaning, in essence perpetuates Black women's subordination. As Black feminist sociologist Deborah K. King succinctly states, "Black feminism asserts self-determination as essential" (1988, 72).

Stressing the importance of Black women's centrality to Black feminist thought does not mean that all African-American women exert this leadership. While being an African-American woman generally provides the experiential base for an Afrocentric feminist consciousness, these same conditions suppress its articulation. It is not acquired as a finished product but must continually develop in relation to changing conditions.

Bonnie Johnson emphasizes the importance of self-definition. In her critique of Patricia Bell Scott's bibliography on Black feminism, she challenges both Scott's categorization of all works by Black women as being Black feminist and Scott's identification of a wide range of African-American women as Black feminists: "Whether I think they're feminists is irrelevant. *They* would not call themselves feminist" (Clarke et al. 1983, 94). As

Patrice L. Dickerson contends, "a person comes into being and knows herself by her achievements, and through her efforts to become and know herself, she achieves" (personal correspondence 1988). Here is the heart of the matter. An Afrocentric feminist consciousness constantly emerges and is part of a self-conscious struggle to merge thought and action.

Third, Black women intellectuals are central in the production of Black feminist thought because we alone can create the group autonomy that must precede effective coalitions with other groups. This autonomy is quite distinct from separatist positions whereby Black women withdraw from other groups and engage in exclusionary politics. In her introduction to *Home Girls, A Black Feminist Anthology*, Barbara Smith describes this difference: "Autonomy and separatism are fundamentally different. Whereas autonomy comes from a position of strength, separatism comes from a position of fear. When we're truly autonomous we can deal with other kinds of people, a multiplicity of issues, and with difference, because we have formed a solid base of strength" (1983, xl). Black women intellectuals who articulate an autonomous, self-defined standpoint are in a position to examine the usefulness of coalitions with other groups, both scholarly and activist, in order to develop new models for social change. However, autonomy to develop a self-defined, independent analysis does not mean that Black feminist thought has relevance only for African-American women or that we must confine ourselves to analyzing our own experiences. As Sonia Sanchez points out, "I've always known that if you write from a black experience, you're writing from a universal experience as well. . . I know you don't have to whitewash yourself to be universal" (in Tate 1983, 142).

While Black feminist thought may originate with Black feminist intellectuals, it cannot flourish isolated from the experiences and ideas of other groups. The dilemma is that Black women intellectuals must place our own experiences and consciousness at the center of any serious efforts to develop Black feminist thought yet not have that thought become separatist and exclusionary. Bell Hooks offers a solution to this problem by suggesting that we shift from statements such as "I am a feminist" to those such as "I advocate feminism." Such an approach could "serve as a way women who are concerned about feminism as well as other political movements could express their support while avoiding linguistic structures that give primacy to one particular group" (1984, 30).

By advocating, refining, and disseminating Black feminist thought, other groups—such as Black men, white women, white men, and other people of color—further its development. Black women can produce an attenuated version of Black feminist thought separated from other groups. Other groups cannot produce Black feminist thought without African-American women. Such groups can, however, develop self-defined knowledge reflecting their own standpoints. But the full actualization of Black feminist thought requires a collaborative enterprise with Black women at the center of a community based on coalitions among autonomous groups.

Coalitions such as these require dialogues among Black women intellectuals and within the larger African-American women's community. Exploring the common themes of a Black women's standpoint is an important first step. Moreover, finding ways of handling internal dissent is especially important for the Black women's intellectual community. Evelynn Hammond describes how maintaining a united front for whites stifles her thinking: "What I need to do is challenge my thinking, to grow. On white publications sometimes I feel like I'm holding up the banner of black womanhood. And that doesn't allow me to be as critical as I would like to be" (in Clarke et al. 1983, 104). Cheryl Clarke observes that she has two dialogues: one with the public and the private ones in which she feels free to criticize the work of other Black women. Clarke states that the private dialogues are the ones that "have changed my life, have shaped the way I feel . . . have mattered to me" (p. 103).

Coalitions also require dialogues with other groups. Rather than rejecting our marginality, Black women intellectuals can use our outsider-within stance as a position of strength in building effective coalitions and stimulating dialogue. Barbara Smith suggests that Black women develop dialogues based on a "commitment to principled coalitions, based not upon expediency, but upon our actual need for each other" (1983, xxxiii). Dialogues among and coalitions with a range of groups, each with its own distinctive set of experiences and specialized thought embedded in those experiences, form the larger, more general terrain of intellectual and political discourse necessary for furthering Black feminism. Through dialogues exploring how relations of domination and subordination are maintained and changed, parallels between Black women's experiences and those of other groups become the focus of investigation.

Dialogue and principled coalition create possibilities for new versions of truth. Alice Walker's answer to the question of what she felt were the major differences between the literature of African-Americans and whites offers a provocative glimpse of the types of truths that might emerge through an epistemology based on dialogue and coalition. Walker did not spend much time considering this question, since it was not the difference between them that interested her, but, rather, the way Black writers and white writers seemed to be writing one immense story, with different parts of the story coming from a multitude of different perspectives. In a conversation with her mother, Walker refines this epistemological vision:

"I believe that the truth about any subject only comes when all sides of the story are put together, and all their different meanings make one new one. Each writer writes the missing parts to the other writer's story. And the whole story is what I'm after" (1983, 49). Her mother's response to Walker's vision of the possibilities of dialogues and coalitions hints at the difficulty of sustaining such dialogues under oppressive conditions: "'Well, I doubt if you can ever get the *true* missing parts of anything away from the white folks,' my mother says softly, so as not to offend the waitress who is mopping up a nearby table; 'they've sat on the truth so long by now they've mashed the life out of it'" (1983, 49).

WHAT CONSTITUTES BLACK FEMINISM? THE RECURRING HUMANIST VISION

A wide range of African-American women intellectuals have advanced the view that Black women's struggles are part of a wider struggle for human dignity and empowerment. In an 1893 speech to women, Anna Julia Cooper cogently expressed this alternative worldview:

> We take our stand on the solidarity of humanity, the oneness of life, and the unnaturalness and injustice of all special favoritisms, whether of sex, race, country, or condition. . . . The colored woman feels that woman's cause is one and universal; and that . . . not till race, color, sex, and condition are seen as accidents, and not the substance of life; not till the universal title of humanity to life, liberty, and the pursuit of happiness is conceded to be inalienable to all; not till then is woman's lesson taught and woman's cause won—not the white woman's nor the black woman's, not the red woman's but the cause of every man and of every woman who has writhed silently under a mighty wrong.(Loewenberg and Bogin 1976, 330–31)

Like Cooper, many African-American women intellectuals embrace this perspective regardless of particular political solutions we propose, our fields of study, or our historical periods. Whether we advocate working through separate Black women's organizations, becoming part of women's organizations, working within existing political structures, or supporting Black community institutions, African-American women intellectuals repeatedly identify political actions such as these as a *means* for human empowerment rather than ends in and of themselves. Thus the primary guiding principle of Black feminism is a recurring humanist vision (Steady 1981, 1987).[7]

Alice Walker's preference for the term *womanist*, a term she describes as "womanist is to feminist as purple is to lavender," addresses this notion of the solidarity of humanity. To Walker, one is "womanist" when one is "committed to the survival and wholeness of entire people, male and female." A womanist is "not a separatist, except periodically for health" and is "traditionally universalist, as is 'Mama, why are we brown, pink, and yellow, and our cousins are white, beige, and black?' Ans.: 'Well, you know the colored race is just like a flower garden, with every color flower represented'" (1983, xi). By redefining all people as "people of color," Walker universalizes what are typically seen as individual struggles while simultaneously allowing space for autonomous movements of self-determination.

In assessing the sexism of the Black nationalist movement of the 1960s, Black feminist lawyer Pauli Murray identifies the dangers inherent in separatism as opposed to autonomy, and also echoes Cooper's concern with the solidarity of humanity:

> The lesson of history that all human rights are indivisible and that the failure to adhere to this principle jeopardizes the rights of all is particularly applicable here. A built-in hazard of an aggressive ethnocentric movement which disregards the interests of other disadvantaged groups is that it will become parochial and ultimately self-defeating in the face of hostile reactions, dwindling allies, and mounting frustrations. . . . Only a broad movement for human rights can prevent the Black Revolution from becoming isolated and can insure ultimate success. (Murray 1970, 102)

Without a commitment to human solidarity, suggests Murray, any political movement—whether nationalist, feminist or antielitist—may be doomed to ultimate failure.

Bell Hook's analysis of feminism adds another critical dimension that must be considered: namely, the necessity of self-conscious struggle against a more generalized ideology of domination:

> To me feminism is not simply a struggle to end male chauvinism or a movement to ensure that women will have equal rights with men; it is a commitment to eradicating the ideology of domination that permeates Western culture on various levels—sex, race, and class, to name a few—and a commitment to reorganizing U.S. society so that the self-development of people can take precedence over imperialism, economic expansion, and material desires. (Hooks 1981, 194)

Former assemblywoman Shirley Chisholm also points to the need for self-conscious struggle against the stereotypes buttressing ideologies of domination. In "working toward our own freedom, we can help others work free from the traps of their stereotypes," she notes. "In the end, antiblack, antifemale, and all forms of discrimination are equivalent to the same thing—antihumanism. . . . We must reject not only the stereotypes that others have of us but also those we have of ourselves and others" (1970, 181).

This humanist vision is also reflected in the growing prominence of international issues and global concerns in the works of contemporary African-American women intellectuals (Lindsay 1980; Steady 1981, 1987). Economists Margaret Simms and Julianne Malveaux's 1986 edited volume, *Slipping through the Cracks: The Status of Black Women*, contains articles on Black women in Tanzania, Jamaica, and South Africa. Angela Davis devotes an entire section of her 1989 book, *Women, Culture, and Politics*, to international affairs and includes essays on Winnie Mandela and on women in Egypt. June Jordan's 1985 volume, *On Call*, includes essays on South Africa, Nicaragua, and the Bahamas. Alice Walker writes compellingly of the types of links these and other Black women intellectuals see between African-American women's issues and those of other groups: "To me, Central America is one large plantation; and I see the people's struggle to be free as a slave revolt" (1988, 177).

The words and actions of Black women intellectuals from different historical times and addressing markedly different audiences resonate with a strikingly similar theme of the oneness of all human life. Perhaps the most succinct version of the humanist vision in Black feminist thought is offered by Fannie Lou Hamer, the daughter of sharecroppers, and a Mississippi civil rights activist. While sitting on her porch, Ms. Hamer observed, "Ain' no such thing as I can hate anybody and hope to see God's face" (Jordan 1981, xi).

Taken together, the ideas of Anna Julia Cooper, Pauli Murray, Bell Hooks, Alice Walker, Fannie Lou Hamer, and other Black women intellectuals too numerous to mention suggest a powerful answer to the question "What is Black feminism?" Inherent in their words and deeds is a definition of Black feminism as a process of self-conscious struggle that empowers women and men to actualize a humanist vision of community.

NOTES

1. For discussions of the concept of standpoint, see Hartsock (1983a, 1983b), Jaggar (1983), and Smith (1987). Even though I use standpoint epistemologies as an organizing concept in this volume, they remain controversial. For a helpful critique of standpoint epistemologies, see Harding (1986). Haraway's (1988) reformulation of standpoint epistemologies approximates my use here.

2. Scott (1985) defines consciousness as the symbols, norms, and ideological forms people create to give meaning to their acts. For de Lauretis (1986), consciousness is

a process, a "particular configuration of subjectivity . . . produced at the intersection of meaning with experience. . . . Consciousness is grounded in personal history, and self and identity are understood within particular cultural contexts. Consciousness . . . is never fixed, never attained once and for all, because discursive boundaries change with historical conditions" (p. 8).

3. The presence of a Black women's culture of resistance (Terborg-Penn 1986; Dodson and Gilkes 1987) that is both Afrocentric and feminist challenges two prevailing interpretations of the consciousness of oppressed groups. One approach claims that subordinate groups identify with the powerful and have no valid independent interpretation of their own oppression. The second assumes the oppressed are less human than their rulers, and are therefore less capable of interpreting their own experiences (Rollins 1985; Scott 1985). Both approaches see any independent consciousness expressed by oppressed groups as being either not of their own making or inferior to that of the dominant group. More important, both explanations suggest that the alleged lack of political activism on the part of oppressed groups stems from their flawed consciousness of their own subordination.

4. Even though I will continue to use the term *Afrocentric feminist thought* interchangeably with the phrase *Black feminist thought*, I think they are conceptually distinct.

5. Canadian sociologist Dorothy Smith (1987) also views women's concrete, everyday world as stimulating theory. But the everyday she examines is individual, a situation reflecting in part the isolation of white, middle-class women. In contrast, I contend that the collective values in Afrocentric communities, when combined with the working-class experiences of the majority of Black women, provide a collective as well as an individual concrete.

6. See Harold Cruse's (1967) analysis of the Black intellectual tradition and John Child's (1984) discussion of the desired relationship of Black intellectuals to African-American culture. Childs argues against a relationship wherein "the people recede. They become merely the raw energy which the intellectuals must reshape, refine, and give voice to. A temptation for these intellectuals is to see themselves as the core formative force through which cultures comes into conscious existence and through which it is returned, now complete, to the people" (p. 69). Like Childs, I suggest that the role of Black women intellectuals is to "illuminate the very intricacy and strength of the peoples' thought" (p. 87).

7. My use of the term *humanist* grows from an Afrocentric historical context distinct from that criticized by Western feminists. I use the term to tap an Afrocentric humanism as cited by West (1977–78), Asante (1987) and Turner (1984) and as part of the Black theological tradition (Mitchell and Lewter 1986; Cannon 1988). See Harris (1981) for a discussion of the humanist tradition in the works of three Black women writers. See Richards (1990) for a discussion of African-American spirituality, a key dimension of Afrocentric humanism. Novelist Margaret Walker offers one of the clearest discussions of Black humanism. Walker claims: "I think it is more important now to emphasize humanism in a technological age than ever before, because it is only in terms of humanism that society can redeem itself. I believe that mankind is only one race—the human race. There are many strands in the family of man—many races. The world has yet to learn to appreciate the deep reservoirs of humanism in all races, and particularly in the Black race" (Rowell 1975, 12).

Part Two

CORE THEMES IN BLACK FEMINIST THOUGHT

Chapter 3

WORK, FAMILY, AND BLACK WOMEN'S OPPRESSION

Honey, de white man is the de ruler of everything as fur as Ah been able tuh find out. Maybe it's some place way off in de ocean where de black man is in power, but we don't know nothin' but what we see. So de white man throw down de load and tell de nigger man tuh pick it up. He pick it up because he have to, but he don't tote it. He hand it to his womenfolks. De nigger woman is de mule uh de world so fur as Ah can see.

—Zora Neale Hurston 1937, 16

With these words Nanny, an elderly African-American woman in Zora Neale Hurston's *Their Eyes Were Watching God*, explains Black women's "place" to her young, impressionable granddaughter. Nanny knows that being treated as "mules uh de world" lies at the heart of Black women's oppression. As mill worker Corine Cannon observes, "your work, and this goes for white people and black, is what you are . . . your work is your life" (Byerly 1986, 156).

One core theme in Black feminist thought consists of analyzing Black women's work, especially Black women's labor market victimization as "mules." As dehumanized objects, mules are living machines and can be treated as part of the scenery. Fully human women are less easily exploited. Documenting Black women's labor market status in order to see the general patterns of race and gender inequality is one primary area of analysis (Wallace 1980; Higginbotham 1983, 1985; Glenn 1985;

Jones 1985). This research is supplemented by studies of Black women's positions in specific occupational niches, such as the attention devoted to Black women domestic workers (Dill 1980, 1988a; Rollins 1985), and during specific historical eras, such as slavery (Jones 1985; D. White 1985) and the urbanizing South (Clark-Lewis 1985). This emerging scholarship provides convincing evidence for Maria Stewart's deft claim that "let our girls possess whatever amiable qualities of soul they may . . . it is impossible for scarce an individual of them to rise above the condition of servants" (Richardson 1987, 46).

More recent scholarship supplements this initial emphasis on oppression by presenting African-American women as constrained but often empowered figures, even in extremely difficult labor market settings (Terborg-Penn 1985). Black women's organizational roles in unions (Lerner 1972; Sacks 1988) and Black women's characteristic forms of everyday resistance (Rollins 1985; Byerly 1986; Dill 1988a) are also receiving increased attention.

Black women intellectuals demonstrate a sustained effort to examine the connections between race and gender oppression in analyzing Black women's work in capitalist political economies (Davis 1981; Higginbotham 1983; Mullings 1986b; Collins 1986a; Brewer 1988). African-American women certainly are not the only group taking this position (see, e.g., Brittan and Maynard 1984; Glenn 1985), but they have consistently done so the longest. While the concept of the interlocking nature of oppression is proposed as a premise, efforts at untangling the nature of the relationships themselves typically yield uneven outcomes (King 1988). As a result, we have a better sense of what these relationships are *not* than of what they are in a political economy of domination.[1]

Research on Black women's unpaid labor within extended families remains less fully developed in Black feminist thought than does that on Black women's paid work. By emphasizing Black women's contributions to Black family well-being, such as keeping families together and teaching children survival skills (Martin and Martin 1978; McCray 1980; Davis 1981), such scholarship suggests that Black women see their unpaid domestic work more as a form of resistance to oppression than as a form of exploitation by men. Less attention is given to ways that Black women's domestic labor is exploited within African-American families, an omission that obscures investigations of families as contradictory locations that simultaneously confine yet allow Black women to develop cultures of resistance.

Afrocentric feminist analyses of Black women's work investigate both the interlocking nature of Black women's oppression in the paid labor market and the dialectical nature of Black women's unpaid family labor. Such analyses stimulate a better appreciation of the powerful and complex interplay between Black women's position as "de mule uh de world" and patterns of capitalist development, racial oppression, and gender subordination.

Afrocentric feminist analyses of Black women's work also promise to shed some light on ongoing debates concerning social class. Black women's experiences have not been adequately explained by the two primary models of social class. In the status attainment model, class sorts out positions in society along a continuum of economic success and social prestige. Social classes become relative rankings and people engage in relative amounts of ascending or descending the ladder of social class. In the class conflict model, class divides society into two or more groups each of which has vested class interests and contends for control of society. Social classes are defined by the social relations of domination and subordination, usually economic and political, and social class always requires a power relation (Vanneman and Cannon 1987).

Neither status attainment nor class conflict models adequately explain Black women's experiences with social class. Status attainment research has relied heavily on occupational prestige of traditionally male jobs. Women's social class position was thought to derive from that of their fathers and husbands. But the higher rates of Black male unemployment, the racial discrimination that has crowded all African-Americans into a narrow set of occupations, and the existence of household arrangements other than two-parent nuclear families among African-Americans have all combined to make status attainment models less suitable for explaining Black social class dynamics. Moreover, the emphasis on *paid* labor and the exclusion of *unpaid* domestic labor have severely limited the ability of status attainment models to explain Black women's social class experiences.

Conflict models have also failed to capture the intersection of race and gender in explaining Black women's social class location. By focusing on paid labor, they too obscure the full range of Black women's work. Moreover, the type of paid work that has long preoccupied conflict theorists—namely, industrial factory jobs, especially unionized jobs—is problematic. African-American women have traditionally worked in agricultural labor or as domestic workers, two occupations resistant to unionization. The result is that Black women's paid work has been neglected in class conflict models.

Placing Black women's work and family experiences at the center of analysis suggests a view of social class other than that offered by status attainment or conflict models. Moreover, understanding the intersection of work and family in Black women's lives is key to clarifying the over-arching political economy of domination. Black women's work remains a fundamental location where the dialectical relationship of oppression and activism occurs.

FAMILY AND WORK: CHALLENGING THE DEFINITIONS

Racially segmented labor markets, gender ideologies in both segmented labor markets and family units, and the overarching capitalist class structure in which Black women's specific race, gender, and social class positions are embedded all structure Black women's work. And yet traditional social science research assesses African-American women's experiences in families using the normative yardstick developed from the experiences of middle-class American and European nuclear families (Billingsley 1968; Ladner 1972; Johnson 1981; Brewer 1988). Three elements of this approach are especially problematic for African-American families. First, this model posits a dichotomous split between the public sphere of economic and political discourse and the private sphere of family and household responsibilities. Contrasting a public political economy to a private, noneconomic and apolitical domestic sphere creates a distinction between the paid labor of the public sphere and the unpaid labor of the domestic sphere. Work and family emerge as separate, discreet spheres, with paid work done outside the household deemed more valuable than unpaid work performed for families. Within the public sphere gradations of pay correspond with differences of status, prestige, and power. For the private sphere, household residency and the family are treated as synonymous. The normative family becomes defined as a heterosexual couple who live together with their dependent children in a self-contained, economically independent household.

Second, under this model the public sphere of political and economic discourse is reserved for men as a "male" domain, leaving the private domestic sphere of family a "female" domain. In spite of claims that the two spheres are separate but equal, in capitalist settings the "female" sphere of family has long been subordinated to the "male" sphere of paid work and political authority. Gender roles are tied to the dichotomous constructions of these two basic societal institutions: men work and women take care of families.

Finally, this public/private dichotomy separating the family/household from the paid labor market shapes sex-segregated gender roles within the private sphere of the family. The archetypal white, middle-class nuclear family divides family life into two oppositional spheres: the "male" sphere of economic providing and the "female" sphere of affective nurturing. This normative family household ideally consists of a working father who earns enough to allow his spouse and dependent children to withdraw from the paid labor force. As head of the household, the father presides over the intimate, private affairs of his own sphere of influence. Guided by the moral influence of the mother, the household/family serves as a haven from the pressures and demands of the impersonal, public sector. All members of the household/family should be glad to retreat from the impersonal public sphere to the warm, supportive environment of "home" (Dill 1988b; Mullings 1986a, 1986b).

Black women's experiences and those of other women of color have never fit this model (Higginbotham 1983; Glenn 1985; Mullings 1986b). Rather than trying to explain why Black women's work and family patterns deviate from the alleged norm, a more fruitful approach lies in challenging the very constructs of work and family themselves. Because household and kin arrangements vary tremendously cross-culturally, the family as described earlier is not a universal institution but is better seen as arising only in particular political and economic contexts (Collier et al. 1982; Oppong 1982; Rapp 1982). Sociologist Rose Brewer (1988) points out that "the nuclear family imperative is rooted in upper-class, white patriarchal prerogatives that are unevenly shared across race and class lines" (p. 332). Because the construct of family/household emerged with the growth of the modern state and is rooted in assumptions about discrete public and private spheres, nuclear families characterized by sex-segregated gender roles are less likely to be found in African-American communities, where political life is radically different.

The family life of poor people challenges these assumptions about universal nuclear family forms because poor families do not exhibit the radical split equating private with home and public with work (Rapp 1982, 179). In order to survive, the family network must share the costs of providing for children. Privatization is less likely when survival depends on rapid circulation of limited resources. African-American families exhibit these fluid public/private boundaries because racial oppression has impoverished disproportionate numbers of Black families (Stack 1974). But they also invoke the Afrocentric worldview that offers alternative definitions of family and community (Surdarkasa 1981a, 1981b).

Like family, work is a highly contested category. In the following discussion of the distinction between work and measures of self, May Madison, a participant in John Gwaltney's study of inner-city African-Americans, alludes to the difference between work as an instrumental activity and work as something for self:

One very important difference between white people and black people is that white people think you *are* your work. . . . Now, a black person has more sense than that because he knows that what I am doing doesn't have anything to do with what I want to do or what I do when I am doing for myself. Now, black people think that my work is just what I have to do to get what I want. (Gwaltney 1980, 174)

Ms. Madison's perspective deconstructs definitions of work that grant white men more status and human worth because they are employed in better-paid occupations. She recognizes that work is a contested construct and that evaluating individual worth by the type of work performed is a questionable practice in systems based on race and gender inequality within segmented labor markets.

Work might be better conceptualized by examining the range of work that Black women actually perform. Work as alienated labor can be economically exploitative, physically demanding, and intellectually deadening—the type of work long associated with Black women's status as "mule." Alienated labor can be either paid, as was the case of domestic service, or unpaid, as was Black women's work under slavery or as is some work within families. But work can also be empowering and creative, even if it is physically challenging and appears to be demeaning. Exploitative wages that Black women were allowed to keep and use for their own benefit or work done out of love for the members of one's family can represent work that is empowering and/or creative. Again, this type of work can be either paid or unpaid.

What is the connection between Black women's work both in the labor market and in African-American family networks? Addressing this question for four key historical periods in Black political economy uses the lens of Black women's work to further an Afrocentric feminist analysis of social class and oppression.

THE PROCESS OF ENSLAVEMENT

Historically African-American families have had a different relationship to capitalist political economies than have middle-class, white families (Cox 1948; Davis 1981; Hogan 1984). This difference provides a context for understanding Black women's work in kin networks and in the wider political economy (Mullings 1986b).

During the transition from competitive to industrial capitalism which characterized the early nineteenth century, white urban middle-class families adopted self-contained nuclear household units. In contrast, the majority of African-American families were enslaved. These families had great difficulty maintaining private households in public spheres controlled by white slaveowners. Enslaved Africans were property (Burnham 1987), and they resisted the dehumanizing effects of slavery by recreating African notions of family as extended kin units (Webber 1978; Sobel 1979). Blood lines carefully monitored in West Africa were replaced by a notion of "blood" whereby enslaved Africans thought of themselves as part of an extended family/community consisting of their Black "brothers" and "sisters" (Gutman 1976). The entire slave community/family stood in opposition to the public sphere of a capitalist political economy controlled by elite white men. For Black women the domestic sphere encompassed a broad range of kin and community relations beyond the nuclear family household. The line separating the Black community from whites served as a more accurate boundary delineating public and private spheres for African-Americans than that separating Black households from the surrounding Black community.

Before enslavement, African women combined work and family without seeing a conflict between the two. In West African societies women routinely joined child care with their contributions to precapitalist political economies (Schildkrout 1983; Ware 1983). In agricultural societies dependent on female farmers, children accompanied their mothers to the fields. Women entrepreneurs took their children with them when conducting business in the marketplace. When old enough, children contributed to family-based production by caring for siblings, running errands, and generally helping out. Working did not detract from West African women's mothering. Instead, being economically productive and contributing to the family-based economy was an integral part of motherhood (Sudarkasa 1981a).

For enslaved African women in the United States, this basic relationship linking work and motherhood was retained, but with two fundamental changes. First, whereas African women worked on behalf of their families and children, enslaved African-American women's labor benefited their owners. Second, the nature of work performed was altered. Women did not retain authority over their time, technology, work mates, or type or amount of work they performed. In essence, the fundamental shift in women's work meant that West African women were forced to serve as economically exploited, politically powerless units of labor.

Gender roles were similarly shaped under slavery. Black women generally performed the same work as men. This enabled them to continue West African traditions whereby women were not limited to devalued domestic labor (Davis 1981; Jones 1985; D. White 1985). This similarity of work coupled with the harshness of racial oppression for all African-Americans suggests that a general equality existed between Black men and women (Webber 1978; Davis 1981).

Unlike African political economies, where women's labor benefited their lineage group and their children, under slavery neither men nor women got to keep what they produced. Slavery also established the racial division of labor whereby African-Americans were relegated to dirty, manual, nonintellectual jobs. As Maria Stewart pointed out, "the Americans have practiced nothing but head-work these 200 years, and we have done their drudgery. And is it not high time for us to imitate their examples, and practice head-work too, and keep what we have got, and get what we can?" (Richardson 1987, 38). In spite of slavery's burdens, African-Americans did not perceive work as the problem but, rather, the exploitation inherent in the work they performed. A saying among enslaved Africans, "it's a poor dog that won't wag its own tail," alludes to popular perceptions among Blacks that whites were lazy and did not value work as much as African-Americans themselves.

Black women's work affected the organization of child care. Perceptions of motherhood and child care as an occupation in the home comparable to male occupations in the public sector popularized by the cult of domesticity never became widespread among the majority of African-American women (Mullings 1986b). Instead, women organized communal child care arrangements such that a few women were responsible for caring for all children too young to work and women as a group felt accountable for one another's children (D. White 1985).

African-American women's experiences as mothers have been shaped by the dominant group's efforts to harness Black women's sexuality and fertility to a system of capitalist exploitation. Efforts to control Black women's reproduction were important to the maintenance of the race, class, and gender inequality characterizing the slave order in at least three ways. First, the biological notions of race underpinning the racial subordination of the slave system required so-called racial purity in order to be effective. Since children followed the condition of their mothers, children born of enslaved Black women were slaves. Forbidding Black men to have sexual relations with white women eliminated the possibility that children of African descent would be born to white mothers. Motherhood and racism were symbolically intertwined, and controlling the sexuality and fertility of both African-American and white women was essential in reproducing notions of "race" as a social and cultural entity (King 1973; Hoch 1979; Mosse 1985).

Second, motherhood as an institution occupies a special place in transmitting values to children about their proper place. On one hand, a mother can foster her children's oppression if she teaches them to believe in their own inferiority. As noted African-American educator Carter G. Woodson contends, "if you can control a man's thinking you do not have to worry about his actions" (1933, 84). On the other hand, the relationship between mothers and children can serve as a private sphere in which cultures of resistance and everyday forms of resistance are learned (Caulfield 1974; Scott 1985). When Black slave mothers taught their children to trust their own self-definitions and value themselves, they offered a powerful tool for resisting oppression.

Finally, controlling Black women's reproduction was essential to the creation and perpetuation of capitalist class relations. Slavery benefited certain segments of the population by economically exploiting others. As Black feminist intellectual Frances Ellen Watkins Harper argued, "How can we pamper our appetites upon luxuries drawn from reluctant fingers. Oh, could slavery exist long if it did not sit on a commercial throne?" (Sterling 1984, 160). Under such a system in which the control of property is fundamental, enslaved African women were valuable commodities. Slaveowners controlled Black women's labor and commodified Black women's bodies as units of capital. Moreover, as mothers, Black women's fertility produced the children who increased their owners' property and labor force (Davis 1981; Burnham 1987).

Efforts to control Black women's sexuality were tied directly to slaveowners' efforts to increase the fertility of their female slaves. Historian Deborah Gray White (1985) claims that "slave masters wanted adolescent girls to have children, and to this end they practiced a passive, though insidious kind of breeding" (p. 98). Techniques such as assigning pregnant women lighter workloads, giving pregnant women more attention and rations, and rewarding prolific women with bonuses were all employed to increase Black women's fertility. Punitive measures were also used. Infertile women could expect to be treated "like barren sows and be passed from one unsuspecting buyer to the next" (D. White 1985, 101).

The relative security that often accompanied motherhood served to reinforce its importance. Childbearing was a way for enslaved Black women to anchor themselves in a given location for an extended period and maintain enduring relationships with husbands, family, and friends. Given the short life expectancy of slave women—33.6 years—and the high mortality rates of Black children—from 1850 to 1860 fewer than two of three Black children survived to the age of ten—the enslaved woman's ability to bear many healthy children was often the critical element in the length and stability of slave marriages (Giddings 1984). Similarly, the refusal of women to bear children and cases of Black infanticide can be interpreted as acts of resistance (Hine and Wittenstein 1981).

Deborah Gray White contends that slaveholders' efforts to increase fertility elevated motherhood over marriage and fostered the continued centrality of women in African-American family networks:

> Relationships between mother and child . . . superseded those between husband and wife. Slaveholder practice encouraged the primacy of the mother-child relationship, and in the mores of the slave community motherhood ranked above marriage. . . . Women in their roles as mothers were the central figures in the nuclear slave family. (1985, 159)

Black women's centrality in Black family networks should not be confused with matriarchal or female-dominated family units (Collins 1989). The conceptual assumption of the matriarchy thesis is that someone must "rule" the household in order for it to function effectively. Neither Black men nor Black women ruled Black family networks (Davis 1981; Burnham 1987). Rather, African-Americans' relationship to the slave political economy made it unlikely that either patriarchal or matriarchal domination could take root.

THE TRANSITION TO "FREE" LABOR

For African-Americans the period between emancipation and subsequent migrations to southern and northern cities was characterized by two distinct models of community. Each offered a different version of the connections between work and family. Within dominant white society the model of community reflected capitalist market economies of competitive, industrial, and monopoly capitalism (Baran and Sweezy 1966; Braverman 1974). Firmly rooted in an exchange-based marketplace with its accompanying assumptions of rational economic decision making and white male control of the marketplace, this model of community stresses the rights of individuals to make decisions in their own self-interest, regardless of the impact on the larger society. Composed of a collection of unequal individuals who compete for greater shares of money as the medium of exchange, this model of community legitimates relations of domination either by denying they exist or by treating them as inevitable but unimportant (Hartsock 1983b).

While enslaved, African-Americans paradoxically were central to yet existed largely outside the market economy and its version of community. Upon emancipation, Blacks became wage laborers and were thrust into these exchange relationships in which individual gain was placed ahead of collective good. Anna Julia Cooper describes this larger setting in which African-Americans found themselves as the Accumulative Period, and challenged its basic assumptions about community and women's role in it:

> At the most trying time of what we have called the Accumulative Period, when internecine war, originated through man's love of gain and his determination to subordinate national interests and black men's rights alike to the considerations of personal profit and loss, was drenching our country with its own best blood, who shall recount the name and fame of the women on both sides of the senseless strife. (Cooper 1892, 128)

Cooper's ideas are key in that they not only link racism, economic exploitation after emancipation, and the violence needed to maintain both, but they clearly label the public sphere and its community as a male-defined arena. By asking, "who shall recount the name and fame of the women?" she questions the role of gender in structuring women's subordination generally, and Black women's work and family roles in particular.

During this period, revitalized political and economic oppression of African-Americans in the South influenced Black actions and ideas about family and community. Notions such as equating family with extended family, of treating community as family, and of seeing dealings with whites as elements of public discourse and dealings with Blacks as part of family business endured. As a result, African-American definitions of community were distinct from public, market-driven, exchange-based community models. Whether adhered to as a remnant of the African past or responding to the exigencies of political and economic disenfranchisement in the post-Reconstruction South, Black communities as places of collective effort and will stood in contrast to the public, market-driven, exchange-based dominant political economy in which they were situated (Bethel 1981).

For African-American women the issue was less one of economic equality with husbands and more the adequacy of overall family income. Denying Black men a family wage meant that women continued working and that motherhood as a privatized, female "occupation" never predominated in the African-American communities (Dill 1988b). Communal child care within extended families continued (Martin and Martin 1978; Jones 1985). Segregation fostered rigid boundaries between African-Americans and whites such that the public/private oppositional dichotomy characterizing racial discourse hardened while fluid boundaries among Black households in the Black family/community continued. Within African-American communities social-class-specific gender ideology developed during this period (Higginbotham 1989).

For at least 75 years after emancipation, the vast majority of Black families worked in southern agriculture (Jones 1985). Black women's work in the public, male-defined sphere of exchange relations took two types. The majority of Black women worked in the fields, with the male head of the extended family unit receiving the wages earned by the family unit. Such work was hard and exhausting and represented little change from the work done by enslaved African-American women. Sara Brooks began full-time work in the fields at age 11 and remembers, "we never was lazy cause we used to really work. We used to work like mens. Oh, fight sometime, fuss sometime, but worked on" (Simonsen 1986, 39).

The other primary occupation for Black women's wage labor was domestic work. Young Black girls were prepared by their families for domestic work. An 87-year-old North Carolina woman remembers her training: "No girl I know wasn't trained for work out by ten. You washed, watched, and whipped somebody the day you stopped crawling. From the time a girl can stand, she's being made to work" (Clark-Lewis 1985, 7). Such work was low paid and exposed Black girls and women to the constant threat of sexual harassment. One African-American woman describes the lack of protection for Black women domestic workers in the South: "I remember . . . I lost my place because I refused to let the madam's husband kiss me. . . . When my husband went to the man who had insulted me, the man cursed him, and slapped him, and—had him arrested!" (Lerner 1972, 155–56). Even though she testified in court, her husband was fined $25 and was told by the presiding judge, "this court will never take the word of a nigger against the word of a white man" (p. 156).

The sexual harassment of African-American women by white men contributed to images of Black women as fair game for all men. The difficulty of the environment prompted one southern Black woman to remonstrate:

> We poor colored women wage-earners in the South are fighting a terrible battle. . . . On the one hand, we are assailed by white men, and on the other hand, we are assailed by black men, who should be our natural protectors; and, whether in the cook kitchen, at the washtub, over the sewing machine, behind the baby carriage, or at the ironing board, we are little more than pack horses, beasts of burden, slaves! (Lerner 1972, 157)

African-American women who were the wives and daughters of able-bodied men withdrew from both field labor and domestic service in order to concentrate on domestic duties in their own homes. In doing so they were "severely criticized by whites for removing themselves from field labor because they were seen to be aspiring to a model of womanhood that was inappropriate to them" (Dill 1988b, 422). Black women wanted to withdraw from the labor force, not to duplicate middle-class white women's cult of domesticity but, rather, to strengthen the political and economic position of their families. Their actions can be seen as a sustained effort to remove themselves from the exploited labor force in order to return the value of their labor to their families and to find relief from the sexual harassment they endured in the marketplace. While many women tried to leave the paid labor force, the limited opportunities available to African-American men made it virtually impossible for the majority of Black families to survive on Black male wages alone. Even though she was offered work only as a maid, Elsa Barkley Brown's college-educated mother was fortunate. From Brown's standpoint, her mother's "decision to be a wife and mother first in a world which defined Black women in so many other ways, the decision to make her family the most important priority, was an act of resistance" (1986, 11). Far too many Black women could not make this choice—they continued to work, and their work profoundly affected African-American family life, communities, and the women themselves (Bethel 1981; Jones 1985).

URBANIZATION AND DOMESTIC WORK

Black women's move to southern and northern cities in the early 1900s continued virtually unabated until after World War II. Migration stimulated substantial shifts in Black women's labor market activities as well as changes in African-American family patterns and community organization. While racial segregation delimited African-American from white physical space, gender relations within Black communities delimited female from male space. Male space included the streets, barber shops, and pool halls: female arenas consisted of households and churches. "Women, who blurred the physical boundaries of gender, did so at the jeopardy of respectability within their communities" (Higginbotham 1989, 59).

Black women migrants encountered urban labor markets segmented along lines of race and gender (Gordon et al. 1982). For the vast majority of African-American women, urbanization meant migration out of agricultural work and into domestic work. In 1910, 38.5 percent of all employed Black women were domestic workers. By 1940 that number had risen to 59.9 percent (Higginbotham 1983).

Black women's confinement in domestic service has attracted the attention of Black women intellectuals who have investigated key dimensions of this special occupational niche. Unlike the life histories of the countless enslaved and emancipated Black women who worked in the fields, Black feminist research on Black domestic workers allows a closer view both of how African-American women perceived their work and of the actions they undertook to resist its exploitative and dehumanizing aspects.

One benefit of urbanization was that it allowed Black domestic workers to shift the conditions of their work from that of live-in servant to day work.

A common migration pattern was for Black girls to train for domestic work in the South by doing chores and taking care of siblings and then go to cities of the North around age ten to assist working relatives (Clark-Lewis 1985). At first girls might take care of their relatives' children. Although it often took years to accomplish, young women eventually found employment in day work. Moving to a larger marketplace where domestics could leave employers when demands were inappropriate allowed African-American women to make the transition from live-in to day work. One 83-year-old respondent in Elizabeth Clark-Lewis's study recounts how she viewed this shift as a move toward better working conditions: "The living-in jobs just kept you running; never stopped. Day or night you'd be getting something for somebody. You'd serve them. It was never a minute's peace. . . . But when I went out days on my jobs, I'd get my work done and be gone. I guess that's it. This work had a end" (Clark-Lewis 1985, 1).

While an improvement, the shift to day work maintained some of the more negative features of the employer/employee relationship. In spite of their removal from the particular form control took in the South, domestic workers in northern cities were economically exploited even under the best of circumstances. At its worst, domestic work approximated conditions the women left behind in the South. Florence Rice describes how the 1930s New York City "Bronx slave market" operated, where women stood in an assigned spot and waited for employers to drive by and offer them day work: "I always remember my domestic days. Some of the women, when they didn't want to pay, they'd accuse you of stealing. . . . It was like intimidation" (Lerner 1972, 275). Although sexual harassment was less pervasive, it too remained a problem. Ms. Rice remembers another male employer who "picked me up and said his wife was ill and then when I got there his wife wasn't there and he wanted to have an affair" (p. 275).

Judith Rollins (1985) contends that what makes domestic work more "profoundly exploitative than other comparable occupations" is the precise element that makes it unique: the personal relationship between employer and employee. Rollins reports that employers do not rank work perfor- mance as their highest priority in evaluating domestic workers. Rather, the "personality of the worker and the kinds of relationships employers were able to establish with them were as or more important considerations" (p. 156).

Deference mattered, and those women who were submissive or who most successfully played the role of obedient servant were most highly valued by their employers, regardless of the quality of the work performed. When domestic worker Hannah Nelson reports, "most people who have worked in service have to learn to talk at great length about nothing," she identified the roles domestics must play in order to satisfy their employers' perceptions of a good Black domestic. She continues, "I never have been very good at that, so I don't speak, normally. . . . Some people I have' worked for think I am slow-witted because I talk very little on the job" (Gwaltney 1980, 6).

Employers used a variety of means to structure domestic work's power relationship and solicit the deference behavior they desired in their domestic employees. Techniques of linguistic deference included addressing domestics by their first names, calling them "girls," and requiring that the domestic call the employer "Ma'am." Employers routinely questioned domestics about their lifestyle, questions they would hesitate to ask members of their own social circle. Gifts of used clothing and other household items highlighted the economic inequality separating domestic and employer. Employers used domestics as confidantes, another behavior that reinforced the notion that domestics were outsiders (Rollins 1985).

Physical markers reinforced the deference relationship. One technique was to require that domestics wear uniforms. One respondent in Clark-Lewis's study explains why her employers liked uniforms: "Them uniforms just seemed to make them know you was theirs. Some say you wore them to show different jobs you was doing. This in grey, other serving in black. But mostly them things just showed you was always at they beck and call. Really that's all them things means!" (Clark-Lewis 1985, 16). The use of space was also a major device in structuring deference behaviors. Domestics were confined to one area of the house, usually the kitchen, and were expected to make themselves invisible when caught in other areas of the house by members of the employer's family. Judith Rollins recounts her reactions to being objectified in this fashion, to being treated as invisible while her employers had a conversation around her:

> It was this aspect of servitude I found to be one of the strongest affronts to my dignity as a human being. To Mrs. Thomas and her son, I became invisible; their conversation was private with me, the black servant, in the room as it would have been with no one in the room. . . . These gestures of ignoring my presence were not, I think, intended as insults; they were expressions of the employers' ability to annihilate the humanness and even, at times, the very existence of me, a servant and a black woman. (Rollins 1985, 209)

Some African-American women were fortunate enough to locate work in manufacturing. In the South, Black women entered tobacco factories, cotton mills, and flour manufacturing. Some of the dirtiest jobs in these industries were offered to African-American women. In the cotton mills Black women were employed as common laborers in the yards, as waste gatherers and as scrubbers of machinery (Glenn 1985). With northern migration, some

Black women entered factory employment, primarily in steam laundries and the rest in unmechanized jobs as sweepers, cleaners, and rag pickers. Regardless of their location, African-American women faced discrimination (Terborg-Penn 1985). For example, Luanna Cooper, an employee for the Winston Leaf Tobacco Storage company, describes her reactions to the effort to organize segregated unions in her plant: "They're trying to have jimcrow unions. But I'm telling you jimcrow unions aren't good. They wanted me to join. I told them: 'I get jimcrow free. I won't pay for that' " (Lerner 1972, 268).

The shift to day work among domestic workers and the incorporation of some Black women into the manufacturing sector paralleled changes in African-American family and community structures. Even though the hours were long and the pay low in the majority of occupations held by Black women, they did have more time to devote to their families and communities than that available to live-in domestic workers. During the first wave of urbanization, African-Americans recreated the types of communities they had known in their southern rural communities (Gutman 1976). De facto segregation in housing and in the labor market meant that African-Americans continued to live in self-contained communities even after migration to northern cities. As a result, the public/private split separating Black communities from what were frequently hostile white neighborhoods remained a salient feature framing Black women's work and family relationships. The cooperative networks among African-American women which were created under slavery and sustained in the rural South endured. Black women domestic workers who rode buses together shared vital information essential to their survival as domestic workers and, on occasion, attempted unionization (Terborg-Penn 1985). Neighbors took care of one anothers' children, and churches typically formed the core of many Black women's community activities (Clark-Lewis 1985; Dill 1988a)

BLACK WOMEN'S WORK AND THE POST-WORLD WAR II POLITICAL ECONOMY

As long as African-Americans lived in self-contained, segregated communities, Afrocentric notions of family and community endured. In the midtwentieth century the post–World War II period brought a shift in this relationship between work and family (Collins 1986a; Brewer 1988).

Dramatic changes in the post–World War II political economy of African-American communities have been stimulated by several factors. One is the restructuring of urban labor markets which has accompanied trends such as job export to nonunionized American locations and foreign markets, job deskilling, the shift from manufacturing to service occupations, and job creation in suburban communities (Baran and Sweezy 1966; Braverman 1974; Gordon et al. 1982; Wilson 1987). Another is the increasing economic marginalization of African-Americans in urban economies, as evidenced in Black unemployment rates double those of whites, and by the increasing dependence of Black households on Aid to Families with Dependent Children (Hogan 1984; Wilson 1987). Changing attitudes in wider society toward the normative nuclear family as expressed in higher divorce rates, more single-parent households, and a rising number of out-of-wedlock births for all groups in the society represent yet another factor (Burnham 1985; Collins 1986a; Claude 1986; Wilson 1987; Brewer 1988).

As a result of these factors, the Black community has become more stratified by social class.[2] A comfortable yet vulnerable Black middle class and a sizable working class segmented by the ability to find steady, well-paying work have emerged. Best estimates place between 25 and 30 percent of African-American families in the middle class (Pinkney 1984, 102). This leaves approximately 70 to 75 percent of African-Americans in the working class. The one-third of African-Americans identified as living below the official poverty line represents the most economically marginalized segment of the Black working class. Each social class has a distinctive relationship to the advanced capitalist welfare state. These relationships frame the changing nature of work and family for African-American women.

These dramatic changes in how racial inequality has been structured should not obscure the overall stability of racial oppression. In 1987 the median Black family income of $18,100 represented 56 percent of the median white family income of $32,270 (U.S. Department of Commerce 1989). In 1985 approximately one of every three African-Americans lived below the official poverty line, as compared with one of every ten whites (U.S. Department of Commerce 1986). These measures of inequality remain constant in spite of emerging social class differences.

Historically the classic pattern of employment for African-American men and women has been higher-paying yet less secure work for Black men as contrasted with lower-paying, more plentiful work for Black women. For example, Black men employed in low-skilled manufacturing occupations typically receive higher wages than their wives working in domestic service. But Black men are more vulnerable to layoffs, and although they make higher wages, few guarantees exist that their wages will be consistently available to their families. In contrast, Black women receive substantially lower wages but can count on receiving them. This classic pattern of exploitation, differentiated by gender, has often been misrepresented in arguments suggesting that Black women or Black men have a labor market "advantage" over the other. What these approaches fail to realize is that both African-American women and men have been disadvantaged in the labor market, with gender differences in employment structuring distinctive patterns of economic vulnerability.

Increased access to managerial and professional positions enabled sizable numbers of African-American individuals and families to move into the middle class. In the post–World War II political economy, owners of capital and labor, the two groups originally forwarded in class conflict theories, have been joined by a new middle class. Members of the new middle class work for owners of productive property just as blue-collar workers do, but they earn generous incomes and enjoy substantial prestige. This new middle class is not merely an arbitrary range along a status scale—it is a genuine class with interests in opposition to the working class (Vanneman and Cannon 1987).

The emerging Black middle class occupies a contradictory location in the American political economy. As is the case for their white counterparts, being middle class requires Black professionals and managers to enter into specific social relations with owners of capital and with workers. In particular, the middle class dominates labor and is itself subordinate to capital. It is this simultaneous dominance and subordination that puts it in the "middle" (Vanneman and Cannon 1987, 57). Like owners, it exercises economic control. Professionals and managers also exercise political controls over the conditions of their own work and that of workers. Finally, members of the new middle class exercise ideological control of knowledge: they are the planners of work and framers of society's ideas.

On all three dimensions of middle-class power—economic, political, and ideological—the Black middle class differs from its white counterpart. Persistent racial discrimination means that Black middle-class families are less economically secure than members of the white middle class (Pinkney 1984). Members of the Black middle class, most of whom became middle class through social mobility from working-class origins, may express more ambivalence concerning their function as controllers of working-class Blacks. While some aspire to manage working-class Blacks, others aim to liberate them from racial oppression and poverty. Similarly, though many middle-class Blacks defend the ideological constructions of the dominant group, others, such as many Black feminist intellectuals, use their minds to challenge race, gender, and class ideologies.

When the traditional gender differences in Black employment patterns are combined with the economic, political, and ideological vulnerability of the Black middle class caused by race, some interesting patterns emerge for African-American women. Black women and men both share the employment vulnerability of being more excluded that whites from these occupations. Fewer Black men have such positions, but when they do get them they acquire higher-paying, higher-status positions. In contrast, greater numbers of Black women than men work in professional and managerial positions, but in lower-paying, lower-status occupations.

For Black women, most of whom are not born into the Black middle class but who have recently arrived in it through social class mobility, dealing with the demands of work and family can be unsettling (Dumas 1980). Consider the case of Leanita McClain, a Black woman journalist raised in segregated Chicago public housing who eventually became a feature writer for a major Chicago newspaper (McClaurin-Allen 1989). In a widely cited piece entitled "The Middle-Class Black's Burden," Ms. McClain laments, "I am not comfortably middle class; I am uncomfortably middle class. I have made it, but where?" (Page 1986, 13). A substantial source of Ms. McClain's frustration stemmed from her marginal status in a range of settings. She notes, "my life abounds in incongruities. . . . Sometimes when I wait at the bus stop with my attaché case, I meet my aunt getting off the bus with other cleaning ladies on their way to do my neighbor's floors" (p.13). No wonder Ms. McClain felt compelled to say, "I am a member of the black middle class who has had it with being patted on the head by white hands and slapped in the face by black hands for my success" (p. 12).

Black women's employment patterns may have significant effects on Black middle-class families especially single-parent households. The smaller number of Black men than Black women in professional and managerial positions represents one important issue facing Black heterosexual women interested in intraracial marriage. This sex ratio imbalance may contribute to an increase in female-headed households among middle-class Black women. Given that separated and divorced Black women professionals are much less likely to remarry than their white counterparts, higher rates of separation and divorce may become a special problem for married Black women professionals. Other factors may also influence the growth of single-parent households among Black professional women. One issue concerns whether African-American women will choose to become mothers when faced with the absence of a suitable marital partner. Another factor is the likely decline in marriages between Black women in professional and managerial jobs and Black men in other segments of the labor market. Another factor may be an increasing tendency by both Black heterosexual women and Black lesbians to head their own households and create alternative family arrangements.

Black working-class families are similarly affected by changing employment patterns. Black women are heavily concentrated in clerical work (50.1 percent), whereas Black men are clustered in factory work (43.2 percent). One of every four African-American women and men in this sector is a skilled crafts worker. The projected patterns of growth for these occupational categories are quite different. Factory work is declining, a trend that is especially problematic for Black men. In contrast, Black women clerical workers are in a growing occupational area.

Studies examining the interaction of race and gender in structuring the work experiences of working-class Black women are sorely needed. Clerical work and other administrative support positions often involve deference relationships reminiscent of Judith Rollins's (1985) study of Black domestic workers. Consider Alice Walker's experiences when trying to visit Dessie Woods, a Black woman incarcerated in the Georgia penal system for defending herself against a white rapist. Walker describes her arrival at the prison, where she was turned away, not by white male guards, but by a Black woman very much like herself:

> We look at each other hard. And I "recognize" her, too. She is very black and her neck is stiff and her countenance has been softened by the blows. All day long, while her children are supported by earnings here, she sits isolated in this tiny glass entranceway, surrounded by white people who have hired her, as they always have, to do their dirty work for them. It is no accident that she is in this prison, too. (Walker 1988, 23).

The disappearance of well-paying manufacturing jobs for Black working-class men suggests that the dual-income, working-class family is becoming less of an option for young African-Americans. The alternative open to past generations of Blacks—intact marriages based on reasonably steady, adequately paid jobs for Black men and reliable yet lesser-paid jobs for Black women—is less available in the advanced capitalist welfare state.

While Black working-class women, especially those in clerical work, are more likely to find steady employment, the income of Black working-class wives cannot compensate for the loss of Black men's incomes. Black working-class families may experience an increase in female-headed households, but for very different reasons from those stimulating a similar trend in the Black middle class. Aggravated by Black men's inability to find well-paying work, rates of separation and divorce may increase, or young Blacks may not be able to marry in the first place. For many Black working-class families, the economic vulnerability of Black men is one fundamental factor spurring increasing poverty among Black working-class women (Burnham 1985; Claude 1986).

Low-income Black families form the economically marginalized, vulnerable segment of the Black working class. Labor market trends as well as changes in federal policies toward the poor have affected this group (Zinn 1989). Ironically, occupational gender differences between Black women and Black men are becoming less pronounced among poor African-Americans. In 1980, 32 percent of Black women and 29 percent of Black men worked in jobs characterized by low wages, job instability, and poor working conditions. These jobs are growing rapidly, with an increasing need for cooks, waitresses, waiters, laundry workers, health aides, and domestic servants to service the needs of affluent middle-class families. While plentiful, many of these jobs are in neighborhoods far from the inner-city communities where poor Black women live. Moreover, few of these jobs offer the wages, stability, or advancement potential of disappearing manufacturing jobs.

The work performed by employed poor Black women parallels their traditional duties in domestic service. In contrast to prior eras, when domestic service was confined to private households, contemporary cooking, cleaning, and child care has been routinized and decentralized in the growing service industry of fast food, cleaning services, and day care centers. Black women perform similar work, but in different settings. The location may have changed, but the treatment of Black women parallels relationships of domination reminiscent of private domestic work. Mabel Lincoln, an inner-city resident, describes how the world looks to her as a working woman:

> If you are a woman slinging somebody else's hash and busting somebody else's suds or doing whatsoever you might do to keep yourself from being a tramp or a willing slave, you will be called out of your name and asked out of your clothes. In this world most people will take whatever they think you can give. It don't matter whether they want it or not, whether they need it or not, or how wrong it is for them to ask for it. (Gwaltney 1980, 68)

Many Black women turn to the informal labor market and to government transfer payments to avoid being called out of their names and asked out of their clothes. In 1980 approximately one-half of all Black women age 16 and over were not in the formal labor force. School attendance, child care responsibilities, retirement, and poor health are all factors affecting nonworking women (McGhee 1984). A considerable proportion supported themselves through varying combinations of low-wage jobs and government transfer payments such as Social Security and Aid to Families with Dependent Children, payments that reduced their dependence on the informal economy.

The employment vulnerability of working-class African-Americans in the post–World War II political economy, the relative employment equality of poor Black women and men, and the gender-specific patterns of dependence on the informal economy all have substantial implications for low-income Black family patterns. One effect has been the growth of female-headed households. That such households are increasing in low-income Black communities (Pinkney [1984] suggests that as much as 70 percent of low-income Black households are headed by women) is commonly accepted. But the more alarming trend is the increasing poverty of African-American women and children living in such households. In 1985, 50 percent of Black families headed by women were below the official poverty line (U.S. Department of Commerce 1986). The situation is more extreme for young African-American women. In 1986, 86 percent of families headed by Black women between the ages of 15 and 24 lived below the poverty line (Simms 1988).

It is important to distinguish explanations of the growing poverty of Black women which stress their preexisting social class position under advanced capitalism (see, for example, Blumberg and Garcia [1977] and Steady [1981, 1987]), from explanations such as "feminization of poverty" analyses prominent in feminist thought.[3] As Linda Burnham (1985) point out, "while poverty has not been 'feminized,' it is true that increasing numbers of working class and minority women are sinking into impoverishment. This is a subtle but crucial distinction" (p. 18). Growing poverty among Black women is attributable less to being a divorce away from poverty and more to the "transformation of the economy and conservative social policies leading to a dismantling of the welfare state" (Ladner 1986, 14). Effects of welfare policies on poor Black women are especially troublesome (Valentine 1981; Pearce 1983; Zinn 1989).

The increase in unmarried Black adolescent parents is only one indication of the effects that changes in the broader political economy are having on work and family patterns of poor Black women. Rates of adolescent pregnancy are actually *decreasing* among young Black women. The real change has been a parallel decrease in marital rates of Black adolescents, a decision linked directly to perceived opportunities to support and sustain an independent household (Simms 1988). A sizable proportion of Black female-headed households are created by unmarried adolescent mothers. This decline in marital rates, a post–World War II trend that accelerated after 1960, is part of changes in African-American community structures overall (Wilson 1987). The communal child care networks of the slave era, the extended family arrangements of the rural South, the importance of grandmothers in child care, and even the recreation of Black community structures during the first wave of urbanization appear to be eroding for poor Black women. These shifts portend major problems for African-American women and point to a continuation of Black women's oppression, but structured through new institutional arrangements.

The effects of these changes are convincingly demonstrated in a replication study conducted by Ladner and Gourdine (1984) of *Tomorrow's Tomorrow*, Joyce Ladner's (1972) ground-breaking study of Black women adolescents. The earlier study examined poor Black teenaged women's values toward motherhood and Black womanhood. The women in the original study encountered the common experiences of urban poverty—they became mothers quite young, lived in substandard housing, attended inferior schools, and generally had to grow up quickly in order to survive. But in spite of the harshness of their environments, the girls in the earlier sample still "had high hopes and dreams that their futures would be positive and productive" (Ladner and Gourdine 1984, 24).

The findings from the replication study are quite different. Ladner and Gourdine maintain that "the assessments the teenagers and their mothers made of the socioeconomic conditions and their futures are harsher and bleaker than a similar population a generation ago" (p. 24). In talking with young grandmothers, all of whom looked older than they were even though the majority were in their 30s and the youngest was age 29, Ladner and Gourdine found that all became single parents through divorce or never being married. The strong Black mothers of prior generations of Black women were not in evidence. Instead, Ladner and Gourdine found that the grandmothers complained about their own unmet emotional and social needs. They appeared to feel "powerless in coping with the demands made by their children. They comment frequently that their children show them no respect, do not listen to their advice, and place little value on their role as parents" (p.23).

Unlike prior eras when Black women's work as "mules uh de world" more uniformly structured Black women's oppression, social class differences increasingly distinguish Black women's experiences with race and gender oppression in the post–World War II era. All African-American women encounter the common theme of having our work and family experiences shaped by the interlocking nature of race, gender, and class oppression. But this commonality is experienced differently by middle-class women such as Leanita McClain and by working-class women such as Mabel Lincoln. Even more ominous are the potentially negative relationships that might develop among Black women of different social classes because of these changes. In prior eras the precarious political and social position of the small numbers of middle-class Black women encouraged them to work on behalf of "race uplift" and fostered racial solidarity among all African-American women. Will middle-class Black women continue to value racial solidarity with their working-class sisters, especially those in poverty, or will they use their newly acquired positions to perpetuate inequalities of social class? Large numbers of poor Black women working as cooks, laundry workers, and in other service occupations serve not only white middle-class individuals but Black ones as well. Countless others living in inner-city neighborhoods are isolated and encounter few middle-class Black women in their daily lives. How will these poor Black women view their more privileged sisters?

There has never been a uniformity of experience among African-American women, and there is less uniformity today. What remains as a challenge to Black feminist scholars is to rearticulate these new and emerging patterns of institutional oppression that differentially affect middle-class and working-class Black women. If this does not occur, each group may in fact become instrumental in fostering the other's oppression.

NOTES

1. Elizabeth Spelman (1982) rejects additive approaches to conceptualizing oppression: "An additive analysis treats the oppression of a black woman in a sexist and racist society as if it were a *further* burden than her oppression in a sexist but non-racist society, when, in fact, it is a *different* burden" (p. 43). Similarly, Brittan and Maynard (1984) argue that separate oppressions cannot be merged under one "grand theory of oppression." Omi and Winant (1986) warn against the tendency to subsume one type of oppression under another—for example, of seeing everything as stemming from class structure. For an incisive discussion of multiple jeopardy as an alternative model, see King (1988).

2. The definition of social class that I use in this section derives from class conflict models, especially those based in labor market segmentation theory (Braverman 1974; Gordon et al. 1982; Vanneman and Cannon 1987). For an extended discussion of labor market segmentation and Black social class structure, see Collins (1986a).

3. Linda Burnham (1985) suggests that the "idea that poverty is being 'feminized' presents a highly distorted picture of the general dynamics that are at the source of poverty in the U.S." (p. 14). By taking an additive approach to oppression, such approaches view poverty as a female problem that is quantitatively intensified for Black women. But as part of a racial group that has experienced traditional racial oppression, the social class patterns of Black women are quite distinct from those of white women. This class difference is key to understanding the statistical disparity between white and Black women, and Black women's poverty is not simply an additional measure of women's oppression. Claude (1986), equally critical of the feminization of poverty thesis, points out that Black female-headed households are not newly poor and that the origins of poverty for white women are profoundly different from those for Black women.

Chapter 4

MAMMIES, MATRIARCHS, AND OTHER CONTROLLING IMAGES

Called Matriarch, Emasculator and Hot Momma. Sometimes Sister, Pretty
Baby, Auntie, Mammy and Girl. Called Unwed Mother, Welfare Recipient
and Inner City Consumer. The Black American Woman has had to admit
that while nobody knew the troubles she saw, everybody, his brother and
his dog, felt qualified to explain her, even to herself.
                                              —Trudier Harris 1982, 4

Race, class, and gender oppression could not continue without powerful
ideological justifications for their existence. As Cheryl Gilkes contends,
"Black women's assertiveness and their use of every expression of racism
to launch multiple assaults against the entire fabric of inequality have been
a consistent, multifaceted threat to the status quo. As punishment, Black
women have been assaulted with a variety of negative images" (1983a,
294). Portraying African-American women as stereotypical mammies,
matriarchs, welfare recipients, and hot mommas has been essential to
the political economy of domination fostering Black women's oppression.
Challenging these controlling images has long been a core theme in Black
feminist thought.

    As part of a generalized ideology of domination, these controlling images
of Black womanhood take on special meaning because the authority to

myths

67

define these symbols is a major instrument of power. In order to exercise power, elite white men and their representatives must be in a position to manipulate appropriate symbols concerning Black women. They may do so by exploiting already existing symbols, or they may create new ones relevant to their needs (Patterson 1982). Hazel Carby suggests that the objective of stereotypes is "not to reflect or represent a reality but to function as a disguise, or mystification, of objective social relations" (1987, 22). These controlling images are designed to make racism, sexism, and poverty appear to be natural, normal, and an inevitable part of everyday life.

Even when the political and economic conditions that originally generated controlling images disappear, such images prove remarkably tenacious because they not only keep Black women oppressed but are key in maintaining interlocking systems of race, class, and gender oppression. The status of African-American women as outsiders or strangers becomes the point from which other groups define their normality. Ruth Shays, a Black inner-city resident, describes how the standpoint of a subordinate group is discredited: "It will not kill people to hear the truth, but they don't like it and they would much rather hear it from one of their own than from a stranger. Now, to white people your colored person is always a stranger. Not only that, we are supposed to be dumb strangers, so we can't tell them anything!" (Gwaltney 1980, 29). As the "Others" of society who can never really belong, strangers threaten the moral and social order. But they are simultaneously essential for its survival because those individuals who stand at the margins of society clarify its boundaries. African-American women, by not belonging, emphasize the significance of belonging.

THE OBJECTIFICATION OF BLACK WOMEN AS THE OTHER

Black feminist critic Barbara Christian asserts that in America, "the enslaved African woman became the basis for the definition of our society's *Other*" (1985, 160). Maintaining images of Black women as the Other provides ideological justification for race, gender, and class oppression. Certain basic ideas crosscut all three systems. Claimed by Black feminist theorist Bell Hooks to be "the central ideological component of all systems of domination in Western society," one such idea is either/or dichotomous thinking (1984, 29). Either/or dichotomous thinking categorizes people, things, and ideas in terms of their difference from one another (Keller 1985, 8). For example, the terms in the dichotomies black/white (Richards 1980; Irele 1983), male/female (Eisenstein 1983), reason/emotion (Hoschschild 1975; Halpin 1989), culture/nature (Asante 1987), fact/opinion (Westkott

1979; Bellah 1983), mind/body (Spelman 1982), and subject/object (Halpin 1989) gain meaning only in *relation* to their counterparts.

Another basic idea concerns the relationship between notions of differences in either/or dichotomous thinking and objectification. In either/or dichotomous thinking, difference is defined in oppositional terms. One part is not simply different from its counterpart; it is inherently opposed to its "other." Whites and Blacks, males and females, thought and feeling are not complementary counterparts—they are fundamentally different entities related only through their definition as opposites. Feeling cannot be incorporated into thought or even function in conjunction with it because in either/or dichotomous thinking, feeling retards thought, values obscure facts, and judgment clouds knowledge.

Objectification is central to this process of oppositional difference. In either/or dichotomous thinking, one element is objectified as the Other, and is viewed as an object to be manipulated and controlled. Social theorist Dona Richards (1980) suggests that Western thought requires objectification, a process she describes as the "separation of the 'knowing self' from the 'known object'" (p. 72). Intense objectification is a "prerequisite for the despiritualization of the universe," notes Richards, "and through it the Western cosmos was made ready for ever increasing materialization" (p. 72). A Marxist assessment of the culture/nature dichotomy argues that history can be seen as one in which human beings constantly objectify the natural world in order to control and exploit it (Brittan and Maynard 1984, 198). Culture is defined as the opposite of an objectified nature that, if left alone, would destroy culture.[1] Feminist scholars point to the identification of women with nature as being central to women's subsequent objectification by men as sex objects (Eisenstein 1983). Black scholars contend that defining people of color as less human, animalistic, or more "natural" denies African and Asian people's subjectivity and supports a political economy of domination (Asante 1987).

Domination always involves attempts to objectify the subordinate group. "As subjects, people have the right to define their own reality, establish their own identities, name their history," asserts Bell Hooks (1989, 42). "As objects, one's reality is defined by others, one's identity created by others, one's history named only in ways that define one's relationship to those who are subject" (p. 42). The treatment afforded Black women domestic workers exemplifies the many forms that objectification can take. Making Black women work as if they were animals or "mules uh de world" represents one form of objectification. Deference rituals such as calling Black domestic workers "girls" and by their first names enable employers to treat their employees like children, as less capable human beings. Objectification can be so severe that the Other simply disappears, as was the case when Judith Rollins's employer treated her as if she were invisible by conducting a conversation while ignoring Rollins's presence in the room. But in spite of these pressures, Black women have insisted on our right to define our own reality, establish our own identities, and name our history. One significant contribution of work by Judith Rollins (1985), Bonnie Thornton Dill (1980, 1988a), Elizabeth Clark-Lewis (1985), and others is that they document Black women's everyday resistance to this attempted objectification.

Finally, because oppositional dichotomies rarely represent different but equal relationships, they are inherently unstable. Tension is resolved by subordinating one half of the dichotomy to the other. Thus whites rule Blacks, men dominate women, reason is thought superior to emotion in ascertaining truth, facts supersede opinion in evaluating knowledge, and subjects rule objects. The foundations of a complex social hierarchy become grounded in the interwoven concepts of either/or dichotomous thinking, oppositional difference, and objectification. With domination based on difference forming an essential underpinning for this entire system of thought, these concepts invariably imply relationships of superiority and inferiority, hierarchical bonds that mesh with political economies of race, gender, and class oppression.

African-American women occupy a position whereby the inferior half of a series of these dichotomies converge, and this placement has been central to our subordination. The allegedly emotional, passionate nature of Black women has long been used to justify Black women's sexual exploitation. Similarly, restricting Black women's literacy, then claiming that we lack the facts for sound judgment, relegates African-American women to the inferior side of the fact/opinion dichotomy. Denying Black women status as fully human subjects by treating us as the objectified Other in a range of such dichotomies demonstrates the power that dichotomous either/or thinking, oppositional difference, and objectification wield in maintaining interlocking systems of oppression. Analyzing the specific, externally defined, controlling images applied to African-American women both reveals the specific contours of Black women's objectification and offers a clearer view of how systems of race, gender, and class oppression actually interlock.

CONTROLLING IMAGES AND BLACK WOMEN'S OPPRESSION

"Black women emerged from slavery firmly enshrined in the consciousness of white America as 'Mammy' and the 'bad black woman,' " contends Cheryl Gilkes (1983a, 294). The dominant ideology of the slave era fostered the creation of four interrelated, socially constructed controlling images of Black womanhood, each reflecting the dominant group's interest in maintaining Black women's subordination. Given that both Black and white women were important to slavery's continuation, the prevailing ideology functioned to mask contradictions in social relations affecting all women. According to the cult of true womanhood, "true" women possessed four cardinal virtues: piety, purity, submissiveness, and domesticity. Elite white women and those of the emerging middle class were encouraged to aspire to these virtues. African-American women encountered a different set of controlling images. The sexual ideology of the period as is the case today "confirmed the differing material circumstances of these two groups of women . . . by balancing opposing definitions of womanhood and motherhood, each dependent on the other for its existence" (Carby 1987, 25).

The first controlling image applied to African-American women is that of the mammy—the faithful, obedient domestic servant. Created to justify the economic exploitation of house slaves and sustained to explain Black women's long-standing restriction to domestic service, the mammy image represents the normative yardstick used to evaluate all Black women's behavior. By loving, nurturing, and caring for her white children and "family" better than her own, the mammy symbolizes the dominant group's perceptions of the ideal Black female relationship to elite white male power. Even though she may be well loved and may wield considerable authority in her white "family," the mammy still knows her "place" as obedient servant. She has accepted her subordination.

Black women intellectuals have aggressively deconstructed the image of African-American women as contented mammies by challenging traditional views of Black women domestics (Dill 1980, 1988a; Clark-Lewis 1985; Rollins 1985). Literary critic Trudier Harris's (1982) volume *From Mammies to Militants: Domestics in Black American Literature* investigates prominent differences in how Black women have been portrayed by others in literature and how they portray themselves. In her work on the difficulties faced by Black women leaders, Rhetaugh Dumas (1980) describes how Black women executives are hampered by being treated as mammies and penalized if they do not appear warm and nurturing. But despite these works, the mammy image lives on in scholarly and popular culture. Audre Lorde's account of a shopping trip offers a powerful example of its tenacity: "I wheel my two-year-old daughter in a shopping cart through a supermarket in . . . 1967, and a little white girl riding past in her mother's cart calls out excitedly, 'Oh look, Mommy, a baby maid!' " (1984, 126).[2]

The mammy image is central to interlocking systems of race, gender, and class oppression. Since efforts to control African-American family life require perpetuating the symbolic structures of racial oppression, the mammy image is important because it aims to shape Black women's behavior as mothers. As the members of African-American families who are most familiar with the skills needed for Black accommodation, Black women are encouraged to transmit to their own children the deference behavior many are forced to exhibit in mammy roles. By teaching Black children their assigned place in white power structures, Black women who internalize the mammy image potentially become effective conduits for perpetuating racial oppression. In addition, employing mammies buttresses the racial superiority of white women employers and weds them more closely to their fathers, husbands, and sons as sources of elite white male power (Rollins 1985).

The mammy image also serves a symbolic function in maintaining gender oppression. Black feminist critic Barbara Christian argues that images of Black womanhood serve as a reservoir for the fears of Western culture, "a dumping ground for those female functions a basically Puritan society could not confront" (1985, 2). Juxtaposed against the image of white women promulgated through the cult of true womanhood, the mammy image as the Other symbolizes the oppositional difference of mind/body and culture/nature thought to distinguish Black women from everyone else. Christian comments on the mammy's gender significance: "All the functions of mammy are magnificently physical. They involve the body as sensuous, as funky, the part of woman that white southern America was profoundly afraid of. Mammy, then, harmless in her position of slave, unable because of her all-giving nature to do harm, is needed as an image, a surrogate to contain all those fears of the physical female" (1985, 2). The mammy image buttresses the ideology of the cult of true womanhood, one in which sexuality and fertility are severed. "Good" white mothers are expected to deny their female sexuality and devote their attention to the moral development of their offspring. In contrast, the mammy image is one of an asexual woman, a surrogate mother in blackface devoted to the development of a white family.

No matter how loved they were by their white "families," Black women domestic workers remained poor because they were economically exploited. The restructured post–World War II economy in which African-American women moved from service in private homes to jobs in the low-paid service sector has produced comparable economic exploitation. Removing Black women's labor from African-American families and exploiting it denies Black extended family units the benefits of either decent wages or Black women's unpaid labor in their homes. Moreover, many white families in both the middle class and working class are able to maintain their class position because they have long used Black women as a source of cheap labor (Rollins 1985; Byerly 1986). The mammy image is designed to mask this economic exploitation of social class (King 1973).

For reasons of economic survival, African-American women may play the mammy role in paid work settings. But within African-American communities these same women often teach their own children something quite different. Bonnie Thornton Dill's (1980) work on child-rearing patterns among Black domestics shows that while the participants in her study showed deference behavior at work, they discouraged their children from believing that they should be deferent to whites and encouraged their children to avoid domestic work. Barbara Christian's analysis of the mammy in Black slave narratives reveals that, "unlike the white southern image of mammy, she is cunning, prone to poisoning her master, and not at all content with her lot" (1985, 5).

The fact that the mammy image cannot control Black women's behavior as mothers is tied to the creation of the second controlling image of Black womanhood. Though a more recent phenomenon, the image of the Black matriarch fulfills similar functions in explaining Black women's placement in interlocking systems of race, gender, and class oppression. Ironically, Black scholars such as William E. B. DuBois (1969) and E. Franklin Frazier (1948) described the connections among higher rates of female-headed households in African-American communities, the importance that women assume in Black family networks, and the persistence of Black poverty. However, neither scholar interpreted Black women's centrality in Black families as a *cause* of African-American social class status. Both saw so-called matriarchal families as an *outcome* of racial oppression and poverty. During the eras when Dubois and Frazier wrote, the oppression of African-Americans was so total that control was maintained without the controlling image of matriarch. But what began as a muted theme in the works of these earlier Black scholars grew into a full-blown racialized image in the 1960s, a time of significant political and economic mobility for African-Americans. Racialization involves attaching racial meaning to a previously racially unclassified relationship, social practice, or group (Omi and Winant 1986). Prior to the 1960s, female-headed households were certainly higher in African-American communities, but an ideology racializing female-headedness as a causal feature of Black poverty had not emerged. Moreover, "the public depiction of Black women as unfeminine, castrating matriarchs came at precisely the same moment that the feminist movement was advancing its public critique of American patriarchy" (Gilkes 1983a, 296).

While the mammy typifies the Black mother figure in white homes, the matriarch symbolizes the mother figure in Black homes. Just as the mammy represents the "good" Black mother, the matriarch symbolizes the "bad" Black mother. The modern Black matriarchy thesis contends that African-American women fail to fulfill their traditional "womanly" duties (Moynihan 1965). Spending too much time away from home, these working mothers ostensibly cannot properly supervise their children and are a major contributing factor to their children's school failure. As overly aggressive, unfeminine women, Black matriarchs allegedly emasculate their lovers and husbands. These men, understandably, either desert their partners or refuse to marry the mothers of their children. From an elite white male standpoint, the matriarch is essentially a failed mammy, a negative stigma applied to those African-American women who dared to violate the image of the submissive, hard-working servant.

Black women intellectuals examining the role of women in African-American families discover few matriarchs and even fewer mammies (Hale 1980; Myers 1980; Sudarkasa 1981b; Dill 1988b). Instead they portray African-American mothers as complex individuals who often show tremendous strength under adverse conditions. In *A Raisin in the Sun*, the first play presented on Broadway written by a Black woman, Lorraine Hansberry (1959) examines the struggles of widow Lena Younger to actualize her dream of purchasing a home for her family. In *Brown Girl, Brownstones*, novelist Paule Marshall (1959) presents Mrs. Boyce, a Black mother negotiating a series of relationships with her husband, her daughters, the women in her community, and the work she must perform outside her home. Ann Allen Shockley's *Loving Her* (1974) depicts the struggle of a lesbian mother trying to balance her needs for self-actualization with the pressures of child-rearing in a homophobic community. Like these fictional analyses, Black women's scholarship on Black single mothers also challenges the matriarchy thesis (Ladner 1972; McCray 1980; Lord 1984; McAdoo 1985; Brewer 1988).

Like the mammy, the image of the matriarch is central to interlocking systems of race, gender, and class oppression. Portraying African-American women as matriarchs allows the dominant group to blame Black women for the success or failure of Black children. Assuming that Black poverty is passed on intergenerationally via value transmission in families, an elite white male standpoint suggests that Black children lack the attention and care allegedly lavished on white, middle-class children and that this deficiency seriously retards Black children's achievement. Such a view diverts attention from the political and economic inequality affecting Black mothers and children and suggests that anyone can rise from poverty if he or she only received good values at home. Those African-Americans who remain poor are blamed for their own victimization. Using Black women's performance as mothers to explain Black economic subordination links gender ideology to explanations of class subordination.

The source of the matriarch's failure is her inability to model appropriate gender behavior. In the post–World War II era, increasing numbers of white women entered the labor market, limited their fertility, and generally challenged their proscribed roles in white patriarchal institutions. The image of the Black matriarch emerged at that time as a powerful symbol for both Black and white women of what can go wrong if white patriarchal power is challenged. Aggressive, assertive women are penalized—they are abandoned by their men, end up impoverished, and are stigmatized as being unfeminine.

The image of the matriarch also supports racial oppression. Much social science research implicitly uses gender relations in African-American communities as one putative measure of Black cultural disadvantage. For example, the Moynihan Report (1965) contends that slavery destroyed Black families by creating reversed roles for men and women. Black family structures are seen as being deviant because they challenge the patriarchal assumptions underpinning the construct of the ideal "family." Moreover, the absence of Black patriarchy is used as evidence for Black cultural inferiority (Collins 1989). Black women's failure to conform to the cult of true womanhood can then be identified as one fundamental source of Black cultural deficiency. Cheryl Gilkes posits that the emergence of the matriarchal image occurred as a counterideology to efforts by African-Americans and women who were confronting interlocking systems of race, gender, and class oppression: "The image of dangerous Black women who were also deviant castrating mothers divided the Black community at a critical period in the Black liberation struggle and created a wider gap between the worlds of Black and white women at a critical period in women's history" (1983a, 297).

Taken together, images of the mammy and the matriarch place African-American women in an untenable position. For Black women workers in domestic work and other occupations requiring long hours and/or substantial emotional labor, becoming the ideal mammy means precious time and energy spent away from husbands and children. But being employed when Black men have difficulty finding steady work exposes African-American women to the charge that Black women emasculate Black men by failing to be submissive, dependent, "feminine" women. Moreover, Black women's financial contributions to Black family well-being have also been cited as evidence supporting the matriarchy thesis (Moynihan 1965). Many Black women are the sole support of their families, and labeling these women "matriarchs" erodes their self-confidence and ability to confront oppression. In essence, African-American women who must work are labeled mammies, then are stigmatized again as matriarchs for being strong figures in their own homes.

A third, externally defined, controlling image of Black womanhood—that of the welfare mother—appears tied to Black women's increasing dependence on the post–World War II welfare state. Essentially an updated version of the breeder woman image created during slavery, this image provides an ideological justification for efforts to harness Black women's fertility to the needs of a changing political economy.

During slavery the breeder woman image portrayed Black women as more suitable for having children than white women. By claiming that Black women were able to produce children as easily as animals, this objectification of Black women as the Other provided justification for interference in the reproductive rights of enslaved Africans. Slaveowners wanted enslaved Africans to "breed" because every slave child born represented a valuable unit of property, another unit of labor, and, if female, the prospects for more slaves. The externally defined, controlling image of the breeder woman served to justify slaveowner intrusion into Black women's decisions about fertility (King 1973; Davis 1981).

The post–World War II political economy has offered African-Americans rights not available in former historical periods (Fusfeld and Bates 1984; Wilson 1987). African-Americans have successfully acquired basic political and economic protections from a greatly expanded welfare state, particularly Social Security, Aid to Families with Dependent Children, unemployment compensation, affirmative action, voting rights, antidiscrimination legislation, and the minimum wage. In spite of sustained opposition by Republican administrations in the 1980s, these programs allow many African-Americans to reject the subsistence-level, exploitative jobs held by their parents and grandparents. Job export, deskilling, and increased use of illegal immigrants have all been used to replace the loss of cheap, docile Black labor (Braverman 1974; Gordon et al. 1982; Nash and Fernandez-Kelly 1983). The large numbers of undereducated, unemployed African-Americans, most of whom are women and children, who inhabit inner cities cannot be forced to work. From the standpoint of the dominant group, they no longer represent cheap labor but instead signify a costly threat to political and economic stability.

Controlling Black women's fertility in such a political economy becomes important. The image of the welfare mother fulfills this function by labeling as unnecessary and even dangerous to the values of the country the fertility of women who are not white and middle class. A closer look at this controlling image reveals that it shares some important features with its mammy and matriarch counterparts. Like the matriarch, the welfare mother is labeled a bad mother. But unlike the matriarch, she is not too aggressive—on the contrary, she is not aggressive enough. While the matriarch's unavailability contributed to her children's poor socialization, the welfare mother's accessibility is deemed the problem. She is portrayed as being content to sit around and collect welfare, shunning work and passing on her bad values to her offspring. The image of the welfare mother represents another failed mammy, one who is unwilling to become "de mule uh de world."

The image of the welfare mother provides ideological justifications for interlocking systems of race, gender, and class oppression. African-Americans can be racially stereotyped as being lazy by blaming Black welfare mothers for failing to pass on the work ethic. Moreover, the welfare mother has no male authority figure to assist her. Typically portrayed as an unwed mother, she violates one cardinal tenet of Eurocentric masculinist thought: she is a woman alone. As a result, her treatment reinforces the dominant gender ideology positing that a woman's true worth and financial security should occur through heterosexual marriage. Finally, in the post–World War II political economy, one of every three African-American families is officially classified as poor. With such high levels of Black poverty, welfare state policies supporting poor Black mothers and their children have become increasingly expensive. Creating the controlling image of the welfare mother and stigmatizing her as the cause of her own poverty and that of African-American communities shifts the angle of vision away from structural sources of poverty and blames the victims themselves. The image of the welfare mother thus provides ideological justification for the dominant group's interest in limiting the fertility of Black mothers who are seen as producing too many economically unproductive children (Davis 1981).

The fourth controlling image—the Jezebel, whore, or sexually aggressive woman—is central in this nexus of elite white male images of Black womanhood because efforts to control Black women's sexuality lie at the heart of Black women's oppression. The image of Jezebel originated under slavery when Black women were portrayed as being, to use Jewelle Gomez's words, "sexually aggressive wet nurses" (Clarke et al. 1983, 99). Jezebel's function was to relegate all Black women to the category of sexually aggressive women, thus providing a powerful rationale for the widespread sexual assaults by white men typically reported by Black slave women (Davis 1981; Hooks 1981; D. White 1985). Yet Jezebel served another function. If Black slave women could be portrayed as having excessive sexual appetites, then increased fertility should be the expected outcome. By suppressing the nurturing that African-American women might give their own children which would strengthen Black family networks, and by forcing Black women to work in the field or "wet nurse" white children, slaveowners effectively tied the controlling images of Jezebel and Mammy to the economic exploitation inherent in the institution of slavery.

The fourth image of the sexually denigrated Black woman is the foundation underlying elite white male conceptualizations of the mammy, matriarch, and welfare mother. Connecting all three is the common theme of Black women's sexuality. Each image transmits clear messages about the proper links among female sexuality, fertility, and Black women's roles in the political economy. For example, the mammy, the only somewhat positive figure, is a desexed individual. The mammy is typically portrayed as overweight, dark, and with characteristically African features—in brief, as an unsuitable sexual partner for white men. She is asexual and therefore is free to become a surrogate mother to the children she acquired not through her own sexuality. The mammy represents the clearest example of the split between sexuality and motherhood present in Eurocentric masculinist thought. In contrast, both the matriarch and the welfare mother are sexual beings. But their sexuality is linked to their fertility, and this link forms one fundamental reason they are negative images. The matriarch represents the sexually aggressive woman, one who emasculates Black men because she will not permit them to assume roles as Black patriarchs. She refuses to be passive and thus is stigmatized. Similarly, the welfare mother represents a woman of low morals and uncontrolled sexuality, factors identified as the cause of her impoverished state. In both cases Black female control over sexuality and fertility is conceptualized as antithetical to elite white male interests.

Taken together, these four prevailing interpretations of Black womanhood form a nexus of elite white male interpretations of Black female sexuality and fertility. Moreover, by meshing smoothly with systems of race, class, and gender oppression, they provide effective ideological justifications for racial oppression, the politics of gender subordination, and the economic exploitation inherent in capitalist economies.

CONTROLLING IMAGES IN EVERYDAY LIFE: COLOR, HAIR TEXTURE, AND STANDARDS OF BEAUTY

Like everyone else, African-American women learn the meaning of race, gender, and social class without obvious teaching or conscious learning. The controlling images of Black women are not simply grafted onto existing social institutions but are so pervasive that even though the images themselves change in the popular imagination, Black women's portrayal as the Other persists. Particular meanings, stereotypes, and myths can change, but the overall ideology of domination itself seems to be an enduring feature of interlocking systems of race, gender, and class oppression (Omi and Winant 1986, 63).

African-American women encounter this ideology through a range of unquestioned, daily experiences. But when the contradictions between Black women's self-definitions and everyday treatment are heightened, controlling images become increasingly visible. Karen Russell, the daughter of basketball great Bill Russell, describes how racial stereotypes affect her:

> How am I supposed to react to well-meaning, good, liberal white people who say things like: "You know, Karen, I don't understand what all the fuss is about. You're one of my good friends, and I never think of you as black." Implicit in such a remark is, "I think of you as white," or perhaps just, "I don't think of your race at all." (Russell 1987, 22).

Ms. Russell was perceptive enough to see that remarks intended to compliment her actually insulted African-Americans. As the Others, African-Americans are assigned all of the negative characteristics opposite and inferior to those reserved for whites. By claiming that Ms. Russell is not really "black," her friends unintentionally validate this system of racial meanings and encourage her to internalize those images.

Although Black women typically resist being objectified as the Other, these controlling images remain powerful influences on our relationships with whites, Black men, and one another. Dealing with issues of beauty—particularly skin color, facial features, and hair texture—is one concrete example of how controlling images denigrate African-American women. A children's rhyme often sung in Black communities proclaims:

> Now, if you're white you're all right,
> If you're brown, stick around,
> But if you're black, Git back! Git back! Git back!

Externally defined standards of beauty long applied to African-American women claim that no matter how intelligent, educated, or "beautiful" a Black woman may be, those Black women whose features and skin color are most African must "git back." Blue-eyed, blond, thin white women could not be considered beautiful without the Other—Black women with classical African features of dark skin, broad noses, full lips, and kinky hair.

Race, gender, and sexuality converge on this issue of evaluating beauty. Judging white women by their physical appearance and attractiveness to men objectifies them. But their white skin and straight hair privilege them in a system in which part of the basic definition of whiteness is its superiority to blackness. Black men's blackness penalizes them. But because they are men, their self-definitions are not as heavily dependent on their physical attractiveness as those of all women. But African-American women experience the pain of never being able to live up to externally defined standards of beauty—standards applied to us by white men, white women, Black men, and, most painfully, one another.

Exploring how externally defined standards of beauty affect Black women's self-images, our relationships with one another, and our relationships with Black men has been one recurring theme in Black feminist thought.[3] The long-standing attention of musicians, writers, and artists to this theme reveals African-American women's deep feelings concerning skin color, hair texture, and standards of beauty. In her autobiography, Maya Angelou records her painful realization that the only way she could become truly beautiful was to become white:

> Wouldn't they be surprised when one day I woke out of my black ugly dream, and my real hair, which was long and blond, would take the place of the kinky mass that Momma wouldn't let me straighten? . . . Then they would understand why I had never picked up a Southern accent, or spoke the common slang, and why I had to be forced to eat pigs' tails and snouts. Because I was really white and because a cruel fairy stepmother . . . had turned me into a too-big Negro girl, with nappy black hair. (Angelou 1969, 2).

Gwendolyn Brooks also explores the meaning of skin color and hair texture for Black women. During Brooks's childhood, having African features was so universally denigrated that she writes, "when I was a child, it did not occur to me even once, that the black in which I was encased . . . would be considered, one day, beautiful" (Brooks 1972, 37). Early on Brooks learned that a clear pecking order existed among African-Americans, one based on one's closeness to whiteness. As a member of the "Lesser Blacks," those farthest from white, Brooks saw first-hand the difference in treatment of her group and the "Brights":

> One of the first "world"-truths revealed to me when I at last became a member of SCHOOL was that, to be socially successful, a little girl must be Bright (of skin). It was better if your hair was curly, too—or at least Good Grade (Good Grade implied, usually, no involvement with the Hot Comb)—but Bright you marvelously *needed* to be. (1972, 37)

 This division of African-Americans into two categories—the "Brights" and the "Lesser Blacks"—affects dark-skinned and light-skinned women differently. Darker women face being judged inferior and receiving the treatment afforded "too-big Negro girls with nappy hair." Institutions controlled by whites clearly show a preference for lighter-skinned Blacks, discriminating against darker ones or against any African-Americans who appear to reject white images of beauty. Sonia Sanchez reports, "sisters tell me today that when they go out for jobs they straighten their hair because if they go in with their hair natural or braided, they probably won't get the job" (Tate 1983, 141).

Sometimes the pain most deeply felt is the pain that Black women inflict on one another. Marita Golden's mother told her not to play in the sun because "you gonna have to get a light husband anyway, for the sake of your children" (1983, 24). In *Color*, a short film exploring the impact of skin color on Black women's lives, the dark-skinned character's mother tries to get her to sit still for the hot comb, asking "don't you want your hair flowing like your friend Rebecca's?" We see the sadness of a young Black girl sitting in a kitchen, holding her ears so they won't get burned by the hot comb that will straighten her hair. Her mother cannot make her beautiful, only "presentable" for church. Marita Golden's description of a Black beauty salon depicts the internalized oppression that some African-American women feel about African features:

> Between customers, twirling in her chair, white-stockinged legs crossed, my beautician lamented to the hairdresser in the next stall, "I sure hope that Gloria Johnson don't come in here asking for me today. I swear 'fore God her hair is this long." She snapped her fingers to indicate the length. Contempt riding her words, she lit a cigarette and finished, "Barely enough to wash, let alone press and curl." (Golden 1983, 25)

African-American women who are members of the "Brights" fare little better, for they too receive special treatment because of their skin color and hair texture. Harriet Jacobs, an enslaved light-skinned woman, was sexually haarassed because she was "beautiful," for a Black woman. Her straight hair and fair skin, her appearance as a dusky white woman, made her physically attractive to white men. But the fact that she was Black, and thus part of a group of sexually denigrated women, made her available to white men as no group of white women had been. In describing her situation, Jacobs notes, "if God has bestowed beauty upon her, it will prove her greatest curse. That which commands admiration in the white woman only hastens the degradation of the female slave" (Washington 1987, 17).

This difference in treatment of dark-skinned and light-skinned Black women creates issues in relationships among African-American women. Toni Morrison's (1970) novel *The Bluest Eye* explores this theme of the tension that can exist among Black women grappling with the meaning of externally defined standards of beauty. Frieda, a dark-skinned, "ordinary" Black girl, struggles with the meaning of these standards. She wonders why adults always got so upset when she rejected the white dolls they gave her and why light-skinned Maureen Peal, a child her own age whose two braids hung like "lynch-ropes down her back," got the love and attention of teachers, adults, and Black boys alike. Morrison explores Freida's attempt not to blame Maureen for the benefits her light skin and long hair afforded her as part of Freida's growing realization that the "Thing" to fear was not Maureen herself but the "Thing" that made Maureen beautiful.

Gwendolyn Brooks (1953) captures the anger and frustration experienced by dark-skinned women in dealing with the differential treatment they and their lighter-skinned sisters receive. In her novel *Maud Martha*, the dark-skinned heroine ponders actions she could take against a red-headed Black woman whom her husband found so attractive. "I could," considered Maud Martha, "go over there and scratch her upsweep down. I could spit on her back. I could scream. 'Listen,' I could scream, 'I'm making a baby for this man and I mean to do it in peace.' " (Washington 1987, 422). But Maud Martha rejects these actions, reasoning "if the root was sour what business did she have up there hacking at a leaf?"

This "sour root" also creates issues in relationships between African-American women and men. Maude Martha explains:

> It's my color that makes him mad. I try to shut my eyes to that, but it's no good. What I am inside, what is really me, he likes okay. But he keeps looking at my color, which is like a wall. He has to jump over it in order to meet and touch what I've got for him. He has to jump away up high in order to see it. He gets awful tired of all that jumping. (Washington 1987, 421)

Her husband's attraction to light-skinned women hurt Maude Martha because his inability to "jump away up high" over the wall of color limited his ability to see her for who she truly was.

ISSUES MERITING FURTHER ATTENTION IN BLACK FEMINIST THOUGHT

Black Women's Reactions to Controlling Images

In *Their Eyes Were Watching God*, Nanny eloquently expresses her standpoint on Black womanhood: "Ah was born back in slavery so it wasn't for me to fulfill my dream of whut a woman oughta be and do. But nothing can't stop you from wishin! You can't beat nobody down so low till you can rob 'em of they will. Ah didn't want to be used for a work-ox and a brood-sow and Ah didn't want mah daughter used dat way neither" (Hurston 1937, 17). Like many African-American women, she resisted the controlling images of "work-ox" and "brood-sow," but her status as a slave prevented her fulfilling her "dreams of whut a woman oughta be and to do." She saw the constraints on her own life but managed to keep the will to resist alive. Moreover, she tried to pass on that vision of freedom from controlling images to her granddaughter.

Despite the pervasiveness of controlling images, African-American women have resisted these ideological justifications for our oppression (Gilkes 1983b). Unlike white women who "face the pitfall of being seduced into joining the oppressor under the pretense of sharing power," and for whom "there is a wider range of pretended choices and rewards for identifying with patriarchal power and its tools," Black women are offered no such possibility (Lorde 1984, 117–18). One theme that merits continued analysis in Black feminist thought—especially by Black feminist sociologists, historians, and psychologists—concerns documenting and explaining Black women's diverse reactions to being objectified as the Other.

Literature by Black women writers provides the most comprehensive view of Black women's struggles to form positive self-definitions in the face of denigrated images of Black womanhood. Portraying the range of ways that African-American women experience internalized oppression is a prominent theme in Black women's writing. Mary Helen Washington's (1982) discussion of the theme of the suspended woman in Black women's literature describes one dimension of Black women's internalized oppression. Pain, violence, and death form the essential content of these women's lives. They are suspended in time and place: their life choices are so severely limited that the women themselves are often destroyed. Pecola Breedlove, an unloved, "ugly" eleven-year-old Black girl in Toni Morrison's novel *The Bluest Eye* (1970), internalizes the denigrated images of African-American women and believes that the absence of blue eyes is central to her "ugliness." Pecola cannot value her Blackness—she longs to be white so that she can escape the pain of being Black, female, poor, and a child. Her mother, Pauline Breedlove, typifies the internalization of the mammy image. Pauline Breedlove neglects her own children, preferring to lavish her concern and attention on the white charges in her care. Only by accepting this subordinate role to white children could she, as a poor Black woman, see a positive place for herself.

Black women writers have chronicled other forms of Black women's attempts to escape from a world predicated upon denigrated images of Black womanhood. Fictional African-American women characters usse drugs, alcohol, excessive religion, and even retreat into madness in an attempt to create other worlds apart from the ones that produced such painful Black female realities. Pauline Breedlove in *The Bluest Eye* and Mrs. Hill in *Meridian* (Walker 1976) both demonstrate an attachment to religion that allows them to ignore their daughters. Eva Medina in Gayl Jones's *Eva's Man* (1976), Merle Kibona in Paule Marshall's *The Chosen Place, the Timeless People* (1976), and Velma Henry in Toni Cade Bambara's *The Salt Eaters* (1980) all experience madness as an escape from pain.

Denial is another characteristic response to the controlling images of Black womanhood and their accompanying conditions. By claiming that they are not like the rest, some African-American women reject connections to other Black women and demand special treatment for themselves. Mary Helen Washington (1982) refers to these characters as assimilated women. They are more aware of their condition than are suspended women, but in spite of their greater potential for shaping their lives, they still feel thwarted because they see themselves as misplaced by time and circumstances. Light-skinned, middle class Cleo, a key figure in Dorothy West's novel *The Living is Easy* (1948), typifies this response. In one scene strong-willed Cleo hustles her daughter past a playground filled with the children of newly arrived southern Blacks, observing that "she wouldn't want her child to go to school with those niggers." Cleo clings to her social class position, one that she sees as separating her from other African-Americans, and tries to muffle the negative status attached to her Blackness by emphasizing her allegedly superior class position. Even though Cleo is more acceptable to the white world, the price she pays for her acceptance is the negation of her racial identity and separation from the sustenance that such an identity might offer.

Black women writers not only portray the range of responses that individual African-American women express concerning their objectification as the Other: they also document the process of personal growth toward positive self-definitions. The personal growth experienced by Renay, the heroine in Ann Allen Shockley's *Loving Her* (1974), illustrates the process of rejecting externally defined controlling images of Black womanhood. Shockley initially presents Renay as a suspended woman who is trapped in a heterosexual marriage to an abusive husband and who tries to deny her feelings for other women. Renay retreats into music and alcohol as temporary spaces where she can escape having her difference—in this case, her Blackness and lesbianism—judged as inferior and deviant. After taking a white woman lover, Renay is initially quite happy, but she grows to realize that she has replaced one set of controlling images—namely, those she experienced with her abusive husband—with another. She leaves her lover to pursue her own self-definition. By the novel's end Renay has begun to resist all external definitions of herself that stem from controlling images applied to Blacks, women, and lesbians.

Renay's experiences typify how Black women writers explore the theme of Black women's resistance to these denigrated images, a resistance typified by the emergent woman in Black women's literature. Sherley Anne Williams's novel *Dessa Rose* (1986) describes a Black slave woman's emerging sense of power after she participates in a slave revolt, runs away, and eventually secures her own freedom. Dorine Davis, the heroine in Rosa Guy's *A Measure of Time* (1983), is raped at age ten by her white employer, subsequently sleeps with men for money, yet retains a core of resistance. Bad things happen to Dorine, but Guy does not portray Dorine as a victim. In *The Bluest Eye* (1970), Toni Morrison presents the character of Claudia, a ten-year-old Black girl who, to the chagrin of grownups, destroys white dolls by tearing off their heads and who refuses to share her classmates' admiration of light-skinned, long-haired Maureen Peal. Claudia's growing awareness of the "Thing that made her [Maureen Peal] beautiful and us ugly" and her rejection of that Thing—racist images of Black women—represents yet another reaction to negative images of Black womanhood. Like Merle Kibona in Paule Marshall's *The Timeless Place, the Chosen People*, Vyry in Margaret Walker's *Jubilee* (1966), Janie Crawford in Zora Neale Hurston's *Their Eyes Were Watching God* (1937), or Meridian in Alice Walker's *Meridian* (1976), Claudia represents a young version of emergent Black women carving out new definitions of Black womanhood.

Institutional Sites for Transmitting Controlling Images

Schools, the media, corporations, and government agencies are essential sites for transmitting ideologies objectifying Black woman as the Other. These institutions are not controlled by African-Americans and are clearly the source of and ultimate beneficiaries of these externally defined controlling images.

Confronting the controlling images forwarded by institutions external to African-American communities should continue as a fundamental concern of Black feminist thought. But this effort should not obscure the equally important issue of examining how African-American institutions also perpetuate notions of Black women as the Other. Although it may be painful to examine—especially in the context of a racially charged society always vigilant for signs of African-American disunity—the question of the role of Black institutions as transmitters of controlling images of Black womanhood merits investigation.

Some Black women are becoming increasingly vocal in describing what they see as sexism in African-American communities (Wallace 1978; Hooks

1981; White 1984). Black feminist Pauline Terrelonge is one of the few Black women who has directly confronted the issue of the Black community's role in the subordination of Black women. Terrelonge asks, "if there is much in the objective condition of black women that warrants the development of a black feminist consciousness, why have so many black women failed to recognize the patterns of sexism that directly impinge on their everyday lives? (1984, 562). To answer this question, Terrelonge contends that a common view within African-American communities is that African-Americans have withstood the long line of abuses perpetuated against us mainly because of Black women's "fortitude, inner wisdom, and sheer ability to survive." Connected to this emphasis on the moral, spiritual, and emotional strength of Black women is the related argument that African-American women play critical roles in keeping Black families together and in supporting Black men. These activities have been important in offsetting the potential annihilation of African-Americans as a "race." As a result, "many blacks regard the role of uniting all blacks to be the primary duty of the black woman, one that should supersede all other roles that she might want to perform, and certainly one that is essentially incompatible with her own individual liberation" (p. 557).

Institutions controlled by African-Americans can be seen as contradictory locations where Black women learn skills of independence and self-reliance which enable African-American families, churches, and civic organizations to endure. But these same institutions may also be locations where Black women learn to subordinate our interests as women to the allegedly greater good of the larger African-American community. Some Black feminist activists claim that relegating Black women to more submissive, supporting roles in African-American organizations has been an obstacle to Black political empowerment. In describing the 1960s nationalist movement, Pauli Murray contends that many Black men misinterpreted Black women's qualities of self-reliance and independence by tacitly accepting the matriarchy thesis. Such a stance was and is highly problematic for Black women. Murray observes, "the black militant's cry for the retrieval of black manhood suggests an acceptance of this stereotype, an association of masculinity with male dominance and a tendency to treat the values of self-reliance and independence as purely masculine traits" (1970, 89).

Sheila Radford-Hill (1986) sees Black women's subordination in African-American institutions as a continuing concern. For Radford-Hill the erosion of Black women's traditional power bases in African-American communities which followed nationalist movements is problematic in that "Black macho constituted a betrayal by black men; a psychosexual rejection of black women experienced as the capstone to our fall from cultural power. . . . Without the power to influence the purpose and direction of our collective experience, without the power to influence our culture from within, we are increasingly immobilized, unable to integrate self and role identities" (p. 168).

Evelyn Brooks (1983) and Jacquelyn Grant (1982) identify the church as one key institution whose centrality to Black community development may have come at the expense of many of the African-American women who constitute the bulk of its membership. Grant asserts, "it is often said that women are the 'backbone' of the church. On the surface, this may appear to be a compliment. . . . It has become apparent to me that most of the ministers who use this term are referring to location rather than function. What they really mean is that women are in the 'background' and should be kept there" (1982, 141).

In their goal of dispelling the myths about African-American women and making Black women acceptable to wider society, some historically Black colleges may also foster Black women's subordination. In *Meridian* Alice Walker describes an elite college for Black women where "most of the students—timid, imitative, bright enough but never daring, were being ushered nearer to Ladyhood every day" (1976, 39). Confined to campus, Meridian, the heroine, had to leave to find the ordinary Black people who exhibited all of the qualities that her elite institution wished to eliminate. Walker's description of the fence surrounding the campus symbolizes how perpetuating the cult of true womanhood was stultifying for Black students. But it also describes the problems African-American institutions create for Black women when they embrace externally defined controlling images:

> The fence that surrounded the campus was hardly noticeable from the street and appeared, from the outside, to be more of an attempt at ornamentation than an effort to contain or exclude. Only the students who lived on campus learned, often painfully, that the beauty of a fence is no guarantee that it will not keep one penned in as securely as one that is ugly. (Walker 1976, 41)

African-American families form another potential location where the objectification of Black women as the Other occurs. Whereas white feminists have actively explored how white, middle-class families perpetuate their subordination (see, for example, Chodorow 1978; Chodorow and Contratto 1982), Black women intellectuals have been less vocal. How do African-American women experience internalized oppression in our families? What is the role of fathers and mothers in this process? We are finally hearing the long hidden stories of those strong Black women whose families truly model cultures of resistance and teach their daughters how to resist (Joseph 1981; Collins 1987). But, with the exception of Black women's fiction, stories expressing the full pain of those Black girls whose mothers, fathers, and significant others told them they were ugly, stupid, or generally undesirable remain largely untold. "It is not that black women have not been and are not strong," maintains Bell Hooks. "It is simply that this is only a part of our story, a dimension, just as the suffering is another dimension—one that has been most unnoticed and unattended to" (1989, 153).

Constructing an Afrocentric Feminist Aesthetic for Beauty

Developing much-needed redefinitions of beauty must involve the critical first step of learning to see African-American women who have classical African features as being capable of beauty. Lorraine Hansberry describes this need for a changed consciousness about African-American women's beauty:

> Sometimes in this country maybe just walking down a Southside street . . . Or maybe suddenly up in a Harlem window . . . Or maybe in a flash turning the page of one of those picture books from the South you will see it—*Beauty* . . . stark and full. . . . No *part* of this—but rather Africa, simply Africa. These thighs and arms and flying winged cheekbones, these hallowed eyes—without negation or apology. *A classical people demand a classical art.* (Hansberry 1969, 106)

But proclaiming Black women "beautiful" and white women "ugly" merely replaces one set of controlling images with another and fails to challenge how Eurocentric masculinist aesthetics foster an ideology of domination. Current standards require either/or dichotomous thinking: in order for one individual to be judged beautiful, another individual—the Other—must be deemed ugly. Accepting this underlying assumption avoids a more basic question concerning the connections among controlling images, either/or dichotomous thinking, and unequal power relationships among groups. Creating an alternative feminist aesthetic involves deconstructing and rejecting existing standards or ornamental beauty that objectify women and judge us by our physical appearance. Such an aesthetic would also reject standards of beauty that commodify women by measuring various quantities of beauty that women broker in the marital marketplace.

African-American women can draw on traditional Afrocentric aesthetics (Gayle 1971; Walton 1971) that potentially free women from standards of ornamental beauty.[4] Though such aesthetics are present in music (Sidran 1971; Cone 1972), dance (Asante 1990), and language (Smitherman 1977; Kochman 1981), quiltmaking offers a suggestive model for an Afrocentric feminist aesthetic (Brown 1989). African-American women quiltmakers do not seem interested in a uniform color scheme but use several methods of playing with colors to create unpredictability and movement (Wahlman and Scully 1983 in Brown 1989, 922). For example, a strong color may be juxtaposed with another strong color, or with a weak one. Contrast is used to structure or organize. Overall, the symmetry in African-American quilts does not come from uniformity as it does in Euro-American quilts. Rather, symmetry comes through diversity. Nikki Giovanni points out that quilts are traditionally formed from scraps. "Quilters teach there is no such thing as waste," she observes, "only that for which we currently see no purpose" (1988, 89). In describing Alice Walker's reaction to a quilt done by an anonymous Black woman, Barbara Christian notes that Walker "brings together . . . the theme of the black woman's creativity, her transformation, despite opposition, of the bits and pieces allowed to her by society into a work of functional beauty" (Christian 1985, 86).

This dual emphasis on beauty occurring via individual uniqueness juxtaposed in a community setting and on the importance of creating functional beauty from the scraps of everyday life offers a powerful alternative to Eurocentric aesthetics. The Afrocentric notions of diversity in community and functional beauty potentially heal many of the oppositional dichotomies inherent in Western social thought. From an Afrocentric perspective, women's beauty is not based solely on physical criteria because mind, spirit, and body are not conceptualized as separate, oppositional spheres. Instead, all are central in aesthetic assessments of individuals and their creations. Beauty is functional in that it has no meaning independent of the group. Deviating from the group "norm" is not rewarded as "beauty." Instead, participating in the group and being a functioning individual who strives for harmony is key to assessing an individual's beauty (Asante 1987). Moreover, participation is not based on conformity but instead is seen as individual uniqueness that enhances the overall "beauty" of the group. Using such criteria, no individual is inherently beautiful because beauty is not a state of being. Instead beauty is always defined in a context as a state of becoming. All African-American women as well as all humans become capable of beauty.

NOTES

1. Dona Richards (1980) offers an insightful analysis of the relationship between Christianity's contributions to an ideology of domination and the culture/nature dichotomy. She notes that European Christianity is predicated on a worldview that sustains the exploitation of nature: "Christian thought provides a view of man, nature, and the

universe which supports not only the ascendancy of science, but of the technical order, individualism, and relentless progress. Emphasis within this world view is placed on humanity's dominance over *all* other beings, which become 'objects' in an 'objectified' universe. There is no emphasis on an awe-inspiring God or cosmos. Being 'made in God's image,' given the European ethos, translates into 'acting *as* God,' recreating the universe. Humanity is separated from nature" (p. 69).

2. Brittan and Maynard (1984) note that ideology (1) is common sense and obvious; (2) appears natural, inevitable, and universal; (3) shapes lived experience and behavior; (4) is sedimented in people's consciousness; and (5) consists of a system of ideas embedded in the social system as a whole. This example captures all dimensions of how racism and sexism function ideologically. The status of Black woman as servant is so "common sense" that even a child knows it. That the child saw a Black female child as a baby maid speaks to the naturalization dimension and to the persistence of controlling images in individual consciousness and the social system overall.

3. While Black women intellectuals have described how these standards affect Black women's relationships, less attention has been given to how skin color, hair texture, and other types of physical markers are used in maintaining systems of oppression. Hair texture and skin color may intersect with gender in structuring systems of oppression. In his exhaustive cross-cultural analysis of slavery, Orlando Patterson notes that dominant groups usually perform elaborate rituals on their subordinates. Shearing of hair is a key part of rituals of domination cross-culturally. But Patterson points out, "it was not so much color differences as differences in hair type that become critical as a mark of servility in the Americas" (1982, 61). To explain this pattern, Patterson contends that hair provides a clearer and more powerful badge of status. Differences between whites and Blacks were sharper in hair quality than in color and persist much longer with miscegenation. Patterson notes, "Hair type rapidly became the real symbolic badge of slavery, although like many powerful symbols, it was disguised . . . by the linguistic device of using the term 'black,' which nominally threw the emphasis to color" (p. 61).

4. Studies of African art and culture indicate that behavior, individuals, and creations deemed "beautiful" from an Afrocentric perspective are valued for qualities other than their appearance and their value in an exchange-based marketplace (Gayle 1971; Asante 1990). For example, the Yoruba assess everything aesthetically, from the taste of food and the qualities of dress to the deportment of a woman or man. Beauty is seen in the mean—in something not too tall or short, not too beautiful (overhandsome people turn out to be skeletons in disguise in many folktales) or too ugly. Moreover, the Yoruba appreciate freshness and improvisation in the arts (Thompson 1983).

Chapter 5

THE POWER OF SELF-DEFINITION

"In order to survive, those of us for whom oppression is as American as apple pie have always had to be watchers," asserts Black feminist poet Audre Lorde (1984, 114). This "watching" generates a dual consciousness in African-American women, one in which Black women "become familiar with the language and manners of the oppressor, even sometimes adopting them for some illusion of protection" (p. 114), while hiding a self-defined standpoint from the prying eyes of dominant groups. Ella Surrey, an elderly Black woman domestic, eloquently summarizes the energy needed to maintain independent self-definitions: "We have always been the best actors in the world. . . . I think that we are much more clever than they are because we know that we have to play the game. We've always had to live two lives—one for them and one for ourselves" (Gwaltney 1980, 238, 240).

Behind the mask of behavioral conformity imposed on African-American women, acts of resistance, both organized and anonymous, have long existed (Davis 1981, 1989; Hine and Wittenstein 1981; Terborg-Penn 1986; Hine 1989). In spite of the strains connected with domestic work, Judith Rollins (1985) asserts that the domestic workers she interviewed appeared to have retained a "remarkable sense of self-worth." They "skillfully deflect these psychological attacks on their personhood, their adulthood, their dignity, these attempts to lure them into accepting employers' definitions of them as inferior" (p. 212). Bonnie Thornton Dill (1988a) found that the domestic workers in her study refused to let their employers push them around. As one respondent declared: "When I went out to work . . . my mother told me, 'Don't let anybody take advantage of you. Speak up for your rights, but do the work right. If they don't give you your rights, you demand that they treat you right. And if they don't, then you quit' " (p. 41). At the turn of the century, a period of heightened racial repression, educator Fannie Barrier Williams viewed the African-American woman not as a defenseless victim but as a strong-willed resister: "As meanly as she is thought of; hindered as she is in all directions, she is always doing something of merit and credit that is not expected of her" (Williams 1905, 151). Williams saw the Black woman as "irrepressible. She is insulted, but she holds up her head; she is scorned, but she proudly demands respect. . . .The most interesting girl of this country is the colored girl" (p. 151).

Resisting by doing something that "is not expected" could not have occurred without Black women's long-standing rejection of mammies, matriarchs, and other controlling images. This tradition of resistance suggests that a distinctive, collective Black women's consciousness exists. Such a consciousness was present in Maria Stewart's 1831 speech advising the "daughters of Africa" to "awake! Arise! No longer sleep nor slumber, but distinguish yourselves. Show forth to the world that ye are endowed with noble and exalted faculties" (Richardson 1987, 30). Such a consciousness is present in the worldview of Johnny Mae Fields, a mill worker from North Carolina possessing few opportunities to resist. Ms. Fields wryly announces, "if they tell me something and I know I ain't going to do it, I don't tell them. I just go on and don't do it" (Byerly 1986, 141).

Silence is not to be interpreted as submission in this tradition of a self-defined Black women's consciousness. In 1925 author Marita Bonner cogently described how consciousness remained the one sphere of freedom available to her in the stifling confines of both her Black middle-class world and a racist white society:

> So—being a woman—you can wait. You must sit quietly without a chip. Not sodden—and weighted as if your feet were cast in the iron of your soul. Not wasting strength in enervating gestures as if two hundred years of bonds and whips had really tricked you into nervous uncertainty. But quiet; quiet. Like Buddha—who brown like I am—sat entirely at ease, entirely sure of himself; motionless and knowing. . . . Motionless on the outside. But inside? (Bonner 1987, 7)

Black women intellectuals have long explored this private, hidden space of Black women's consciousness, the "inside" ideas that allow

Black women to cope with and, in most cases, transcend the confines of race, class, and gender oppression. How have African-American women as a group found the strength to oppose our objectification as "de mule uh de world?" How do we account for the voices of resistance of Audre Lorde, Ella Surrey, Maria Stewart, Fannie Barrier Williams, and Marita Bonner? What foundation sustained Sojourner Truth so that she could ask, "ain't I a woman?" The voices of these African-American women are not those of victims but of survivors. Their ideas and actions suggest that not only does a self-defined, articulated Black women's standpoint exist, but its presence has been essential to Black women's survival.

"A system of oppression," claims Black feminist activist Pauli Murray, "draws much of its strength from the acquiescence of its victims, who have accepted the dominant image of themselves and are paralyzed by a sense of helplessness" (1987, 106). Black women's ideas and actions force a rethinking of the concept of hegemony, the notion that Black women's objectification as the Other is so complete that we become willing participants in our own oppression. Most African-American women simply do not define ourselves as mammies, matriarchs, welfare mothers, mules, or sexually denigrated women. The ideology of domination in which these controlling images are embedded is much less cohesive or uniform than imagined.

African-American women encounter these controlling images, not as disembodied symbolic messages but as ideas that should provide meaning in our daily lives (Scott 1985). Black women's work and family experiences create the conditions whereby the contradictions between everyday experiences and the controlling images of Black womanhood become visible. Seeing the contradictions in the ideologies opens them up for demystification. Just as Sojourner Truth deconstructed the term *woman* by using her own concrete experiences to challenge it, so in a variety of ways do everyday African-American women do the same thing. That fewer Maria Stewarts, Sojourner Truths, Ella Surreys, or Johnny Mae Fieldses are heard from is less a statement about the existence of Black women's ideas than it is a reflection of the suppression of ideas that do exist. As Nancy White, an inner-city resident points out, "I like to say what I think. But I don't do that much because most people don't care what I think" (Gwaltney 1980, 156). Like Marita Bonner, far too many Black women remain motionless on the outside . . . but inside?

FINDING A VOICE: COMING TO TERMS WITH CONTRADICTIONS

"To be able to use the range of one's voice, to attempt to express the totality of self, is a recurring struggle in the tradition of [Black women] writers" maintains Black feminist literary critic Barbara Christian (1985, 172). African-American women have certainly expressed our individual voices. Black women have been described as generally outspoken and self-assertive speakers, and as a consequence of an Afrocentric expectation that both men and women participate in the public sphere, Black women communicate more nearly as equals with Black men (Stanback 1985). But despite this tradition, the overarching theme of finding a voice to express a self-defined Black women's standpoint remains a core theme in Black feminist thought.

Why this theme of self-definition should preoccupy African-American women is not surprising. Black women's lives are a series of negotiations that aim to reconcile the contradictions separating our own internally defined images of self as African-American women with our objectification as the Other. The struggle of living two lives, one for "them and one for ourselves" (Gwaltney 1980, 240) creates a peculiar tension to extract the definition of one's true self from the treatment afforded the denigrated categories in which all Black women are placed.

Much of the best of Black feminist thought reflects this effort to find a self-defined voice and express a fully articulated Afrocentric feminist standpoint. Audre Lorde observes that "within this country where racial difference creates a constant, if unspoken, distortion of vision, Black women have on the one hand always been highly visible, and so, on the other hand, have been rendered invisible through the depersonalization of racism" (1984, 42). Lorde also points out that the "visibility which makes us most vulnerable"—that accompanying being black—"is that which is also the source of our greatest strength" (p. 42). The category of "Black woman" makes all Black women especially visible and open to the objectification afforded Black women as a category. This group treatment renders each Black woman invisible as a fully human individual. But paradoxically, being treated as an invisible Other gives Black women a peculiar angle of vision, the outsider-within stance that has served so many African-American women intellectuals as a source of tremendous strength.

Resolving contradictions of this magnitude takes considerable inner strength. In describing the development of her own racial identity, Pauli Murray remembers: "My own self-esteem was elusive and difficult to sustain. I was not entirely free from the prevalent idea that I must prove myself worthy of the rights that white individuals took for granted. This psychological conditioning along with fear had reduced my capacity for resistance to racial injustice" (1987, 106). Murray's quest was for constructed knowledge (Belenky et al. 1986), a type of knowledge essential to resolving contradictions. To learn to speak in a "unique and authentic voice, women must 'jump outside' the frames and systems authorities provide and create their own frame" (p. 134). Unlike white women's images attached to the cult of true womanhood, the controlling images applied to Black women are so uniformly negative that they almost necessitate resistance if Black women are to have any positive self-images. For Black women, constructed knowledge of self emerges from the struggle to reject controlling images and integrate knowledge deemed personally important, usually knowledge essential to Black women's survival.[1]

SAFE SPACES AND FINDING A VOICE

While domination may be inevitable as a social fact, it is unlikely to be hegemonic as an ideology within that social space where Black women speak freely. This realm of relatively safe discourse, however narrow, is a necessary condition for Black women's resistance. Extended families, churches, and African-American community organizations are important locations where safe discourse potentially can occur. Sondra O'Neale describes the workings of this Black women's space: "Beyond the mask, in the ghetto of the black women's community, in her family, and, more important, in her psyche, is and has always been another world, a world in which she functions—sometimes in sorrow but more often in genuine joy . . . —by doing the things that 'normal' black women do" (1986, 139). This space is not only safe—it forms a prime location for resisting objectification as the Other. In this space Black women "observe the feminine images of the 'larger' culture, realize that these models are at best unsuitable and at worst destructive to them, and go about the business of fashioning themselves after the prevalent, historical black female role models in their own community" (O'Neale 1986, 139). By advancing Black women's empowerment through self-definition, the safe spaces housing this culture of resistance help Black women resist the dominant ideology promulgated not only outside Black communities but within African-American institutions.

These institutional sites where Black women construct independent self-definitions reflect the dialectical nature of oppression and activism. Institutions controlled by the dominant group such as schools, the media, literature, and popular culture are the initial source of externally defined, controlling images. African-American women have traditionally used Black families and community institutions as places where they could develop a Black women's culture of resistance. But African-American institutions such as churches and extended families can also perpetuate this dominant ideology. The resulting reality is much more complex than one of an external white society objectifying Black women as the Other with a unified Black community staunchly challenging these external assaults through its "culture of resistance." Instead, African-American women find themselves in a web of cross-cutting relationships, each presenting varying combinations of controlling images and Black women's self-definitions.

Historian Darlene Clark Hine suggests that the complexity of these institutional arrangements has profoundly affected Black women's consciousness and its articulation in a self-defined standpoint:

> Because of the interplay of racial animosity, class tensions, gender role differentiation, and regional economic variation, Black women, as a rule, developed and adhered to a cult of secrecy, a culture of dissemblance, to protect the sanctity of inner aspects of their lives. The dynamics of dissemblance involved creating the appearance of disclosure, an openness about themselves and their feelings, while actually remaining an enigma. Only with secrecy, thus achieving a self-imposed invisibility, could ordinary Black women accrue the psychic space and harness the resources needed to hold their own. (1989, 915)

What have been the primary focal points where Black women's consciousness has been nurtured and where African-American women have spoken freely in order to articulate a self-defined standpoint?

Black Women's Relationships with One Another

Black women's efforts to find a voice have occurred in at least three safe spaces. One location involves Black women's relationships with one another. In some cases, such as friendships and family interactions, these relationships are informal, private dealings among individuals. In others, as was the case during slavery (D. White 1985), in Black churches (Gilkes 1985), or in Black women's organizations (Gilkes 1982; Giddings 1988), more formal organizational ties have nurtured powerful Black women's communities. As mothers, daughters, sisters, and friends to one another, African-American women affirm one another (Myers 1980).

The mother/daughter relationship is one fundamental relationship among Black women. Countless Black mothers have empowered their daughters by passing on the everyday knowledge essential to survival as African-American women (Joseph 1981; Collins 1987). Mothers and mother figures emerge as central figures in autobiographies such as Maya Angelou's *I Know Why the Caged Bird Sings* (1969), Bebe Moore Campbell's

Sweet Summer (1989), and Mamie Garvin Fields and Karen Fields's *Lemon Swamp and Other Places* (1983). Alice Walker attributes the trust she has in herself to her mother. Walker "never doubted her powers of judgment because her mother assumed that they were sound; she never questioned her right to follow her intellectual bent, because her mother implicitly entitled her to it" (Washington 1984, 145). By giving her daughter a library card, Walker's mother knew the value of a free mind.

In the comfort of daily conversations, through serious conversation and humor, African-American women as sisters and friends affirm one another's humanity, specialness, and right to exist. Black women's fiction, such as Toni Cade Bambara's short story "The Johnson Girls" (1981) and Toni Morrison's novels *Sula* (1974), *The Bluest Eye* (1970), and *Beloved* (1987), is the primary location where Black women's friendships are taken seriously. In a dialogue with four other Black women, Evelyne Hammond describes this special relationship that Black women can have with one another: "I think most of the time you have to be there to experience it. When I am with other black women I always laugh. I think our humor comes from a shared recognition of who we all are in the world" (Clarke et al. 1983, 114).

This shared recognition often operates among African-American women who do not know one another but who see the need to value Black womanhood. Marita Golden describes her efforts in 1968 to attend a college which was "nestled . . . in the comfortable upper reaches of northwest Washington, surrounded by . . . the manicured, sprawling lawns of the city's upper class." To enter this world, Golden caught the bus downtown with "black women domestic workers who rode to the end of the line to clean house for young and middle-aged white matrons." Golden describes her fellow travelers' reaction to her acquiring a college education:

> They gazed proudly at me, nodding at the books in my lap. . . . I accepted their encouragement and hated America for never allowing them to be selfish or greedy, to feel the steel-hard bite of ambition. . . . They had parlayed their anger, brilliantly shaped it into a soft armor of survival. The spirit of those women sat with me in every class I took. (Golden 1983, 21)

My decision to pursue my doctorate was stimulated by a similar experience. In 1978 I offered a seminar as part of a national summer institute for teachers and other school personnel. After my Chicago workshop, an older Black woman participant whispered to me, "Honey, I'm real proud of you. Some folks don't want to see you up there [in the front of the classroom] but you belong there. Go back to school and get your Ph.D. and then they won't be able to tell you nothing!" In talking with other Black women, I have discovered that many of us have had similar experiences.

This issue of Black women being the ones who really listen to one another is an important one, particularly given the importance of voice in Black women's lives (Hooks 1989).[2] Audre Lorde describes the importance of voice in self-affirmation: "Of course I am afraid, because the transformation of silence into language and action is an act of self-revelation, and that always seems fraught with danger" (1984, 42). One can write for a nameless, faceless audience, but the act of using one's voice requires a listener. For African-American women the listener most able to move beyond the invisibility created by objectification as the Other in order to see and hear the fully human Black woman is another Black woman. This process of trusting one another can seem dangerous because only Black women know what it means to be Black women. But if we will not listen to one another, then who will?

While social science research on Black women's relationships remains scarce, Black women writers have recognized their importance. Mary Helen Washington points out that one distinguishing feature of Black women's literature is that it is about African-American women. Women talk to one another, and "their friendships with other women—mothers, sisters, grandmothers, friends, lovers—are vital to their growth and well-being" (1987, xxi). This emphasis on Black women's relationships is so striking that novelist Gayl Jones suggests that women writers select different themes from those of their male counterparts. In the work of many Black male writers, the significant relationships are those that involve confrontation with individuals outside the family and community. But among Black women writers, relationships within family and community, between men and women, and among women are treated as complex and significant (Tate 1983, 92).

Black women writers have explored themes such as the difficulties inherent in affirming Black women in a society that denigrates African-American women (Claudia's use of her relationship with her sister in searching for positive Black women's images in Toni Morrison's *The Bluest Eye*); of how Black women's relationships can support and renew (the relationship between Celie and Shug in Alice Walker's *The Color Purple*); or how such relationships can control and repress (Audre Lorde's relationship with her mother in *Zami* [1982]). Perhaps Ntozake Shange best summarizes the importance that Black women can have for one another in resisting oppressive conditions. Shange gives the following reason for why she writes: "When I die, I will not be guilty of having left a generation

denigrate = belittle

of girls behind thinking that anyone can tend to their emotional health other than themselves" (in Tate 1983, 162).

The Black Women's Blues Tradition

African-American music as art has provided a second location where Black women have found a voice. "Art is special because of its ability to influence feelings as well as knowledge," suggests Angela Davis (1989, 200). Davis contends that the dominant group failed to grasp the social function of music in general and particularly the central role music played in all aspects of life in West African society. As a result, "Black people were able to create with their music an aesthetic community of resistance, which in turn encouraged and nurtured a political community of active struggle for freedom" (1989, 201). Spirituals, blues, jazz, and the progressive raps of the 1980s all form part of a "continuum of struggle which is at once aesthetic and political" (p. 201).

Afrocentric communication maintains the integrity of the individual and his or her personal voice, but does so in the context of group activity (Smitherman 1977; Kochman 1981; Asante 1987; Cannon 1988; Brown 1989). In music one effect of this oral mode of discourse is that individuality, rather than being stifled by group activity or being equated with specialization, actually flourishes in a group context (Sidran 1971).[3] "There's something about music that is so penetrating that your soul gets the message. No matter what trouble comes to a person, music can help him face it," claims Mahalia Jackson (1985, 454). "A song must do something for me as well as for the people that hear it. I can't sing a song that doesn't have a message. If it doesn't have the strength it can't lift you" (p. 446).

The blues tradition is an essential part of African-American music.[4] Blues singer Alberta Hunter explains the importance of the blues as a way of dealing with pain: "To me, the blues are almost religious . . . almost sacred—when we sing the blues, we're singing out of our own hearts . . . our feelings" (Harrison 1978, 63). Black people's ability to cope with and even transcend trouble without ignoring it means that it will not destroy us (Cone 1972).

Traditionally, blues assumed a similar function in African-American oral culture as that played by print media for white, visually based culture. Blues was not just entertainment—it was a way of solidifying community and commenting on the social fabric of Black life in America. Sherley Anne Williams contends that "the blues records of each decade explain something about the philosophical basis of our lives as black people. If we don't understand that as so-called intellectuals, then we don't really understand anything about ourselves" (in Tate 1983, 208). For African-American women, blues seemed to be everywhere. Mahalia Jackson describes its pervasiveness during her childhood in New Orleans: "The famous white singers like Caruso—you might hear them when you went by a white folk's house, but in a colored house you heard blues. You couldn't help but hear blues—all through the thin partitions of the houses—through the open windows—up and down the street in the colored neighborhoods—everybody played it real loud" (1985, 447).

Black women have been central in maintaining, transforming, and recreating the blues tradition of African-American culture (Harrison 1978, 1988; Russell 1982). Michele Russell asserts that "blues, first and last, are a familiar idiom for Black women, even a staple of life" (1982, 130). Blues has occupied a special place in Black women's music as a site of the expression of Black women's self-definitions. The blues singer strives to create an atmosphere in which analysis can take place, and yet this atmosphere is intensely personal and individualistic. When Black women sing the blues, we sing our own personalized, individualistic blues while simultaneously expressing the collective blues of African-American women.

Michele Russell's (1982) analysis of five Black women blues singers' music demonstrates how the texts of blues singers can be seen as expressions of a Black women's standpoint. Russell claims that the works of Bessie Smith, Bessie Jackson, Billie Holiday, Nina Simone, and Esther Phillips help Black women "own their past, present, and future." To Russell, these women are primary because "the content of their message, combined with the form of their delivery, make them so" (p. 130).

The music of the classic blues singers of the 1920s—almost exclusively women—marks the early written record of this dimension of Afrocentric oral culture. The songs themselves were originally sung in small communities, where boundaries distinguishing singer from audience, call from response, and thought from action were fluid and permeable. These records were made exclusively for the "race market" of African-Americans. Because literacy was not possible for large numbers of Black women, these recordings represented the first permanent documents expressing a Black women's standpoint accessible to Black women in diverse communities. The songs can be seen as poetry, as expressions of ordinary Black women rearticulated through the Afrocentric oral tradition.

The lyrics sung by many of the Black women blues singers challenge the externally defined controlling images used to justify Black women's objectification as the Other. The songs of Ma Rainey, dubbed "Queen of the Blues" and the first major female blues singer to be extensively recorded, validate the Black feminist intellectual tradition. In contrast to the ingenues of most white popular music of the same period, Ma Rainey and her contemporaries sing of mature, sexual women (Lieb 1981). For example, Sara Martin's "Mean Tight Mama" rejects the cult of true womanhood and its confining images of beauty:

> Now my hair is nappy and I don't wear no clothes of silk
> Now my hair is nappy and I don't wear no clothes of silk
> But the cow that's black and ugly has often got the sweetest milk.
> (Harrison 1978, 69)

Bessie Smith's "Get It, Bring It, and Put It Right Here"—like the words of Maria Stewart—advises Black women to possess the spirit of independence. She sings to her man:

> I've had a man for fifteen years, give him his room and his board
> Once he was like a Cadillac, now he's like an old worn-out Ford.
> He never brought me a lousy dime, and put it in my hand
> Oh, there'll be some changes from now on, according to my plan.
> He's got to get it, bring it, and put it right here
> Or else he's gonna keep it out there.
> If he must steal it, beg it, or borrow it somewhere
> Long as he gets it, I don't care. (Russell 1982, 133)

Sometimes the texts of Black women blues singers take overtly political forms. Billie Holiday recorded "Strange Fruit" in 1939 during a decade rife with racial unrest:

> Southern trees bear a strange fruit, blood on the leaves and blood at
>   the root
> Black body swinging in the Southern breeze, strange fruit hanging from
>   the poplar trees.
> Pastoral scene of the gallant South, the bulging eyes and the twisted
>   mouth,
> Scent of magnolia sweet and fresh, and the sudden smell of burning
>   flesh!
> Here is a fruit for the crows to pluck, for the rain to gather, for the wind
>   to suck, for the sun to rot, for a tree to drop,
> Here is a strange and bitter crop. (*Billie Holiday Anthology* 1976, 111).

Through her powerful rendition of these lyrics, Billie Holiday demonstrated a direct connection to the antilynching political activism of Ida B. Wells and other better-known Black feminists.

The emergence of professional songwriters modified the very close and personal relationship among Black women blues singers, their songs, and the Afrocentric group tradition on which all depended for the act of creation and which the act of creation affirms and extends (Williams 1979). Commodification of the blues and its transformation into marketable crossover music has virtually stripped it of its close ties to the African-American oral tradition. Thus the expression of a Black women's voice in the oral blues tradition is being supplemented and may be supplanted by a growing Black women's voice in a third location, the space created by Black women writers.[5]

The Voices of Black Women Writers

During the summer of 1944, recent law school graduate Pauli Murray returned to her California apartment and found the following anonymous note from the "South Crocker Street Property Owner's Association" tacked to her door: "We . . . wish to inform you the flat you now occupy . . . is restricted to the white or Caucasian race only. . . . We intend to uphold these restrictions, therefore we ask that you vacate the above mentioned flat . . . within seven days" (1987, 253). Murray's response was to write. She remembers: "I was learning that creative expression is an integral part of the equipment needed in the service of a compelling cause; it is another form of activism. Words poured from my typewriter" (p. 255).

Increased literacy among African-Americans has provided new opportunities for Black women to transform former institutional sites of domination such as scholarship and literature into institutional sites of resistance. Trudier Harris (1988) suggests that a community of Black women writers has emerged since 1970, one in which African-American women engage in dialogue among one another in order to explore formerly taboo subjects. Black feminist literary criticism is documenting the intellectual and personal space created for African-American women in this emerging body of ideas (Washington 1980, 1982; Tate 1983; Evans 1984; Christian 1985; McDowell 1985; Pryse and Spillers 1985; O'Neale 1986). Especially noteworthy are the ways in which this emerging community of Black women writers builds on former themes and approaches of the Black women's blues tradition (Williams 1979) and of earlier Black women writers (Cannon 1988). Also key are the new themes raised by contemporary Black women writers. For example, Trudier Harris (1988) contends that a variety of taboos are violated in contemporary Black women's literature, among them the taboos that Black women were not allowed to leave their children, have interracial affairs, have lesbian relationships, be the victims of incest, or generally escape the confining image of "long-suffering commitment to Black people." In all, the emerging work of this growing community potentially offers another safe space where Black women can articulate a self-defined standpoint.

Not everyone agrees that Black women writers are using the full range of their voices to create safe spaces. In discussing the potential for systems of domination to harness the creative potential of Black music, Angela Davis observes, "some of the superstars of popular-musical culture today are unquestionably musical genuises, but they have distorted the Black music tradition by brilliantly developing its form while ignoring its content of struggle and freedom" (1989, 208). Black literary critic Sondra O'Neale suggests that a similar process may be affecting Black women's writing. "Where are the Angela Davises, Ida B. Wellses, and Daisy Bateses of black feminist literature?" she asks (1986, 144). O'Neale contends that one of the tasks of the Black woman critic is to assess whether contemporary Black women's literature reveals those strengths that have furthered Black women's survival. "Lamentably," O'Neale points out, "we are still seeing the black women in roles that the prevailing cultural manipulators ascribe to her—always on the fringes of society, always alone" (p. 153).

The specialized thought of contemporary Black feminist writers and scholars should be able to draw on the long-standing Afrocentric tradition of struggle in order to produce "progressive art." As Angela Davis observes, "progressive art can assist people to learn not only about the objective forces at work in the society in which they live, but also about the intensely social character of their interior lives. Ultimately it can propel people toward social emancipation" (1989, 200). This type of art is emancipatory because it fuses thought, feeling, and action and helps its participants see their world differently and act to change it. Traditionally, everyday thought expressed in Black women's music approximated this definition of *progressive*. It remains to be seen whether the specialized thought generated by contemporary Black feminist thinkers in very different institutional locations is capable of creating safe spaces that will carry African-American women even further.

CONSCIOUSNESS AS A SPHERE OF FREEDOM

Taken together, Black women's relationships with one another, the Black women's blues tradition, and the emerging influence of Black women writers coalesce to offer an alternative worldview to that embedded in institutional locations of domination. These three sites offer safe spaces that nurture the everyday and specialized thought of African-American women and where Black women intellectuals can absorb ideas and experiences for the task of rearticulating Black women's experiences and infusing them with new meaning. More important, these new meanings offer African-American women potentially powerful tools to resist the controlling images of Black womanhood. Far from being a secondary concern in bringing about social change, challenging controlling images and replacing them with a Black women's standpoint is an essential component in resisting systems of race, gender, and class oppression (Thompson-Cager 1989). What are some of the fundamental themes developed in these safe spaces?

The Importance of Self-Definition

"Black groups digging on white philosophies ought to consider the source. Know who's playing the music before you dance," cautions poet Nikki Giovanni (1971, 126). Her advice is especially germane for African-American women. Giovanni suggests: "We Black women are the single group in the West intact. And anybody can see we're pretty shaky. We are . . . the only group that derives its identity from itself. I think it's been rather unconscious but we measure ourselves by ourselves, and I think that's a practice we can ill afford to lose" (1971, 144). Black women's survival is at stake, and creating self-definitions reflecting an independent Afrocentric feminist consciousness is an essential part of that survival.

The issue of the journey from internalized oppression to the "free mind" of a self-defined, Afrocentric feminist consciousness is a prominent theme in the works of Black women writers. Author Alexis DeVeaux notes that there is a "great exploration of the self in women's work. It's the self in relationship with an intimate other, with the community, the nation and the world" (in Tate 1983, 54). Far from being a narcissistic or trivial concern, this placement of self at the center of analysis is critical for understanding a host of other relationships. DeVeaux continues, "you have to understand what your place as an individual is and the place of the person who is close to you. You have to understand the space between you before you can understand more complex or larger groups" (p. 54).

Black women have also stressed the importance of self-definition as part of the journey from victimization to a free mind in their blues. Sherley Anne Williams's analysis of the affirmation of self in the blues make a critical contribution in understanding the blues as a Black women's text. In discussing the blues roots of Black literature, Williams notes, "the assertion of individuality and the implied assertion—as action, not mere verbal statement—of self is an important dimension of the blues" (1979, 130).

The assertion of self usually comes at the end of a song, after the description or analysis of the troublesome situation. This affirmation of self is often the only solution to that problem or situation. Nina Simone's (1985) classic blues song "Four Women" illustrates this use of the blues to affirm self. Simone sings of three Black women whose experiences typify controlling images—Aunt Sarah, the mule, whose back is bent from a lifetime of hard work; Sweet Thing, the Black prostitute who will belong to anyone who has money to buy; and Saphronia, the mulatto whose Black mother was raped late one night. Simone explores Black women's objectification as the Other by invoking the pain these three women actually feel. But Peaches, the fourth woman, is an especially powerful figure, because Peaches is angry. "I'm awfully bitter these days," Peaches cries out, "because my parents were slaves." These words and the feelings they invoke demonstrate her growing awareness and self-definition of the situation she encountered and offer to the listener, not sadness and remorse, but an anger that leads to action. This is the type of individuality Williams means—not that of talk but self-definitions that foster action.

While the theme of the journey also appears in the work of Black men, African-American women writers and musicians explore this journey toward freedom in ways that are characteristically female (Thompson-Cager 1989). Black women's journeys, though at times embracing political and social issues, basically take personal and psychological forms and rarely reflect the freedom of movement of Black men who hop "trains," "hit the road," or in other ways physically travel in order to find that elusive sphere of freedom from racial oppression. Instead, Black women's journeys often involve "the transformation of silence into language and action" (Lorde 1984, 40). Typically tied to children and/or community, fictional Black women characters search for self-definition within close geographical boundaries. Even though physical limitations confine the Black heroine's quest to a specific area, "forming complex personal relationships adds depth to her identity quest in lieu of geographical breadth" (Tate 1983, xxi). In their search for self-definition and the power of a free mind, Black heroines may remain "motionless on the outside . . . but inside?"

Given the physical limitations on Black women's mobility, the conceptualization of self that is part of Black women's self-definitions is distinctive. Self is not defined as the increased autonomy gained by separating oneself from others. Instead, self is found in the context of family and community—as Paule Marshall describes it, "the ability to recognize one's continuity with the larger community" (Washington 1984, 159). By being accountable to others, African-American women develop more fully human, less objectified selves. Sonia Sanchez points to this version of self by stating, "we must move past always focusing on the 'personal self' because there's a larger self. There's a 'self' of black people" (Tate 1983, 134). Rather than defining self in opposition to others, the connectedness among individuals provides Black women deeper, more meaningful self-definitions.[6]

This journey toward self-definition has political significance. As Mary Helen Washington observes, Black women who struggle to "forge an identity larger than the one society would force upon them . . . are aware and conscious, and that very consciousness is potent" (1980, xv). Identity is not the goal but rather the point of departure in the process of self-definition. In this process Black women journey toward an understanding of how our personal lives have been fundamentally shaped by interlocking systems of race, gender, and class oppression. Peaches's statement, "I'm awfully bitter these days because my parents were slaves," illustrates this transformation.

The journey toward self-definition offers a powerful challenge to the externally defined, controlling images of African-American women. Replacing negative images with positive ones can be equally problematic if the function of stereotypes as controlling images remains unrecognized. John Gwaltney's (1980) interview with Nancy White, a 73-year-old Black woman, suggests that ordinary Black women can be acutely aware of the power of these controlling images. To Nancy White the difference between the controlling images applied to African-American and white women are those of degree, not of kind:

> My mother used to say that the black woman is the white man's mule and the white woman is his dog. Now, she said that to say this: we do the heavy work and get beat whether we do it well or not. But the white woman is closer to the master and he pats them on the head and lets them sleep in the house, but he ain't gon' treat neither one like he was dealing with a person. (p. 148)

Although both groups are objectified, albeit in different ways, the function of the images is to dehumanize and control both groups. Seen in this light, it makes little sense in the long run for Black women to exchange one set of controlling images for another even if positive stereotypes bring better treatment in the short run.

The insistence on Black female self-definition reframes the entire dialogue from one of protesting the technical accuracy of an image—namely, refuting the Black matriarchy thesis— to one stressing the power dynamics underlying the very process of definition itself. By insisting on self-definition, Black women question not only what has been said about African-American women but the credibility and the intentions of those possessing the power to define. When Black women define ourselves, we clearly reject the assumption that those in positions granting them the authority to interpret our reality are entitled to do so. Regardless of the actual content of Black women's self-definitions, the act of insisting on Black female self-definition validates Black women's power as human subjects.

Self-Valuation and Respect

While self-definition speaks to the power dynamics involved in rejecting externally defined, controlling images of Black womanhood, the theme of Black women's self-valuation addresses the actual content of these self-definitions. Through relationships with one another, music, and literature, African-American women create self-valuations that challenge externally defined notions of Black womanhood.

Many of the controlling images applied to African-American women are actually distorted renderings of those aspects of our behavior that threaten existing power arrangements (Gilkes 1983a; D. White 1985). For example, strong mothers are threatening because they contradict elite white male definitions of femininity. To ridicule strong, assertive Black mothers by labeling them matriarchs reflects an effort to control a dimension of Black women's behavior that threatens the status quo. African-American women who value those aspects of Black womanhood that are stereotyped, ridiculed, and maligned in scholarship and the popular media challenge some of the basic ideas inherent in an ideology of domination.

The significance of self-valuation is illustrated through the emphasis that Black feminist thinkers place on respect. In a society in which no one is obligated to respect African-American women, we have long admonished one another to have self-respect and to demand the respect of others. Black women's voices from a variety of sources resonate with this demand for respect. Katie G. Cannon (1988) suggests that Black womanist ethics embraces three basic dimensions of "invisible dignity," "quiet grace," and "unstated courage," all qualities essential for self-valuation and self-respect. Black feminist critic Claudia Tate (1983) reports that the issue of self-esteem is so primary in the writing of Black women that it deserves special attention. Tate claims that what the writers seem to be saying is that "women must assume responsibility for strengthening their self-esteem by learning to love and appreciate themselves" (p. xxiii). Her analysis is certainly borne out in Alice Walker's comments to an audience of women. Walker cautioned, "please remember, especially in these times of group-think and the right-on chorus, that no person is your friend (or kin) who demands your silence, or denies your right to grow and be perceived as fully blossomed as you were intended. Or who belittles in any fashion the gifts you labor so to bring into the world" (Walker

1983, 36). The right to be Black *and* female *and* respected pervades everyday conversations among African-American women. In describing the importance self-respect has for her, elderly domestic worker Sara Brooks notes, "I may not have as much as you, I may not have the education you got, but still, if I conduct myself as a decent person, I'm just as good as anybody" (Simonsen 1986, 132).

Respect from others—especially from Black men—is a recurring theme in Black women's writing. In describing the things a woman wants out of life, middle-class Marita Bonner lists "a career as fixed and as calmly brilliant as the North Star. The one real thing that money buys. Time . . . And of course, a husband you can look up to without looking down on yourself" (Bonner 1987, 3). Black women's belief in respect also emerges in the works of a variety of Black women blues singers. Perhaps the best-known popular statement of Black women's demand for self-respect and that of others is found in Aretha Franklin's (1967) rendition of the Otis Redding song "Respect." Aretha sings to her man:

> What you want? Baby I got it.
> What you need? You know I got it.
> All I'm asking for is a little respect when you come home.

Even though the lyrics can be sung by anyone, they take on special meaning when sung by Aretha in the way that she sings them. On one level the song functions as a metaphor for the condition of African-Americans in a racist society. But Aretha's being a Black woman enables the song to tap a deeper meaning. Within the blues tradition, the listening audience of African-American women assumes "we" Black women, even though Aretha as the blues singer sings "I." Sherley Anne Williams describes the power of Aretha's blues: "Aretha was right on time, but there was also something about the way Aretha characterized respect as something given with force and great effort and cost. And when she even went so far as to spell the word 'respect,' we just knew that this sister wasn't playing around about getting Respect and keeping it" (Williams 1979, 124).

June Jordan suggests that this emphasis on respect is tied to a distinctive Black feminist politic. For Jordan, a "morally defensible Black feminism" is verified in the ways Black women present ourselves to others, and in the ways in which Black women treat people different from ourselves. While self-respect is essential, respect for others is key. "As a Black feminist," claims Jordan, "I cannot be expected to respect what somebody else calls self-love if that concept of self-love requires my suicide to any degree" (1981, 144).

Self-Reliance and Independence

In her 1831 essay Black feminist thinker Maria Stewart not only encouraged Black women's self-definition and self-valuations but linked Black women's self-reliance with issues of survival:

> We have never had an opportunity of displaying our talents; therefore the world thinks we know nothing. . . . Possess the spirit of independence. The Americans do, and why should not you? Possess the spirit of men, bold and enterprising, fearless and undaunted: Sue for your rights and privileges. . . . You can but die if you make the attempt; and we shall certainly die if you do not. (Richardson 1987, 38)

Whether by choice or circumstance, African-American women have "possessed the spirit of independence," have been self-reliant, and have encouraged one another to value this vision of womanhood that clearly challenges prevailing notions of femininity (Steady 1987). These beliefs apparently find wide support among African-American women. For example, when asked what they admired about their mothers, the women in Gloria Joseph's (1981) study of the Black mother/daughter relationship recounted their mothers' independence and ability to provide in the face of difficulties. Participants in Lena Wright Myers's (1980) study of Black women's coping skills respected women who were resourceful and self-reliant. Black women's autobiographies, such as Shirley Chisholm's *Unbought and Unbossed* (1970) and Maya Angelou's *I Know Why the Caged Bird Sings* (1969), typify Black women's self-valuation of self-reliance. As elderly domestic worker Nancy White cogently explains, "most black women can be their own boss, so that's what they be" (Gwaltney 1980, 149).

The works of prominent Black women blues singers also counsel the importance of self-reliance and independence for African-American women. In her classic ballad "God Bless the Child That Got His Own," Billie Holiday sings:

> The strong gets more, while the weak ones fade,
> Empty pockets don't ever make the grade;
> Mama may have, Papa may have,
> But God bless the child that got his own!
> (*Billie Holiday Anthology* 1976, 12)

In this mournful song Billie Holiday offers an insightful analysis of the need for autonomy and self-reliance. "Money, you got lots of friends, crowdin' 'round the door," she proclaims. But "when you're gone and spendin' ends they don't come no more." In these passages Holiday admonishes Black women to become financially independent because having one's "own" allows women to choose their relationships. In "Tain't Nobody's Business if I Do," Holiday offers a vision of the type of freedom Black women will have if we become self-reliant and independent:

> If I should take a notion, to jump into the ocean,
> If I dislike my lover and leave him for another,
> If I go to church on Sunday then cabaret on Monday,
> If I should get the feeling to dance upon the ceilin'.
> Tain't nobody's business if I do! (*Billie Holiday Anthology* 1976, 119)

The linking of economic self-sufficiency as one critical dimension of self-reliance with the demand for respect permeates Black feminist thought. For example, in "Respect" when Aretha sings, "your kisses sweeter than honey, but guess what, so is my money," she demands respect on the basis of her economic self-reliance. Perhaps this connection between respect, self-reliance, and assertiveness is best summarized by Nancy White, who declares, "there is a very few black women that their husbands can pocketbook to death because we can do for ourselves and will do so in a minute!" (Gwaltney 1980, 149).

Self, Change, and Empowerment

"The master's tools will never dismantle the master's house. They may allow us temporarily to beat him at his own game, but they will never enable us to bring about genuine change" (Lorde 1984, 112). In this passage Audre Lorde explores how independent self-definitions empower Black women to bring about social change. By struggling for a self-defined Afrocentric feminist consciousness that rejects the "master's" images, African-American women change ourselves. This changed consciousness in turn is a fundamental factor in empowering Black women to change the conditions of our lives.

Nikki Giovanni illuminates these connections among self, change, and empowerment. She admonishes that people are rarely powerless, no matter how stringent the restrictions on our lives: "We've got to live in the real world. If we don't like the world we're living in, change it. And if we can't change it, we change ourselves. We can do something" (in Tate 1983, 68). Giovanni recognizes that effective change occurs through action. The multiple strategies of resistance that Black women have employed, such as withdrawing from postemancipation agricultural work in order to return their labor to their families, ostensibly conforming to the deference rituals of domestic work, protesting male bias in African-American organizations, or creating the progressive art of Black women's blues all represent physical actions to bring about change. Here is the connected self and the empowerment that comes from change in the context of community.

But change can also occur in the private, personal space of an individual woman's consciousness. Equally fundamental, this type of change is also empowering. If a Black woman is forced to remain "motionless on the outside," she can always develop the "inside" of a changed consciousness as a sphere of freedom. Becoming empowered through self-knowledge, even within conditions that severely limit one's ability to act, is essential. In Black women's literature

> this type of change . . . occurs because the heroine recognizes, and more importantly respects her inability to alter a situation. . . . This is not to imply that she is completely circumscribed by her limitations. On the contrary, she learns to exceed former boundaries but only as a direct result of knowing where they lie. In this regard, she teaches her readers a great deal about constructing a meaningful life in the midst of chaos and contingencies, armed with nothing more than her intellect and emotions. (Tate 1983, xxiv)

In this passage Claudia Tate demonstrates the significance of rearticulation. But rearticulation does not mean reconciling Afrocentric feminist ethics and values with opposing Eurocentric masculinist ones. Instead, as Chezia Thompson-Cager contends, rearticulation "confronts them in the tradition of 'naming as power' by revealing them very carefully" (1989, 590). Naming daily life by putting language to everyday experience infuses it with the new meaning of an Afrocentric feminist consciousness and becomes a way of transcending the limitations of race, gender, and class subordination.

Black women's literature contains many examples of how Black women are empowered by a changed consciousness. Barbara Christian maintains that the heroines of 1940s Black women's literature, such as Lutie Johnson in Ann Petry's *The Street* (1946) and Cleo Judson in Dorothy West's *The Living Is Easy* (1948), are defeated not only by social reality but by their "lack of self-knowledge." In contrast, the heroines from the 1950s to the present represent a significant shift toward self-knowledge as a sphere of freedom. Christian dates the shift from Gwendolyn Brooks's *Maud Martha* (1953) and claims, "because Maud Martha constructs her own standards, she manages to transform that 'little life' into so much more despite the limits set on her. . . . [she] emerges neither crushed nor triumphant" (1985, 176).

No matter how oppressed an individual woman may be, contemporary

African-American women writers place the power to save the self within the self (Harris 1988). Other Black women may assist a Black woman in this journey toward empowerment, but the ultimate responsibility for self-definitions and self-valuations lies within the individual woman herself. An individual woman may use multiple strategies in her quest for the constructed knowledge of an independent voice. Like Celie in Alice Walker's *The Color Purple*, some women write themselves free. Sexually, physically, and emotionally abused, Celie writes letters to God when no one else will listen. The act of acquiring a voice through writing, of breaking silence with language, eventually moves her to the action of talking with others. Other women talk themselves free. In *Their Eyes Were Watching God*, Janie tells her story to a good friend, a prime example of the rearticulation process essential for Black feminist thought (Hurston 1937). Ntozake Shange's *For Colored Girls* (1975) also captures this journey toward self-definition, self-valuation, and an empowered self. At the end of the play the women gather around one woman who shares the pain she experienced at seeing her children killed. They listen until she says "I found God in myself and I loved her fiercely." These words, expressing her ability to define herself as worthwhile, draw them together. They touch one another as part of a Black women's community that heals the member in pain, but only after she has taken the first step of wanting to be healed, of wanting to make the journey toward finding the voice of empowerment.

Persistence is a fundamental requirement of this journey from silence to language to action. Black women's blues contains numerous messages to Black women to keep on pushing despite the difficulties. When Sweet Honey in the Rock (1985) sing the traditional African-American song "We'll Understand It Better By and By," they sing of hope in times of trouble. When Aretha Franklin (1967) sings that change has been a "long time comin' " but that she knows her "change is gonna come," she acknowledges the difficulties of the present and holds out hope for the future, but only for those who persist. These songs tap deep roots in African-American women. The message is to continue the connectedness of self with others, to persist through the responsibilities of hard times, because understanding and change will come.

Black women's persistence is fostered by the strong belief that to be Black and female is valuable and worthy of respect. In a song "A Change Is Gonna Come," Aretha Franklin (1967) expresses this feeling of enduring in spite of the odds. She sings that there were times that she thought that she would not last for long. She sings of how it has been an "uphill journey all the way" to find the strength to carry on. But in spite of the difficulties, Aretha "knows" that "a change is gonna come."

Actions to bring about change, whether the struggle for an Afrocentric feminist consciousness or the persistence needed for institutional transformation, empower African-American women. Because our actions change the world from one in which we merely exist to one over which we have some control, they enable us to see everyday life as being in process and therefore amenable to change. By persisting in the journey toward self-definition we are changed, and this change empowers us. Perhaps this is why so many African-American women have managed to persist and "make a way out of no way." Perhaps they knew the power of self-definition.

NOTES

1. Belenky et al. (1986) suggest that achieving constructed knowledge requires self-reflection about and distancing from familiar situations, whether psychological and/or physical. For Black women intellectuals, being outsiders within may provide the distance from and angle of vision on the familiar that can be used to "find a voice" or create constructed knowledge. Belenky et al. describe this process as affecting individuals. I suggest that a similar argument can be applied to Black women as a group.

2. Belenky et al. (1986) report that women repeatedly use the metaphor of voice to depict their intellectual and ethical development: "The tendency for women to ground their epistemological premises in metaphors suggesting speaking and listening is at odds with the visual metaphors (such as equating knowledge with illumination, knowing with seeing, and truth with light) that scientists and philosophers most often use to express their sense of mind" (p. 16). This emphasis on voice in women's culture parallels the importance of oral communication in African-American culture (Sidran 1971; Smitherman 1977).

3. Sidran (1971) suggests that to get one's own "sound" is a key part of vocalized Black music. Black theologian James Cone has also written about Black music as carrier of the values of African-American culture. Cone notes that Black music is "unity music. It unites the joy and the sorrow, the love and the hate, the hope and the despair of black people. . . . Black music is unifying because it confronts the individual with the truth of black existence and affirms that black being is possible only in a communal context. Black music is functional. Its purposes and aims are directly related to the consciousness of the black community" (1972, 5). Note the both/and orientation of Cone's description, an analysis rejecting the either/or dichotomous thinking of Western societies. Moreover, Cone's discussion of functionality reinforces the discussion of functional beauty presented in Chapter 4.

4. Black women have participated in all forms of Black music but have been especially central in vocal music such as spirituals, gospel, and the blues (Jackson 1981). I focus on the blues because of its association with the Black women's secular tradition. Though a more recent phenomenon, gospel music is also "a Black feminine musical tradition" (Jackson 1981). With roots in the urban Black folk church, the text of gospel songs could also be examined.

5. Another emerging location for Black women's voice is in the works of African-American women filmmakers. Julie Dash's *Illusions* and *Diary of an African Nun*, Michelle Parkerson's *Gotta Make That Journey: Sweet Honey in the Rock*, Ayoka Chenzira's satiric

Hair Piece, and Kathleen Collins's *Losing Ground* all explore different facets of Black women's reality. For information on Black women filmmakers, see Campbell (1983). More general information on Black women in film can be found in Mapp (1973).

6. Afrocentric scholars have examined this conceptualization of the self in African and African-American communities. See Smitherman (1977), Asante (1987), Myers (1988), and Brown (1989). For feminist analyses of women's development of self as a distinctive process, see especially Evelyn Keller's (1985) discussion of dynamic autonomy and how it relates to relationships of domination, and Benhabib and Cornell's (1987) discussion of the unencumbered self.

Chapter 6

BLACK WOMEN AND MOTHERHOOD

Just yesterday I stood for a few minutes at the top of the stairs leading to a white doctor's office in a white neighborhood. I watched one Black woman after another trudge to the corner, where she then waited to catch the bus home. These were Black women still cleaning somebody else's house or Black women still caring for somebody else's sick or elderly, before they came back to the frequently thankless chores of their own loneliness, their own families. And I felt angry and I felt ashamed. And I felt, once again, the kindling heat of my hope that we, the daughters of these Black women, will honor their sacrifice by giving them thanks. We will undertake, with pride, every transcendent dream of freedom made possible by the humility of their love.

—June Jordan 1985, 105

June Jordan's words poignantly express the need for Black feminists to honor our mothers' sacrifice by developing an Afrocentric feminist analysis of Black motherhood. Until recently analyses of Black motherhood have largely been the province of men, both white and Black, and male assumptions about Black women as mothers have prevailed. Black mothers have been accused of failing to discipline their children, of emasculating their sons, of defeminizing their daughters, and of retarding their children's academic achievement (Wade-Gayles 1980). Citing high rates of divorce, female-headed households, and out-of-wedlock births, white male scholars and their representatives claim that African-American mothers wield unnatural power in allegedly deteriorating family structures (Moynihan 1965; Zinn 1989). The African-American mothers observed by Jordan vanish from these accounts.

White feminist work on motherhood has failed to produce an effective critique of elite white male analyses of Black motherhood. Grounded in a white, middle-class women's standpoint, white feminist analyses have been profoundly affected by the limitations that this angle of vision has on race (Chodorow 1974, 1978; Flax 1978; Chodorow and Contratto 1982). While white feminists have effectively confronted white male analyses of their own experiences as mothers, they rarely challenge controlling images such as the mammy, the matriarch, and the welfare mother and therefore fail to include Black mothers "still cleaning somebody else's house or . . . caring for somebody else's sick or elderly." As a result, white feminist theories have had limited utility for African-American women (Joseph 1984).

In African-American communities the view has been quite different. As Barbara Christian contends, the "concept of motherhood is of central importance in the philosophy of both African and Afro-American peoples" (1985, 213). But in spite of its centrality, Black male scholars in particular typically glorify Black motherhood by refusing to acknowledge the issues faced by Black mothers who "came back to the frequently thankless chores of their own loneliness, their own families." By claiming that Black women are richly endowed with devotion, self-sacrifice, and unconditional love—the attributes associated with archetypal motherhood—Black men inadvertently foster a different controlling image for Black women, that of the "superstrong Black mother" (Staples 1973; Dance 1979). In many African-American communities so much sanctification surrounds Black motherhood that "the idea that mothers should live lives of sacrifice has come to be seen as the norm" (Christian 1985, 234).

Far too many Black men who praise their own mothers feel less accountable to the mothers of their own children. They allow their wives and girlfriends to support the growing numbers of African-American children living in poverty (Frazier 1948; Burnham 1985; U.S. Department of Commerce 1986, 1989). Despite the alarming deterioration of economic and social supports for Black mothers, large numbers of young men encourage their unmarried teenaged girlfriends to give birth to children whose futures are at risk (Ladner 1972; Ladner and Gourdine 1984; Simms 1988). Even when they are aware of the poverty and struggles these women face, many Black men cannot get beyond the powerful controlling image of the superstrong Black mother in order to see the very real costs of mothering to African-American women. Michele Wallace describes the tenacity of this controlling image:

I remember once I was watching a news show with a black male friend of mine who had a Ph.D. in psychology and was the director of an out-patient clinic. We were looking at some footage of a black woman. . . . She was in bed wrapped in blankets, her numerous small, poorly clothed children huddled around her. Her apartment looked rat-infested, cramped, and dirty. She had not, she said, had heat and hot water for days. My friend, a solid member of the middle class now but surely no stranger to poverty in his childhood, felt obliged to comment . . . "That's a *strong* sister," as he bowed his head in reverence. (1978, 108–9)

The absence of a fully articulated Afrocentric feminist standpoint on motherhood is striking but not particularly surprising. While Black women have produced insightful critiques of both white male and white feminist analyses of motherhood (King 1973; Davis 1981; Gilkes 1983a; Hooks 1981), we have paid far less attention to Black male views. This silence partly reflects the self-imposed restrictions that accompany African-Americans' efforts to present a united front to the dominant group. Part of Black women's reluctance to challenge Black men's ideas in particular stems from the vehement attacks sustained by those Black feminist scholars, such as Michele Wallace, Alice Walker, and Ntozake Shange, who have been perceived as critical of Black men (see, for example, Staples 1978). But much of our silence emanates from an unwillingness to criticize Black men's well-intentioned efforts to defend and protect Black womanhood. Glorifying the strong Black mother represents Black men's attempts to replace negative white male interpretations with positive Black male ones. But no matter how sincere, externally defined definitions of Black womanhood—even those offered by sympathetic African-American men—are bound to come with their own set of problems.

In the case of Black motherhood, the problems have been a stifling of dialogue among African-American women and the perpetuation of ttroublesome, controlling images, both negative and positive. As Renita Weems observes: "We have simply sat and nodded while others talked about the magnificent women who bore and raised them and who, along with God, made a way out of no way. . . . We paid to hear them lecture about the invincible strength and genius of the Black mother, knowing full well that the image can be as bogus as the one of the happy slave" (1984, 27).

African-American women need an Afrocentric feminist analysis of motherhood that debunks the image of "happy slave," whether the white-male-created "matriarch" or the Black-male-perpetuated "superstrong Black mother." Some of the classic sociological and ethnographic work on African-American families gives a comprehensive sense of how Black women mother (Herskovits 1941; Young 1970; Ladner 1972; Stack 1974; Aschenbrenner 1975; Dougherty 1978; Dill 1980). This emphasis on Black women's actions has recently been enriched by an outpouring of research on Black women's ideas by Black women scholars (McCray 1980; Joseph 1981, 1984; Rollins 1985; D. White 1985; *Sage* 1984, 1987). When coupled with the explorations of Black women's consciousness extant in Black women's autobiographies, fiction, and Black feminist literary criticism (Walker 1983; Washington 1984; Christian 1985), these sources offer the rich conceptual terrain of a Black women's standpoint from which an Afrocentric feminist analysis of African-American motherhood can emerge.

EXPLORING A BLACK WOMEN'S STANDPOINT ON MOTHERING

The institution of Black motherhood consists of a series of constantly renegotiated relationships that African-American women experience with one another, with Black children, with the larger African-American community, and with self. These relationships occur in specific locations such as the individual households that make up African-American extended family networks, as well as in Black community institutions (Martin and Martin 1978; Sudarkasa 1981b). Moreover, just as Black women's work and family experiences varied during the transition from slavery to the post–World War II political economy, how Black women define, value, and shape Black motherhood as an institution shows comparable diversity.

Black motherhood as an institution is both dynamic and dialectical. An ongoing tension exists between efforts to mold the institution of Black motherhood to benefit systems of race, gender, and class oppression and efforts by African-American women to define and value our own experiences with motherhood. The controlling images of the mammy, the matriarch, and the welfare mother and the practices they justify are designed to oppress. In contrast, motherhood can serve as a site where Black women express and learn the power of self-definition, the importance of valuing and respecting ourselves, the necessity of self-reliance and independence, and a belief in Black women's empowerment. This tension leads to a continuum of responses. Some women view motherhood as a truly burdensome condition that stifles their creativity, exploits their labor, and makes them partners in their own oppression. Others see motherhood as providing a base for self-actualization, status in the Black community, and a catalyst for social activism. These alleged contradictions can exist side by side in African-American communities and families and even within individual women.

Embedded in these changing relationships are five enduring themes that characterize a Black women's standpoint on Black motherhood. For any given historical moment, the particular form that Black women's relationships with one another, children, community, and self actually take depends on how this dialectical relationship between the severity of oppression facing African-American women and our actions in resisting that oppression is expressed.

BLOODMOTHERS, OTHERMOTHERS, AND WOMEN-CENTERED NETWORKS

In African-American communities, fluid and changing boundaries often distinguish biological mothers from other women who care for children. Biological mothers, or bloodmothers, are expected to care for their children. But African and African-American communities have also recognized that vesting one person with full responsibility for mothering a child may not be wise or possible. As a result, othermothers—women who assist bloodmothers by sharing mothering responsibilities—traditionally have been central to the institution of Black motherhood (Troester 1984).

The centrality of women in African-American extended families reflects both a continuation of West African cultural values and functional adaptations to race and gender oppression (Tanner 1974; Stack 1974; Aschenbrenner 1975; Martin and Martin 1978; Sudarkasa 1981b; Reagon 1987). This centrality is not characterized by the absence of husbands and fathers. Men may be physically present and/or have well-defined and culturally significant roles in the extended family and the kin unit may be woman-centered. Bebe Moore Campbell's (1989) parents separated when she was small. Even though she spent the school year in the North Philadelphia household maintained by her grandmother and mother, Campbell's father assumed an important role in her life. "My father took care of me," Campbell remembers. "Our separation didn't stunt me or condemn me to a lesser humanity. His absence never made me a fatherless child. I'm not fatherless now" (p. 271). In woman-centered kin units such as Campbell's—whether a mother-child household unit, a married couple household, or a larger unit extending over several households—the centrality of mothers is not predicated on male powerlessness (Tanner 1974, 133).

Organized, resilient, women-centered networks of bloodmothers and othermothers are key in understanding this centrality. Grandmothers, sisters, aunts, or cousins act as othermothers by taking on child-care responsibilities for one another's children. When needed, temporary child-care arrangemennts can turn into long-term care or informal adoption (Stack 1974; Gutman 1976). Despite strong cultural norms encouraging women to becomee biological mothers, women who choose not to do so often receive recognition and status from othermother relationships that they establish with Black children.

In African-American communities these women-centered networks of community-based child care often extend beyond the boundaries off biologically related individuals and include "fictive kin" (Stack 1974). Civil rights activist Ella Baker describes how informal adoption by othermothers functioned in the rural southern community of her childhood:

> My aunt who had thirteen children of her own raised three more. She had become a midwife, and a child was born who was covered with sores. Nobody was particularly wanting the child, so she took the child and raised him . . . and another mother decided she didn't want to be bothered with two children. So my aunt took one and raised him . . . they were part of the family. (Cantarow 1980, 59)

Even when relationships are not between kin or fictive kin, African-American community norms traditionally were such that neighbors cared for one anothers' children. Sara Brooks, a southern domestic worker, describes the importance that the community-based child care a neighbor offered her daughter had for her: "She kept Vivian and she didn't charge me nothin either. You see, people used to look after each other, but now its not that way. I reckon its because we all was poor, and I guess they put theirself in the place of the person that they was helpin" (Simonsen 1986, 181). Brooks's experiences demonstrate how the African-American cultural value placed on cooperative child care traditionally found institutional support in the adverse conditions under which so many Black women mothered.

Othermothers are key not only in supporting children but also in helping bloodmothers who, for whatever reason, lack the preparation or desire for motherhood. In confronting racial oppression, maintaining community-based child care and respecting othermothers who assume child-care responsibilities serve a critical function in African-American communities. Children orphaned by sale or death of their parents under slavery, children conceived through rape, children of young mothers, children born into extreme poverty or to alcoholic or drug-addicted mothers, or children who for other reasons cannot remain with their bloodmothers have all been supported by othermothers, who, like Ella

Baker's aunt, take in additional children even when they have enough of their own.

Young women are often carefully groomed at an early age to become othermothers. As a ten-year-old, civil rights activist Ella Baker learned to be an othermother by caring for the children of a widowed neighbor: "Mama would say, 'You must take the clothes to Mr. Powell's house, and give so-and-so a bath.' The children were running wild. . . . The kids . . . would take off across the field. We'd chase them down, and bring them back, and put 'em in the tub, and wash 'em off, and change clothes, and carry the dirty ones home, and wash them. Those kind of things were routine" (Cantarow 1980, 59).

Many Black men also value community-based child care but exercise these values to a lesser extent. Young Black men are taught how to care for children (Young 1970; Lewis 1975). During slavery, for example, Black children under age ten experienced little division of labor. They were dressed alike and performed similar tasks. If the activities of work and play are any indication of the degree of gender role differentiation that existed among slave children, "then young girls probably grew up minimizing the difference between the sexes while learning far more about the differences between the races" (D. White 1985, 94). Differences among Black men and women in attitudes toward children may have more to do with male labor force patterns. As Ella Baker observes, "my father took care of people too, but . . . my father had to work" (Cantarow 1980, 60).

Historically, community-based child care and the relationships among bloodmothers and othermothers in women-centered networks have taken diverse institutional forms. In some polygynous West African societies, the children of the same father but different mothers referred to one another as brothers and sisters. While a strong bond existed between the biological mother and her child—one so strong that, among the Ashanti for example, "to show disrespect towards one's mother is tantamount to sacrilege" (Fortes 1950, 263)—children could be disciplined by any of their other "mothers." Cross-culturally, the high status given to othermothers and the cooperative nature of child-care arrangements among bloodmothers and othermothers in Caribbean and other Black societies gives credence to the importance that people of African descent place on mothering (Clarke 1966; Shimkin et al. 1978; Sudarkasa 1981a, 1981b).

Although the political economy of slavery brought profound changes to enslaved Africans, cultural values concerning the importance of motherhood and the value of cooperative approaches to child care continued. While older women served as nurses and midwives, their most common occupation was caring for the children of parents who worked (D. White

1985). Informal adoption of orphaned children reinforced the importance of social motherhood in African-American communities (Gutman 1976).

The relationship between bloodmothers and othermothers survived the transition from a slave economy to postemancipation southern rural agriculture. Children in southern rural communities were not solely the responsibility of their biological mothers. Aunts, grandmothers, and others who had time to supervise children served as othermothers (Young 1970; Dougherty 1978). The significant status women enjoyed in family networks and in African-American communities continued to be linked to their bloodmother and othermother activities.

The entire community structure of bloodmothers and othermothers is under assault in many inner-city neighborhoods, where the very fabric of African-American community life is being eroded by illegal drugs. But even in the most troubled communities, remnants of the othermother tradition endure. Bebe Moore Campbell's 1950s North Philadelphia neighborhood underwent some startling changes when crack cocaine flooded the streets in the 1980s. Increases in birth defects, child abuse, and parental neglect left many children without care. But some residents, such as Miss Nee, continue the othermother tradition. After raising her younger brothers and sisters and five children of her own, Miss Nee cares for three additional children whose families fell apart. Moreover, on any given night Miss Nee's house may be filled by up to a dozen children because she has a reputation for never turning away a needy child ("Children of the Underclass" 1989).

Traditionally, community-based child care certainly has been functional for African-American communities and for Black women. Black feminist theorist Bell Hooks suggests that the relationships among bloodmothers and othermothers may have greater theoretical importance than currently recognized:

> This form of parenting is revolutionary in this society because it takes place in opposition to the ideas that parents, especially mothers, should be the only childrearers. . . . This kind of shared responsibility for child care can happen in small community settings where people know and trust one another. It cannot happen in those settings if parents regard children as their "property," their possession. (1984, 144)

The resiliency of women-centered family networks illustrates how traditional cultural values—namely, the African origins of community-based child care—can help people cope with and resist oppression. By continuing community-based child care, African-American women challenge one fundamental assumption underlying the capitalist system itself: that children are "private property" and can be disposed of as such. Notions of property, child care, and gender differences in parenting styles are embedded in the institutional arrangements of any given political economy. Under the property model stemming from capitalist patriarchal families, parents may not literally assert that their children are pieces of property, but their parenting may reflect assumptions analogous to those they make in connection with property (J. Smith 1983). For example, the exclusive parental "right" to discipline children as parents see fit, even if discipline borders on abuse, parallels the widespread assumption that property owners may dispose of their property without consulting members of the larger community. By seeing the larger community as responsible for children and by giving othermothers and other nonparents "rights" in child rearing, African-Americans challenge prevailing property relations. It is in this sense that traditional bloodmother/othermother relationships in women-centered networks are "revolutionary."

MOTHERS, DAUGHTERS, AND SOCIALIZATION FOR SURVIVAL

Black mothers of daughters face a troubling dilemma. On one hand, to ensure their daughters' physical survival, mothers must teach them to fit into systems of oppression. For example, as a young girl Black activist Ann Moody questioned why she was paid so little for the domestic work she began at age nine, why Black women domestics were sexually harassed by their white male employers, why no one would explain the activities of the National Association for the Advancement of Colored People to her, and why whites had so much more than Blacks. But her mother refused to answer her questions and actually chastised her for questioning the system and stepping out of her "place" (Moody 1968). Like Ann Moody, Black daughters learn to expect to work, to strive for an education so they can support themselves, and to anticipate carrying heavy responsibilities in their families and communities because these skills are essential to their own survival and those for whom they will eventually be responsible (Ladner 1972; Joseph 1981). New Yorker Michele Wallace recounts: "I can't remember when I first learned that my family expected me to work, to be able to take care of myself when I grew up. . . . It had been drilled into me that the best and only sure support was self-support" (1978, 89–90). Mothers also know that if their daughters uncritically accept the limited opportunities offered Black women, they become willing participants in their own subordination. Mothers may have ensured their daughters' physical survival, but at the high cost of their emotional destruction.

On the other hand, Black daughters with strong self-definitions and self-valuations who offer serious challenges to oppressive situations may not physically survive. When Ann Moody became active in the early 1960s in sit-ins and voter registration activities, her mother first begged her not to participate and then told her not to come home because she feared the whites in Moody's hometown would kill her. Despite the dangers, mothers routinely encourage Black daughters to develop skills to confront oppressive conditions. Learning that they will work and that education is a vehicle for advancement can also be seen as ways of enhancing positive self-definitions and self-valuations in Black girls. Emotional strength is essential, but not at the cost of physical survival.

Historian Elsa Barkley Brown captures this delicate balance Black mothers negotiate by pointing out that her mother's behavior demonstrated the "need to teach me to live my life one way and, at the same time, to provide all the tools I would need to live it quite differently" (1989, 929). Black daughters must learn how to survive in interlocking structures of race, class, and gender oppression while rejecting and transcending those same structures. In order to develop these skills in their daughters, mothers demonstrate varying combinations of behaviors devoted to ensuring their daughters' survival—such as providing them with basic necessities and protecting them in dangerous environments—to helping their daughters go further than mothers themselves were allowed to go.

This special vision of Black mothers may grow from the nature of work women have done to ensure Black children's survival. These work experiences have provided Black women with a unique angle of vision, a particular perspective on the world to be passed on to Black daughters. African and African-American women have long integrated economic self-reliance with mothering. In contrast to the cult of true womanhood, in which work is defined as being in opposition to and incompatible with motherhood, work for Black women has been an important and valued dimension of Afrocentric definitions of Black motherhood. Sara Brooks describes the powerful connections that economic self-reliance and mothering had in her childhood: "When I was about nine I was nursin my sister Sally—I'm about seven or eight years older than Sally. And when I would put her to sleep, instead of me goin somewhere and sit down and play, I'd get my little old hoe and get out there and work right in the field around the house"(in Simonsen 1986, 86).

Mothers who are domestic workers or who work in proximity to whites may experience a unique relationship with the dominant group. For example, African-American women domestics are exposed to all the intimate details of the lives of their white employers. Working for whites offers domestic workers a view from the inside and exposes them to ideas and resources that might aid in their children's upward mobility. In some cases domestic workers form close, long-lasting relationships with their employers. But domestic workers also encounter some of the harshest exploitation confronting women of color. The work is low paid, has few benefits, and exposes women to the threat and reality of sexual harassment. Black domestics could see the dangers awaiting their daughters.

Willi Coleman's mother used a Saturday-night hair-combing ritual to impart a Black women's standpoint on domestic work to her daughters:

> Except for special occasions mama came home from work early on Saturdays. She spent six days a week mopping, waxing and dusting other women's houses and keeping out of reach of other women's husbands. Saturday nights were reserved for "taking care of them girls" hair and the telling of stories. Some of which included a recitation of what she had endured and how she had triumphed over "folks that were lower than dirt" and "no-good snakes in the grass." She combed, patted, twisted and talked, saying things which would have embarrassed or shamed her at other times. (Coleman 1987, 34)

Bonnie Thornton Dill's (1980) study of the child-rearing goals of domestic workers illustrates how African-American women see their work as both contributing to their children's survival and instilling values that will encourage their children to reject their proscribed "place" as Blacks and strive for more. Providing a better chance for their children was a dominant theme among Black women. Domestic workers described themselves as "struggling to give their children the skills and training they did not have; and as praying that opportunities which had not been open to them would be open to their children" (p. 110). But the women also realized that while they wanted to communicate the value of their work as part of the ethics of caring and personal accountability, the work itself was undesirable. Bebe Moore Campbell's (1989) grandmother and college-educated mother stressed the importance of education. Campbell remembers, "[they] wanted me to Be Somebody, to be the second generation to live out my life as far away from a mop and scrub brush and Miss Ann's floors as possible" (p. 83).

Understanding this goal of balancing the need for the physical survival of their daughters with the vision of encouraging them to transcend the boundaries confronting them explains many apparent contradictions in Black mother-daughter relationships. Black mothers are often described as strong disciplinarians and overly protective; yet these same women manage to raise daughters who are self-reliant and assertive. To explain this apparent contradiction, Gloria Wade-Gayles suggests that Black mothers

> do not socialize their daughters to be "passive" or "irrational." Quite the contrary, they socialize their daughters to be independent, strong and self-confident. Black mothers are suffocatingly protective and domineering

precisely because they are determined to mold their daughters into whole and self-actualizing persons in a society that devalues Black women. (1984, 12)

African-American mothers place a strong emphasis on protection, either by trying to shield their daughters as long as possible from the penalties attached to their race, class, and gender status or by teaching them skills of independence and self-reliance so that they will be able to protect themselves. Consider the following verse from a traditional blues song:

I ain't good lookin' and ain't got waist-long hair
I say I ain't good lookin' and I ain't got waist-long hair
But my mama gave me something that'll take me anywhere.
(Washington 1984, 144)

Unlike white women, symbolized by "good looks" and "waist-long hair," Black women have been denied male protection. Under such conditions it becomes essential that Black mothers teach their daughters skills that will "take them anywhere."

Black women's autobiographies and fiction can be read as texts revealing the multiple ways that African-American mothers aim to shield their daughters from the demands of being Black women in oppressive conditions. Michele Wallace describes her growing understanding of how her mother viewed raising Black daughters in Harlem: "My mother has since explained to me that since it was obvious her attempt to protect me was going to prove a failure, she was determined to make me realize that as a black girl in white America I was going to find it an uphill climb to keep myself together" (1978, 98). In discussing the mother-daughter relationship in Paule Marshall's *Brown Girl, Brownstones*, Rosalie Troester catalogues the ways mothers have aimed to protect their daughters and the impact this may have on relationships themselves:

Black mothers, particularly those with strong ties to their community, sometimes build high banks around their young daughters, isolating them from the dangers of the larger world until they are old and strong enough to function as autonomous women. Often these dikes are religious, but sometimes they are built with education, family, or the restrictions of a close-knit and homogeneous community. . . . This isolation causes the currents between Black mothers and daughters to run deep and the relationship to be fraught with an emotional intensity often missing from the lives of women with more freedom. (1984, 13)

Michele Wallace's mother built banks around her headstrong adolescent daughter by institutionalizing her in a Catholic home for troubled girls.

Wallace went willingly, believing "I thought at the time that I would rather live in hell than be with my mother" (1978, 98). But years later Wallace's evaluation of her mother's decision changed: "Now that I know my mother better, I know that her sense of powerlessness made it all the more essential to her that she take radical action" (p. 98).

African-American mothers try to protect their daughters from the dangers that lie ahead by offering them a sense of their own unique self-worth. Many contemporary Black women writers report the experience of being singled out, of being given a sense of specialness at an early age which encouraged them to develop their talents. My own mother marched me to the public library at age five, helped me get my first library card, and told me that I could do anything if I learned how to read. In discussing the works of Paule Marshall, Dorothy West, and Alice Walker, Mary Helen Washington observes that all three writers make special claims about the roles their mothers played in the development of their creativity: "The bond with their mothers is such a fundamental and powerful source that the term 'mothering the mind' might have been coined specifically to define their experiences as writers" (1984, 144).

Black women's efforts to provide a physical and psychic base for their children can affect mothering styles and the emotional intensity of Black mother-daughter relationships. As Gloria Wade-Gayles points out, "mothers in Black women's fiction are strong and devoted . . . they are rarely affectionate" (1984, 10). For example, in Toni Morrison's *Sula* (1974), Eva Peace's husband ran off, leaving her with three small children and no money. Despite her feelings, "the demands of feeding her three children were so acute she had to postpone her anger for two years until she had both the time and energy for it" (p. 32). Later in the novel Eva's daughter Hannah asks, "Mamma, did you ever love us?" (p. 67). Eva angrily replies, "What you talkin' bout did I love you girl I stayed alive for you" (p. 69). For far too many Black mothers, the demands of providing for children in interlocking systems of oppression are sometimes so demanding that they have neither the time nor the patience for affection. And yet most Black daughters love and admire their mothers and are convinced that their mothers truly love them (Joseph 1981).

Black daughters raised by mothers grappling with hostile environments have to come to terms with their feelings about the difference between the idealized versions of maternal love extant in popular culture and the strict and often troubled mothers in their lives. For a daughter, growing up means developing a better understanding that even though she may desire more affection and greater freedom, her mother's physical care and protection are acts of maternal love. Ann Moody describes her growing awareness of the cost her mother paid as a domestic worker who was a single mother of three. Watching her mother sleep after the birth of another child, Moody remembers:

> For a long time I stood there looking at her. I didn't want to wake her up. I wanted to enjoy and preserve that calm, peaceful look on her face, I wanted to think she would always be that happy. . . . Adline and Junior were too young to feel the things I felt and know the things I knew about Mama. They couldn't remember when she and Daddy separated. They had never heard her cry at night as I had or worked and helped as I had done when we were starving. (1968, 57)

Moody initially sees her mother as a strict disciplinarian, a woman who tries to protect her daughter by withholding information. But as Moody matures and better understands the oppression in her community, her ideas change. On one occasion Moody left school early the day after a Black family had been brutally murdered by local whites. Moody's description of her mother's reaction reflects her deepening understanding: "When I walked in the house Mama didn't even ask me why I came home. She just looked at me. And for the first time I realized she understood what was going on within me or was trying to anyway" (1968, 136).

Another example of a daughter's efforts to understand her mother is offered in Renita Weems's account of coming to grips with maternal desertion. In the following passage Weems struggles with the difference between the stereotypical image of the superstrong Black mother and her own alcoholic mother's decision to leave her children: "My mother loved us. I must believe that. She worked all day in a department store bakery to buy shoes and school tablets, came home to curse out neighbors who wrongly accused her children of any impropriety (which in an apartment complex usually meant stealing), and kept her house cleaner than most sober women" (1984, 26). Weems concludes that her mother loved her because she provided for her to the best of her ability.

Othermothers often help to defuse the emotional intensity of relationships between bloodmothers and their daughters. In recounting how she dealt with the intensity of her relationship with her mother, Weems describes the women teachers, neighbors, friends, and othermothers she turned to—women who, she observes, "did not have the onus of providing for me, and so had the luxury of talking to me" (1984, 27). Cheryl West's household included her brother, her lesbian mother, and Jan, her mother's lover. Jan became an othermother to West: "Yellow-colored, rotund and short in stature, Jan was like a second mother. . . . Jan braided my hair in the morning, mother worked two jobs and tucked me in at night. Loving, gentle, and fastidious in the domestic arena, Jan could be a rigid disciplinarian. . . . To the outside world . . . she was my 'aunt' who happened to live with us. But she was much more involved and nurturing than any of my 'real' aunts" (1987, 43).

June Jordan offers an eloquent analysis of one daughter's realization of the high personal cost African-American women can pay in providing an economic and emotional foundation for their children. In the following passage Jordan offers a powerful testament of how she came to see that her mother's work was an act of love:

> As a child I noticed the sadness of my mother as she sat alone in the kitchen at night. . . . Her woman's work never won permanent victories of any kind. It never enlarged the universe of her imagination or her power to influence what happened beyond the front door of our house. Her woman's work never tickled her to laugh or shout or dance. But she did raise me to respect her way of offering love and to believe that hard work is often the irreducible factor for survival, not something to avoid. Her woman's work produced a reliable home base where I could pursue the privileges of books and music. Her woman's work invented the potential for a completely different kind of work for us, the next generation of Black women: huge, rewarding hard work demanded by the huge, new ambitions that her perfect confidence in us engendered. (1985, 105)

COMMUNITY OTHERMOTHERS AND POLITICAL ACTIVISM

Black women's experiences as othermothers provide a foundation for Black women's political activism. Nurturing children in Black extended family networks stimulates a more generalized ethic of caring and personal accountability among African-American women who often feel accountable to all the Black community's children.

This notion of Black women as community othermothers for all Black children traditionally allowed African-American women to treat biologically unrelated children as if they were members of their own families. For example, sociologist Karen Fields describes how her grandmother, Mamie Garvin Fields, draws on her power as a community othermother when dealinig with unfamiliar children: "She will say to a child on the street who looks up to no good, picking out a name at random, 'Aren't you Miz Pinckney's boy?' in that same reproving tone. If the reply is, 'No, *ma'am*, my mother is Miz Gadsden,' whatever threat there was dissipates" (Fields and Fields 1983, xvii).

The use of family language in referring to members of the African-American community also illustrates this dimension of Black motherhood. In the following passage, Mamie Garvin Fields describes how she became active in surveying substandard housing conditions among African-Americans in Charleston. Note her explanation of why she uses family language:

> I was one of the volunteers they got to make a survey of the places where we were paying extortious rents for indescribable property. I said "we," although it wasn't Bob and me. We had our own home, and so did many of the Federated Women. Yet we still felt like it really was "we" living in those terrible places, and it was up to us to do something about them. (Fields and Fields 1983, 195)

Black women frequently describe Black children using family language. In recounting her increasingly successful efforts to teach a boy who had given other teachers problems, my daughter's kindergarten teacher stated, "You know how it can be—the majority of children in the learning disabled classes are *our children*. I know he didn't belong there, so I volunteered to take him." In their statements both women use family language to describe the ties that bind them as Black women to their responsibilities as members of an African-American community/family.

In explaining why the South Carolina Federation of Colored Women's Clubs founded a home for girls, Mrs. Fields observes, "We all could see that we had a responsibility for those girls: they were the daughters of our community coming up" (Fields and Fields 1983, 197). Ms. Fields's activities as a community othermother on behalf of the "daughters" of her community represent an established tradition among educated Black women. Serving as othermothers to women in the Black community has a long history. A study of 108 of the first generation of Black club women found that three-quarters were married, three-quarters worked outside the home, but only one-fourth had children (Giddings 1984). These women emphasized self-support for Black women, whether married or not, and realized that self-sufficient community othermothers were important. "Not all women are intended for mothers," declares an 1894 edition of the *Woman's Era*. "Some of us have not the temperment for family life. . . . Clubs will make women think seriously of their future lives, and not make girls think their only alternative is to marry" (Giddings 1984, 108).

Black women writers also explore this theme of the African-American community othermother who nurtures the Black community. One of the earliest examples is found in Frances Ellen Watkins Harper's 1892 novel *Iola Leroy*. By rejecting an opportunity to marry a prestigious physician and dissociate herself from the Black community, nearly white Iola, the main character, chooses instead to serve the African-American community. Similarly, in Alice Walker's *Meridian* (1976), the main character rejects the controlling image of the "happy slave," the self-sacrificing Black mother, and chooses to become a community othermother. Giving up her biological child to the care of an othermother, Meridian gets an education, works in the civil rights movement, and eventually takes on responsibility for the children of a small southern town. She engages in a "quest that will take her beyond the society's narrow meaning of the word *mother* as a physical state and expand its meaning to those who create, nurture, and save life in social and psychological as well as physical terms" (Christian 1985, 242).

Sociologist Cheryl Gilkes (1980, 1982, 1983b) suggests that community othermother relationships can be key in stimulating Black women's decisions to become community activists. Gilkes asserts that many of the Black women community activists in her study became involved in community organizing in response to the needs of their own children and of those in their communities. The following comment is typical of how many of the Black women in Gilkes's study relate to Black children: "There were alot of summer programs springing up for kids, but they were exclusive . . . and I found that most of *our kids* were excluded" (1980, 219). For many women what began as the daily expression of their obligations as community othermothers, as was the case for the kindergarten teacher, developed into full-fledged actions as community leaders.

This community othermother tradition also explains the "mothering the mind" relationships that can develop between Black women teachers and their Black women students. Unlike the traditional mentoring so widely reported in educational literature, this relationship goes far beyond that of providing students with either technical skills or a network of academic and professional contacts. Bell Hooks shares the special vision that teachers who see our work in community othermother terms can pass on to our students: "I understood from the teachers in those segregated schools that the work of any teacher committed to the full self-realization of students was necessarily and fundamentally radical, that ideas were not neutral, that to teach in a way that liberates, that expands consciousness, that awakens, is to challenge domination at its very core" (1989, 50). Like the mother-daughter relationship, this "mothering the mind" amongg Black women seeks to move toward the mutuality of a shared sisterhood that binds African-American women as community othermothers.

Community othermothers have made important contributions in building a different type of community in often hostile political and economic surroundings (Reagon 1987). Community othermothers' actions demonstrate a clear rejection of separateness and individual interest as the basis of either community organization or individual self-actualization. Instead, the connectedness with others and common interest expressed by community othermothers models a very different value system, one whereby

Afrocentric feminist ethics of caring and personal accountability move communities forward.

MOTHERHOOD AS A SYMBOL OF POWER

Motherhood—whether bloodmother, othermother, or community other-mother—can be invoked by African-American women as a symbol of power. Much of Black women's status in African-American communities stems not only from actions as mothers in Black family networks but from contributions as community othermothers.

Black women's involvement in fostering African-American community development forms the basis for community-based power. This is the type of power many African-Americans have in mind when they describe the "strong Black women" they see around them in traditional African-American communities. Community othermothers work on behalf of the Black community by expressing ethics of caring and personal account-ability which embrace conceptions of transformative power and mutuality (Kuykendall 1983). Such power is transformative in that Black women's relationships with children and other vulnerable community members is not intended to dominate or control. Rather, its purpose is to bring people along, to—in the words of late-nineteenth-century Black feminists—"uplift the race" so that vulnerable members of the community will be able to attain the self-reliance and independence essential for resistance.

When older African-American women invoke their power as community othermothers, the results can be quite striking. Karen Fields recounts a telling incident:

> One night . . . as Grandmother sat crocheting alone at about two in the morning, a young man walked into the living room carrying the portable TV from upstairs. She said, "Who are you looking for *this* time of night?" As Grandmother [described] the incident to me over the phone, I could hear a tone of voice that I know well. It said, "Nice boys don't do that." So I imagine the burglar heard his own mother or grandmother at that moment. He joined in the familial game just created: "Well, he told me that I could borrow it." "*Who* told you?" "John." "Um um, no *John* lives here. You got the wrong house." (Fields and Fields 1983, xvi)

After this dialogue, the teenager turned around, went back upstairs, and returned the television.

In local African-American communities, community othermothers be-come identified as powerful figures through furthering the community's well-being. Sociologist Charles Johnson (1934/1979) describes the behavior of an elderly Black woman at a church service in rural 1930s Alabama. Even though she was not on the program, the woman stood up to speak. The master of ceremonies rang for her to sit down, but she refused to do so claiming, "I am the mother of this church, and I will say what I please" (p. 172). The master of ceremonies offered the following explanation to the congregation as to why he let the woman continue: "Brothers, I know you all honor Sister Moore. Course our time is short but she has acted as a mother to me. . . . Any time old folks get up I give way to them" (p. 173).

THE VIEW FROM THE INSIDE: THE PERSONAL MEANING OF MOTHERING

Within African-American communities, women's innovative and practical approaches to mothering under oppressive conditions often bring power and recognition. But this situation should not obscure the costs of motherhood to many Black women. Black motherhood is fundamentally a contradictory institution. African-American communities value motherhood, but Black mothers' ability to cope with race, class, and gender oppression should not be confused with transcending those conditions. Black motherhood can be rewarding, but it can also extract high personal costs. The range of Black women's reactions to motherhood and the ambivalence that many Black women feel about mothering reflect motherhood's contradictory nature.

Certain dimensions of Black motherhood are clearly problematic. Coping with unwanted pregnancies and being unable to care for one's children is oppressive. Sara Brooks remembers, "I had babies one after another because I never knew how to avoid havin babies and I didn't ask nobody, so I didn't know nothin. . . . After I separated from my husband, I *still* didn't know nothin, so there come Vivian" (Simonsen 1986, 174). Brooks became pregnant again even though she was unmarried and had three children from a previous marriage whom she could not support. Brooks describes the strain placed on Black women who must mother under oppressive conditions: "I hated it. . . . I didn't want no other baby. I couldn't hardly take care of myself, and I had other kids I'da loved to have taken care of, and I couldn't do that" (p. 177). Like Brooks, many Black women have children they really do not want. When combined with Black community values claiming that good Black women always want their children, ignorance about reproductive issues leaves many Black women with unplanned pregnancies and the long-term responsibilities of parenting.

Ann Moody's mother also did not celebrate her repeated pregnancies. Moody remembers her mother's feelings when her mother started "getting fat" and her boyfriend stopped coming by: "Again Mama started crying every night. . . . When I heard Mama crying at night, I felt so bad. She wouldn't cry until we were all in bed and she thought we were sleeping. Every night I would lie awake for hours listening to her sobbing quietly in her pillow. The bigger she got the more she cried, and I did too" (Moody 1968, 46). To her children, Moody's mother may have appeared to be the stereotypical strong Black mother, but Ann Moody was able to see the cost her mother paid for living with this controlling image.

Dealing with an unwanted pregnancy can have tragic consequences. All Sara Brooks could think about was "doing away with this baby." She self-medicated herself and almost died. But she was luckier than her mother. As Brooks recalls, "my momma, she got pregnant too close behind me—it was an unwanted pregnancy—and so she taken turpentine and she taken too much, I guess, and she died. She bled to death and died" (Simonsen 1986, 160). She was not alone. Prior to the 1973 *Roe v. Wade* U.S. Supreme Court decision that a woman's right to personal privacy gave her the right to decide whether or not to have an abortion, large numbers of women who died from illegal abortions were Black. In New York, for example, during the several years preceding the decriminalization of abortions, 80 percent of the deaths from illegal abortions involved Black and Puerto Rican women (Davis 1981).

Strong pronatalist values in African-American communities may stem in part from traditional Black values that vest adult status on women who become biological mothers. For many, becoming a biological mother is often seen as a significant first step toward womanhood. Annie Amiker, an elderly Black woman, describes the situation in the rural Mississippi of her childhood. When asked if there were many girls with out-of-wedlock children, she replied, "there was some but not many—not many because when you run upon a girl who had a child the other girls wouldn't have nothing to do with her . . . she was counted as a grown person so she wasn't counted among the young people" (Parker 1979, 268). Joyce Ladner describes how this link between adult status and motherhood operates in low-income, urban communities: "If there was one common standard for becoming a woman that was accepted by the majority of the people in the community, it was the time when girls gave birth to their first child. This line of demarcation was extremely clear and separated the *girls* from the *women*" (1972, 212).

In spite of the high personal costs, Ann Moody's mother, Sara Brooks, and an overwhelming majority of unmarried Black adolescent mothers choose to keep their children (Simms 1988). Those women who give up their children can also pay high personal costs. In Alice Walker's *Meridian*, the fact that mothers cannot attend her prestigious, Black women's college forces Meridian to choose between keeping her child and going to college. After relinquishing her child, Meridian suffers physiological and psychological illness. Although she knows that her son is better cared for by others, she feels "condemned, consigned to penitence for life," for she has committed the ultimate sin against Black motherhood. Knowing that she had parted with her baby when her enslaved maternal ancestors had done anything and everything to keep their children was almost too much for Meridian to bear (Christian 1985).

The pain of knowing what lies ahead for Black children while feeling powerless to protect them is another problematic dimension of Black mothering. Michele Wallace remembers, "I can understand why my mother felt desperate. No one else thought it would be particularly horrible if I got pregnant or got married before I had grown up, if I never completed college. I was a black girl" (1978, 98). Nineteen-year-old Harriet Jacobs, a slave mother, articulates the feelings of Black mothers who must raise their children in dangerous and impoverished environments: "When they told me my new-born babe was a girl, my heart was heavier than it had ever been before. Slavery is terrible for men; but it is far more terrible for women" (1860/1987, 46). In a 1904 letter, a Black mother in the South wrote to a national magazine:

> I dread to see my children grow. I know not their fate. Where the white girl has one temptation, mine will have many. Where the white boy has every opportunity and protection, mine will have few opportunities and no protection. It does not matter how good or wise my children may be, they are colored. When I have said that, all is said. Everything is forgiven in the South but color. (Lerner 1972, 158)

Protecting Black children remains a primary concern of African-American mothers because Black children are at risk. Nearly 40 percent of all Black mothers receive no prenatal care in the first trimester of pregnancy. One in every eight Black infants has a low birth weight, a factor contributing to an infant mortality rate among Black babies that remains twice that for white infants. During the first year of life Black babies die from fires and burns at a rate 4.5 times greater than that of white infants. The number of cases of pediatric AIDS has doubled between 1986 and 1989, and more than 75 percent of children with AIDS are Black or Hispanic, more than half of them the offspring of intravenous drug users ("Children of the Underclass" 1989, 27). An anonymous mother expresses her concern for Black children:

> I turn my eyes on the little children, and keep on praying that one of them will grow up at the right second, when the schoolteachers have time to say hello and give him the lessons he needs, and when they get rid of the building

here and let us have a place you can breathe in and not get bitten all the time, and when the men can find work—because *they* can't have children, and so they have to drink or get on drugs to find some happy moments, and some hope about things. (Lerner 1972, 315)

To this mother, even though her children are her hope, the conditions under which she must mother are intolerable.

Black mothers also pay the cost of giving up their own dreams of achieving full creative ability. Because many spend so much time feeding the physical needs of their children, as Alice Walker queries, "when . . . did my over-worked mother have time to know or care about feeding the creative spirit?" (1983, 239). Much of that creativity goes into dimensions of Black culture that are relatively protected from the incursions of the dominant group. Many Black women blues singers, poets, and artists manage to incorporate their art into their daily responsibilities as bloodmothers and othermothers. But for far too many African-American women who are weighed down by the incessant responsibilities of mothering others, that creative spark never finds full expression.

Harriet Jacobs's autobiography gives a clear example of one mother's denial of her own self-actualization and illustrates the costs paid by Black mothers who assume the heavy responsibilities inherent in their blood-mother and othermother relationships. Jacobs desperately wanted to escape slavery but explains how having children created a particular dilemma:

> I could have made my escape alone; but it was more for my helpless children than for myself that I longed for freedom. Though the boon would have been precious to me, above all price, I would not have taken it at the expense of leaving them in slavery. Every trial I endured, every sacrifice I made for their sakes, drew them closer to my heart, and gave me fresh courage. (1860/1987, 59)

Black mothers like those of Ann Moody and June Jordan and women like Harriet Jacobs and Sara Brooks are examples of women who gave up their freedom for the sake of their children. Community othermothers like Mamie Fields and Miss Nee pay a similar cost, not for the sakes of their own biological children but for the Black community's children.

Despite the obstacles and costs, motherhood remains a symbol of hope for many of even the poorest Black women. One anonymous mother describes how she feels about her children:

> To me, having a baby inside me is the only time I'm really alive. I know I can make something, do something, no matter what color my skin is, and what names people call me. . . . You can see the little one grow and get larger and

start doing things, and you feel there must be some hope, some chance that things will get better; because there it is, right before you, a real, live, growing baby. . . . The baby is a good sign, or at least he's *some* sign. If we didn't have that, what would be the difference from death? (Lerner 1972, 314)

Given the harshness of this mother's environment, her children offer hope. They are all she has.

Mothering is an empowering experience for many African-American women. Gwendolyn Brooks (1953) explores this issue of reproductive power in her novel *Maud Martha*. Maud Martha is virtually silent until she gives birth to her daughter, when "pregnancy and the birth of a child connect Maud to some power in herself, some power to speak, to be heard, to articulate feelings" (Washington 1987, 395). Her child serves as a catalyst for her movement into self-definition, self-valuation, and eventual empowerment. Marita Golden describes a similar experience that illustrates how the special relationship between mother and child can foster a changed definition of self and an accompanying empowerment:

Now I belonged to me. No parents or husband claiming me. . . . There was only my child who consumed and replenished me . . . my son's love was unconditional and, as such, gave me more freedom than any love I had known. . . . I at last accepted mama as my name. Realized that it did not melt down any other designations. Discovered that it expanded them—and me. (1983, 240–41)

This special relationship that Black mothers have with their children can also foster a creativity, a mothering of the mind and soul, for all involved. It is this gift that Alice Walker alludes to when she notes, "and so our mothers and grandmothers have, more often than not anonymously, handed on the creative spark, the seed of the flower they themselves never hoped to see" (1983, 240).

But what cannot be overlooked in work emphasizing mothers' influences on their children is how Black children affirm their mothers and how important that affirmation can be in a society that denigrates Blackness and womanhood. In her essay "One Child of One's Own," Alice Walker offers a vision of what African-American mother-child relationships can be:

It is not my child who tells me: I have no femaleness white women must affirm. Not my child who says: I have no rights black men must respect. It is not my child who has purged my face from history and herstory, and left mystory just that, a mystery; my child loves my face and would have it on every page, if she could, as I have loved my own parents' faces above all others. . . . We are together, my child and I. Mother and child, yes, but *sisters* really, against whatever denies us all that we are. (Walker 1979b, 75)

Chapter 7

RETHINKING BLACK WOMEN'S ACTIVISM

> The way I looked at it, a white person might be judgin me, but I'm judgin them, too. If they seem as if they was scornful of a colored person, at the same time that they was scornful of me, I'm the same way about them . . . if my place ain't good enough for you—[if] I ain't good enough to drink out of a glass that you got because I'm black, I don't want to do it.
>
> —Sara Brooks, in Simonsen 1986, 199

Sara Brooks is not typically seen as a political activist. Her long hours as a domestic worker left her little time to participate in unions, community groups, demonstrations, or other forms of organized political activity. Her lifelong struggle was not for political causes but to garner sufficient resources to reunite her children and provide a home for them. To outsiders Sara Brooks may appear to be an exploited domestic worker victimized by the racial politics of a segmented labor market and the sexual politics of having too many children. But when she states "if they was scornful of me, I'm the same way about them," she taps a powerful yet overlooked part of a Black women's activist tradition. She has not only survived her experiences with race, gender, and class oppression, but she clearly rejects their ideological justifications. "If my place ain't good enough for you—[if] I ain't good enough to drink out of a glass that you got because I'm black, I don't want to do it," she proclaims. Self-definition, self-valuation, and movement toward self-reliance inform her worldview, beliefs that stem from her struggles to *survive*.

To Sara Brooks survival is a form of resistance, and her struggles to provide for the survival of her children represent the foundation for a powerful Black women's activist tradition. Historically African-Americans' resistance to racial oppression could not have occurred without an accompanying struggle for group survival. Sara Brooks's contributions in caring for her children and in rejecting the controlling images of herself as the objectified Other represent the unacknowledged yet essential actions taken by countless Black women to ensure this group survival. Without this key part of Black women's activism, struggles to transform American educational, economic, and political institutions could not have been sustained. Yet as Cheryl Gilkes (1988) points out, "popular perspectives on Black communities and their problems often fail to comprehend the tremendous efforts at internal transformation that exist alongside persistent efforts to combat racism" (p. 53).

Social science research has ignored Black women's actions in both the struggle for group survival and institutional transformation. In part this neglect stems from the exclusion of Black women's experiences as a subject of serious study from both traditional scholarship and its Afrocentric and feminist critiques. But this omission also reflects problems plaguing existing scholarly conceptualizations of power, political resistance, and political activism.[1]

Contested definitions of power, activism, and resistance have influenced scholarship in Black women's studies. On one hand, recent research on African-American women stresses the ways in which Black women are oppressed, especially by interlocking structures of oppression (Beale 1970; Davis 1981; Hooks 1981; Dill 1983). On the other hand, the literature simultaneously explores Black women's strength and resiliency in the face of hardship and despair, features thought to characterize Black women's resistance to oppression (Davis 1981, 1989; Steady 1981; Terborg-Penn 1986). As a result, recent Black feminist works portray African-American women as empowered individuals within multiple structures of domination. But in spite of this promising approach, theoretical analyses of African-American women's power, activism, and resistance remain elusive.

White male conceptualizations of the political process produce definitions of power, activism, and resistance that fail to capture the meaning of these concepts in Black women's lives. Social science research typically focuses on public, official, visible political activity even though unofficial, private, and seemingly invisible spheres of social life and organization may be equally important (Millman and Kanter 1975; Bookman and Morgen 1988). For example, conflict approaches to social class see labor unions and political parties—two modes of political activism dominated by white males—as the two fundamental mechanisms for working-class activism (Vanneman and Cannon 1987). African-American women have been excluded from both of these arenas, leaving conflict models bereft of a theoretical analysis of Black women's social class protest. Such approaches assess Black women's absence from both positions of formal authority and the membership rosters of political organizations as indicating low levels of Black women's activism. These definitional limitations also influence analyses of Black women's actions in resistance struggles. For example, historian Rosalyn Terborg-Penn defines resistance as "women's involvement in the organized struggle against slavery, peonage, and imperialism. Strategies included open and guerrilla warfare, maroonage, slave revolts, and peasant revolts" (1986, 190). Terborg-Penn uncovers important and much-needed information about these specific types of Black women's resistance. But the limits of her definition lead her to overlook less visible but equally important forms of Black women's political activity within African-American communities.

Black feminist scholars are investigating how African-American women are activists in formal organizational settings, in areas of overt political resistance such as those described by Terborg-Penn, and in the context of everyday life (see e.g., Gilkes 1980; Steady 1981; Bush 1986; and Fox-Genovese 1986). Reclaiming this Black women's activist tradition not only reconceptualizes Black women's activism and resistance but may point the way toward a comprehensive analysis of the very nature of power itself.

CONCEPTUALIZING BLACK WOMEN'S ACTIVISM

The Black women's activist tradition of individual and group actions designed to bring about social change has occurred along two primary dimensions. The struggle for group survival is the first dimension. Consisting of actions taken to create Black female spheres of influence within existing structures of oppression, this dimension does not directly challenge oppressive structures because, in many cases, direct confrontation is neither preferred nor possible. Instead, women engaged in creating Black female spheres of influence indirectly resist oppressive structures by undermining them. Jualyne Dodson and Cheryl Gilkes contend that the "ties that bind the black community together exist primarily because of the vigilant action of black women. Black women are, in a very profound sense, the 'something within' that shaped the 'culture of resistance,' the patterns of consciousness and self-expression, and the social organizational framework of local and national expressions of community" (1987, 81).

The second dimension of Black women's activism consists of the struggle for institutional transformation—namely, those efforts to change existing structures of oppression. All individual and group actions that directly challenge the legal and customary rules governing African-American women's subordination can be seen as part of the struggle for institutional transformation. Participating in civil rights organizations, labor unions, feminist groups, boycotts, and revolts exemplify this dimension of the Black women's activist tradition.

While conceptually distinct, these two dimensions of Black women's activism are actually interdependent. For example, Black domestic workers have traditionally drawn on both dimensions of a Black women's activist tradition while appearing to be doing neither (Rollins 1985; Dill 1988a). Most Black women domestic workers neither organize for better working conditions nor confront their employers by demanding better pay—actions representing the struggle for institutional transformation—because they need their jobs in order to provide for their families. Rather, Black domestic workers find other ways to resist. Many women superficially adhere to the prevailing rules and thus appear to be endorsing them. Black women domestic workers report that they are often called by their white employers to play roles as deferent, contented servants grateful for handouts of old clothes in place of decent wages.

But these women simultaneously resist these ongoing attempts to dehumanize them. The childlike, obedient servants they pretend to be masks a very different analysis and worldview. The women share stories of *acting* grateful for the handouts given them by their employers while throwing the things away as soon as they leave their jobs (Rollins 1985). They tell of deliberately altering their physical appearance to look worse than normal. One woman actually reports concealing her children's college attendance from her employer in order not to appear out of her "place." But had these women fully accepted their "place," they would not encourage their children to attend college, they would not improve their physical appearance when out of view of their employers, and they would be truly grateful to receive handouts instead of raises. The Black female sphere of influence created in this case was Black women's refusal to relinquish control over their self-definitions. While they pretend to be mules and mammies and thus appear to conform to institutional rules, they resist by creating their own self-definitions and self-valuations in the safe spaces they create among one another.

Sustaining an independent consciousness as a sphere of freedom enables African-American women to engage in additional forms of resistance. Bonnie Thornton Dill recounts numerous stories of how Black domestic workers undermine the rules governing their employment by creating Black female spheres of influence and control over the conditions of their work. The following case reveals one woman's strategies in resisting her employer's attempts to supervise her work too closely:

> She [the employer] told me what she wanted done and then she said, "My girl always scrubs the floor." Well, I noticed down in the basement that she had a mop, and she had taken the mop and hid it. So I cleaned the whole house and everything, but I didn't mop the floors. And when I got ready to go, I took the bucket, the brush, and the knee-pad and set them in the corner. When she came in she was very pleased. . . . She went into the kitchen and she looked and she said, "But you didn't scrub the floor." She had a daughter who was ten years old, and I know I'm not her girl, I'm just the lady who came to do the days' work. So I said, "Well, you said your girl cleans the floor, and I'm not your girl . . . and I don't scrub floors on my hands and knees." "Well," she said, "tomorrow I'll go out and buy a mop." So, I got my coat on and I said, "Why don't you just let me go down in the basement and bring the mop up?" (Dill 1988a, 40)

This domestic worker avoided direct actions to change the rules. She did not form a union, confront her employer about the power inequities involved in calling her "girl" and asking her to scrub floors on her knees when a mop was available, or engage in other forms of overt political resistance. Yet even though her actions were constrained by the need to ensure her family's economic survival, she did challenge the rules that governed her work. Her participation in a Black female sphere of influence gave her different tools to resist, and she stimulated institutional transformation by undermining the rules governing her work.

Black women's community work, with its duality of internal and external efforts, also incorporates the interdependence of these two dimensions of a Black women's activist tradition. Dodson and Gilkes (1987) contend that Black women's centrality in African-American families/communities reflects the both/and conceptual orientation of a Black women's standpoint. Black women's actions to maintain community integrity through the struggle for group survival is both conservative and radical. As cultural workers, Black women thwarted European efforts to eliminate African culture (Reagon 1987). The survival of certain African customs was not an accident but instead resulted from "continual resistance" whereby the women in particular "took it upon themselves to preserve certain customs" (Thiam 1978, 123). Algerian feminist Awa Thiam asserts, "in refusing to allow Black African civilization to be destroyed, our mothers were revolutionary. Yet some people describe this attitude as conservative" (1978, 123).

By conserving and recreating an Afrocentric worldview, women expressing this dimension of activism subtly undermine oppressive institutions by rejecting the anti-Black and antifemale ideologies they promulgate. Although the importance of Black women in fashioning an Afrocentric culture that resists white racism has been acknowledged (Terborg-Penn 1986; Radford-Hill 1986; Dodson and Gilkes 1987; Reagon 1987), the importance of a Black *women's* culture of resistance is often overlooked. But a culture of resistance that is simultaneously Afrocentric and feminist is essential because the Black feminist consciousness nurtured and articulated in this safe space may be all that stands between many Black women and the internalized oppression fostered by our status as the Other. For example, the domestic workers in Judith Rollins's (1985) study retain their sense of self-worth by adhering to an alternative value system that "measures an individual's worth less by material success than by 'the kind of person you are.' " These women judge themselves "by the quality of one's interpersonal relationships and by one's standing in the community" (1985, 212). This moral system is what gives domestics the strength to accept what is beneficial to them in their employers' treatment while not being profoundly damaged by the negative conceptualizations on which such treatment is based (Cannon 1988). The presence of a culture of resistance allows Black women to live with the contradictions inherent in being valued individuals in a devalued occupation.

At the same time that African-American women engage in cultural maintenance that is both conservative and radical, Black women's political struggles to transform racist institutions represent a radical political thrust. "Any description of the roles of Black women in their communities . . . must incorporate an understanding of this seeming contradiction," suggest Dodson and Gilkes (1987, 82). Black women cannot be content with merely creating culture and providing for families and communities because the welfare of those families and communities is profoundly affected by American political, economic, and social institutions. Because African-Americans must function in schools and labor markets controlled by unsympathetic officials, Black women often find themselves working for institutional transformation. Katie Murray, a sheet metal worker, only wanted to earn a decent wage so that she could be economically self-reliant. But she found herself increasingly described as a troublemaker because she refused to ignore an incident in which her white coworkers were invited to attend a three-day workshop with pay while she was never included: "It's sad; we're all out there workin' together, payin' our union dues just like the whites are except they haven't asked a black person to go. And whenever I bring up something like this, they say I'm trying to cause trouble. But it is not that I wanna cause trouble. It's just that I wanna be treated equally" (Schroedel 1985, 137).

The dual nature of the Black women's activist tradition illustrates the necessity of both types of political action in efforts to bring about social change. In a 1981 speech at a women's music festival, Bernice Johnson Reagon, a long-time activist in the Black civil rights and women's movements and a founding member of the musical group, Sweet Honey In the Rock, describes the necessity of linking the struggle for group survival with that for institutional transformation. Reagon compared building community institutions with being in a barred room offering nurturance and a safe space: "That space while it lasts should be a nurturing space where you sift out what people are saying about you and decide who you really are . . . in that little barred room where you check everybody at the door, you act out community. You pretend that your room is a world" (Reagon 1983, 358). But while the barred room of community is necessary and often may be the only form of resistance available, it cannot be sufficient to bring about fundamental social change. Reagon continues:

> The problem with the experiment is that there ain't nobody in there but folk like you. . . . Now that's nationalism . . . it's nurturing, but it is also nationalism. At a certain stage nationalism is crucial to a people if you are going to ever impact as a group in your own interest. Nationalism at another point becomes reactionary because it is totally inadequate for surviving in the world with many peoples. (Reagon 1983, 358)

To Reagon the struggle for group survival is designed to foster autonomy, not separatism. Moreover, this autonomy provides the foundation for the principled coalitions with other groups that are essential for institutional transformation.[2]

THE STRUGGLE FOR GROUP SURVIVAL

The external constraints of racism, sexism, and poverty have been so severe that, like Sara Brooks, the majority of African-American women have found it difficult to participate in organized political activities. Possessing neither the opportunity nor the resources to confront oppressive institutions directly, the majority of Black women have engaged in the struggle for group survival. Our strategies of everyday resistance have largely consisted of trying to create spheres of influence, authority, and power within institutions that traditionally have allowed African-Americans and women little formal authority or real power.

Ranging from the private, individual actions of Black mothers within their homes to the more organized group behavior of Black churchwomen and sorority sisters, Black women use a variety of strategies to undermine oppressive institutions. These strategies occur in three primary settings: political and economic institutions, Black extended families, and the African-American community as "family."

African-American women's actions in political and economic institutions typify the struggle for group survival. Rosalyn Terborg-Penn (1986) asserts that directly confronting the slave system by waging war against it was a much less successful strategy of resistance than establishing maroon societies on the fringe of slave communities. Women were usually involved in the leadership of these maroon societies, and as was the case in their African societies of origin, women cultivated and produced the food consumed by the community and thus were essential to this type of resistance. Using examples from Brazil, Jamaica, Surinam, and the United States, Terborg-Penn suggests that "day-to-day survival was imperative to these communities, and women provided the stability for the community" (p. 199). Black women's efforts after the Civil War to remove themselves from the labor market and direct the benefits of their labor to their families also reflect Black women's resistance in the political economy. Similarly, the constant pressure exerted by domestic workers to control the conditions of their work (Dill 1980, 1988a; Clark-Lewis 1985) illustrates strategies of everyday resistance among Black women workers.[3]

As bloodmothers and othermothers in Black extended families, women are key to transmitting an Afrocentric worldview (Steady 1981; Bush 1986; Fox-Genovese 1986). Like Sara Brooks, Black women confined to underpaid, demanding, menial jobs resisted passing on to their children externally defined images of Black women as mules, mammies, matriarchs, and sexually denigrated women. Rather, they used their families as effective Black female spheres of influence to foster their children's self-valuation and self-reliance (Dill 1980). In some cases Black women's centrality in Black family networks led them to exert their political power through existing family structures without appearing to do so. Anna Julia Cooper (1892) reports that even though nineteenth-century Black women were disenfranchised, they were not without political influence: "It is notorious that ignorant black women in the South have actually left their husband's homes and repudiated their support for what was understood by the wife to be race disloyalty, or 'voting away,' as she expresses it, the privileges of herself and little ones" (p. 139).

Traditionally women's activism within Black families meshed smoothly with activism as community othermothers in the wider Black community as "family." In both types of "family," African-American women worked to create Black female spheres of influence, authority, and power that produced a worldview markedly different from that advanced by the dominant group. Within African-American communities Black women's activities as cultural workers is empowering (Reagon 1987). "The power of black women was the power to make culture, to transmit folkways, norms, and customs, as well as to build shared ways of seeing the world that insured our survival," observes Sheila Radford-Hill. "This power . . . was neither economic nor political; nor did it translate into female dominance" (1986, 168). This culture was a culture of resistance, essential to the struggle for group survival. Examining one specific version of the community othermother role—namely, Black women's standpoint on education—reveals a fundamental dimension of Black women's political activism.

Education has long served as a powerful symbol for the important connections among self, change, and empowerment in African-American communities (Lerner 1972, 83–149; Webber 1978; Davis 1981; Neverdon-Morton 1989). The commitment to the value of education by prominent Black women such as Anna Julia Cooper, whose 1892 book *A Voice from the South* championed the cause of Black women's education; Mary McLeod Bethune, the founder of a college; Nannie Burroughs, a vigorous campaigner for Black women's education; and Johnetta Cole, the first Black woman president of Spelman College, goes far beyond the themes of gaining the technical skills essential to African-American employability, or mastering the social skills required for white acceptance (Barnett 1978; Harley 1978). In describing the purpose of the education offered at the Institute for Colored Youth, a school founded to educate the children of emancipated African-Americans, principal Fanny Jackson Coppin was "not interested in producing 'mere scholars' at the Institute, but rather students who would be committed to race 'uplift' " (Perkins 1982, 190). Like their anonymous slave foremothers, these women saw the activist potential of education and skillfully used this Black female sphere of influence to foster a definition of education as a cornerstone of Black community development.

African-American women have long realized that ignorance doomed Black people to powerlessness. Under slavery it was illegal to teach African-Americans to read and write. Mastering these skills was an expression of political activism not because education allowed slaves to become better slaves but because it offered skills essential in challenging the very tenets of slavery itself. One elderly ex-slave recalls the importance that reading held for enslaved African-Americans:

> I couldn't read, but my uncle could. I was a waiting-maid, an' used to help missis to dress in the morning. If massa wanted to tell her something he didn't want me to know, he used to spell it out. I could remember the letters, an' as soon as I got away I ran to uncle an' spelled them over to him, an' he told me what they meant. (Lerner 1972, 29–30)

When she became a mother, this anonymous African-American woman encouraged her children to become educated, and they were among the first to enter freedman's schools during the Civil War. Holding high expectations for her children, she was heard to comment about her son in particular, "Why, if I had his chance, do you think I would not learn!" For this mother education was clearly a powerful tool for liberation. Denied the opportunity to read and write, this Black woman resisted by remembering the letters and asking her uncle what they meant. She thus appeared to be conforming to the rules of slavery—she remained illiterate—while rejecting the rules themselves. Not only did this mother resist slavery in this way, she passed on her conceptions of resistance to her children through her role as educator.

Bell Hooks encountered a similar belief in education in her southern community: "Growing up in a community where I would be sent here and there to read the Bible to Miss Zula because she does not know how, to read this and that, a letter, words on a detergent box—to read—to write for others. How could I not understand the need for literacy? How could I not long to know?" (1989, 62). These examples not only illustrate the importance of education as a liberating force in African-American communities, but they also portray the centrality of Black women as everyday political activists.

This overall philosophy of education as a group effort has its roots in the slave experience. In early nineteenth-century African-American communities, education was not for individual gain but was for "race uplift" (Perkins 1983). This education was for the entire race, and its purpose was to assist in the economic, political, and social improvement of the enslaved and later emancipated African-Americans. As explained by Fanny Jackson Coppin, "our idea of getting an education did not come out of wanting to imitate anyone whatever. It grew out of the uneasiness and the restlessness of the desires we felt within us; the desire to know, not just a little, but a great deal" (Loewenberg and Bogin 1976, 316).

The activities of prominent Black female educators rest on the foundation established by the collective actions of Black women like anonymous slave mothers and the members of Bell Hooks's segregated African-American community. It is no accident that many well-known Black women activists were either teachers or somehow involved in struggling for educational opportunities for African-Americans of both sexes (Perkins 1983; Neverdon-Morton 1989). Limited professional opportunities pushed Black women together and fostered a sense of collective vision about education and political activism for race uplift. But the traditional role of women as educators and the power and status earned from women's roles as cultural workers also served to reinforce the importance of Black women's roles as educators. Black men and women who were perceived by the community as leaders of the struggle for group survival were described as "educators." Historian Sharon Harley notes that an integral element of Black feminist activist Anna Julia Cooper's "fight for women's rights and the elevation of the entire Black race was her commitment to the education of black youth" (1978, 92). Working for race uplift and education became intertwined.

While race uplift was the expected objective of all educated African-Americans, after the Civil War the implementation of this philosophy primarily fell to Black women (Perkins 1983). Given the small numbers of educated Black women in the late nineteenth century, the importance of their education for race uplift was clearly evident. The first college degree earned by a Black woman in the United States was acquired by Mary Jane Paterson from Oberlin College in 1862. In 1865 Fanny Jackson Coppin became the second Black woman to earn a degree. By 1890 only thirty Black women in the United States held baccalaureate degrees as compared with 300 Black men and 2500 white women (Perkins 1983). African-American women saw their performance as students and educators in broadly political terms (Neverdon-Morton 1989). Coppin describes the importance of her school performance: "I never rose to recite in my classes at Oberlin but I felt that I had the honor of the whole African race upon my shoulders. I felt that, should I fail, it would be ascribed to the fact that I was colored" (Loewenberg and Bogin 1976, 306).

Educated Black women traditionally were brought up to see their education as something gained not just for their own development but for the purpose of race uplift. This feeling was so strong that the women founding the National Association of Colored Women's Clubs chose as their motto "Lifting As We Climb." Coppin describes this deep commitment on the part of Black women as teachers/activists in this arena of the struggle for group survival: "It was in me to get an education and to teach my people. This idea was deep in my soul. Where it came from I cannot tell, for I had never had any exhortations, nor any lectures which influenced me to take this course" (Loewenberg and Bogin 1976, 307). Mary McLeod Bethune echoes a similar sentiment: "I am my mother's daughter, and the drums of Africa still beat in my heart. They will not let me rest while there is a single Negro boy or girl without a chance to prove his worth" (Lerner 1972, 143).

This belief in education for race uplift and in the special role of Black women in this struggle continued well into the twentieth century. In a 1938 article in the *Journal of Negro History*, Mary McLeod Bethune argued, "if our people are to fight their way up and out of bondage we must arm them with the sword and the shield . . . of pride—belief in themselves and their possibilities, based upon a sure knowledge of the achievements of the past" (Lerner 1972, 544). More recently that belief and pride has come through the struggle to secure our own educations. Struggles around educational issues have politicized Black women. A 23-year-old Black woman participant in the 1982 struggle for better education at the predominantly Black and female Medgar Evers College at the City College of New York taps this meaning of education in what was formerly called race uplift but what is now called Black community development:

> I learned so much—more than I could ever learn in the classroom! I learned that there's a whole lot more than getting a degree and getting ahead financially. You must do so with principle and dignity. You can't just sit back and watch all the atrocious things continue to happen, take your little class notes, read your books, and do nothing to change conditions. (Nicola-McLaughlin and Chandler 1988, 195)

Traditionally, being a teacher in the Black community meant the kind of visibility that emerged as community leadership (Neverdon-Morton 1989). In describing her role as a teacher, Fanny Jackson Coppin stated that "she had always taught two schools—the students of the Institute and the Black community" (Perkins 1982, 190). Black women used their classrooms and status as educators for African-American community development. In comparing the letters of Black and white women applying to missionary societies to become teachers in the South after the Civil War, historian Linda Perkins (1983) uncovered some significant differences. Overwhelmingly single, upper- and middle-class, unemployed, and educated in New England colleges and at Oberlin, white women wrote of the "deep need to escape idleness and boredom" brought on by their placement in the cult of true womanhood. In contrast, the Black women who applied were employed and financially supported families, and their letters consistently reflected themes of duty and race uplift. While white women working in the South generally did so for two to three years, Black women expressed the desire to "devote their entire lives to their work." Perkins points out that most did. Formally educated Black women teachers in early twentieth-century Washington, D.C., also believed that they had a special responsibility to their respective communities which they alone could fulfill (Harley 1982). Such women "often saw themselves more as 'uplifters' than as working women. . . . Educating the children of poor unlettered blacks was considered part of their moral and social obligations as educated women" (Harley 1982, 257). In describing the work of one of her teachers who expressed this type of political leadership, Alice Walker notes, "mostly she taught by the courage of her own life, which to me is the highest form of teaching" (1983, 38).

This kind of teaching reflects a form of Afrocentric feminist political activism essential to the struggle for group survival. By placing family, children, education, and community at the center of our political activism, African-American women draw on Afrocentric conceptualizations of mothering, family, community, and empowerment. Moreover, offering a vision of what is possible in human relationships furthers the recurring humanist vision in Black feminist thought. Alice Walker describes the impact a white teacher had in her life and, in doing so, taps an Afrocentric feminist perspective on education and the politics of empowerment:

> Muriel viewed the Child as, I think, she viewed herself: as teacher, student, poet, and friend. And to the Child, she held herself, her life, accountable. I do not know what struggles brought Muriel to her belief in the centrality of the Child. For me, there has been conflict, struggle, occasional defeat—not only in affirming the life of my own child (children) at all costs, but also in seeing in that affirmation a fond acceptance and confirmation of myself in a world that would deny me the untrampled blossoming of my own existence. Not surprisingly, I have found this to be political in the deepest sense. (Walker 1983, 362)

Teaching becomes an arena for political activism wherever it occurs.

Black women's activities in the Black church have also been profoundly influenced by the vision of Black women as educators of African-American families and communities. Dodson and Gilkes (1987) suggest "if any one ministry could be identified as central to the black sacred cosmos of the twentieth century, it would be education. . . . Black people . . . defined education of the oppressed and the oppressors as central tasks of Christian mission" (p. 84). Black churches have been central in supporting a variety of social, economic, political, and ethical actions essential to Black community development (Sobel 1979; Lincoln 1984; Mitchell and

Lewter 1986). While men dominate positions of formal authority in church hierarchies, women make up a large percentage of the congregations, hold positions of authority, and generally exert a powerful influence on African-American church communities across denominations (Dodson and Gilkes 1987). The situation is far more complex than that proposed by traditional models arguing that female "followers" obey the orders of male "leaders." Rather, emerging research in Black women's studies indicates that men and women exert different types of leadership within Black church communities.

"It was biblical faith grounded in the prophetic tradition," declares Katie Cannon, that helped Black women "devise strategies and tactics to make Black people less susceptible to the indignities and proscriptions of an oppressive white social order" (1985, 35). Cheryl Gilkes's (1985) work on the turn-of-the-century Sanctified Church describes how African-American women used this prophetic tradition to create and maintain a sophisticated community of sisterhood. Gilkes contends that "women's concentration in educational roles . . . was not simply a form of female segregation: instead it was the basis for alternative structures of authority, career pathways, and spheres of influence" (1985, 689). During a time when dominant society denigrated African-American women, Black women in the Sanctified Church referred to one another as "saints." In doing this they clearly rejected their societally defined "place" in favor of creating their own self-definitions. Their emphasis on biblical authority made learning "the Word" an important means for living a sanctified life and offered a powerful rationale for getting an education. During a time when educated African-American women were scarce, the largely working-class women in the church encouraged one another to become educated. As fund raisers women made essential economic contributions to Sanctified churches. Strong Women's Departments retained control over the disbursement and allocation of their funds. The women "believed in economic cooperation with men, not in economic dependence on them" (Gilkes 1985, 690). By giving advice to their younger "sisters," older women taught less experienced women the skills necessary for their survival as African-American women. Sisterhood did not occur at the expense of Black men or children. Rather, it meshed with the needs of these groups so that the church practiced unity without uniformity.

A similar standpoint on the importance of education, sisterhood, self-definitions, self-valuations, and economic self-reliance permeated other Black women's organizations. Through advocacy and education the turn-of-the-century Black women's club movement aimed to address a broad spectrum of Black women's issues (Neverdon-Morton 1989). The original departments of the National Association of Colored Women, the first national organization of Black women's organizations, included the following units: Woman Suffrage, Patriotism, Education, Conditions in Rural Life, Music, Literature and Art, Gainful Occupation and Business, Better Railroad Conditions, Mothers Meetings and Night Schools, Public Speaking, and Child Welfare (Lerner 1972, 445). Black sororities also listed as part of their mission attending to the special needs of Black women as a key part of the struggle for group survival (Giddings 1988).

Not all African-American women were welcomed as equal participants in middle-class Black women's organizations. While working on behalf of all Black women, members of the Black Women's Club Movement did not work with them as equals. The general thinking among many middle-class reformers "was that most uneducated, unskilled women were in need of social and moral uplift and, therefore, lacked the refinement . . . to join in the uplift process, at least as members of their organizations" (Harley 1982, 258). Early twentieth-century Black churches were key locations where Black women who were less educated and less financially secure than the better-educated teachers who populated Black women's organizations could exert leadership. Working-class and poor Black women took up membership in church women's groups, female auxiliaries to fraternal orders, and benevolent societies. These organizations generally required less affluent life styles and less active public roles and had more practical benefits for their members than did predominantly middle-class reform organizations (Harley 1982).

In spite of social class differences among Black women, this tradition of becoming educated for Black community development has permeated the Black women's activist tradition. Cheryl Gilkes's (1983b) study of 25 Black women community leaders documents Black women's continued rejection of more limited definitions of education. In assessing their own educational experiences, these Black women were highly critical of the functions of higher education as an agency of socialization into a white middle-class worldview. They perceived higher education in white institutions as a "form of pacification and mystification," education that "teaches you not to fight." These women rejected this form of education in favor of "focused educations" within the same white institutions that would allow them to continue the tradition of Black women working for race uplift.

Depending on their social class backgrounds, the women in Gilkes's study followed different routes to acquiring a focused education. For middle-class women becoming "race women" was stressed by their parents. These women were taught to adhere to the long tradition of educated Black women working on behalf of the race. In contrast, working-class women went to school for the credentials and information they felt they needed for specific community problems. One respondent from a working-class background recounts her reasons for returning to school:

> I heard people talking about how black parents were apathetic and I never believed that black parents were apathetic. . . . Parents had always had the feeling, and I was under the same impression until I became involved with the teachers, that teachers were always right because we (black people) always have this great respect for education. . . . I felt even though I worked with a parents' group that because I wasn't a teacher no one took my words very seriously. And I decided that I was going to become a teacher, not to work in the classroom, but to work with parents. (Gilkes 1983b, 121)

This woman's focused education empowered her by granting her the credentials she felt she needed to organize parents. Her education was designed to further African-Americans as a group, not solely for her own personal development.

Acquiring a focused education demonstrates the significance of self, change, and empowerment for Black women. A 38-year-old-mother of five who participated in the struggle at Medgar Evers College describes the importance the struggle for an education had for her: "More than anything, I learned that I am a powerful person! You see, it's important to realize that no matter what your age or what you've been through, each person can make a contribution to changing the conditions of our people" (Nicola-McLaughlin and Chandler 1988, 194). Perhaps Black women's empowerment through education is best summarized by another participant in that same political movement. She asserts, "I was basically a shy and reserved person prior to the struggle at Medgar, but I found my voice—and I used it! Now, I will never lose my voice again!" (Nicola-McLaughlin and Chandler 1988, 195).

THE STRUGGLE FOR INSTITUTIONAL TRANSFORMATION

Actions taken to eliminate discriminatory legislation in the areas of housing, employment, education, public accommodations, and political representation as well as those aimed at combating discriminatory customs in these same areas represent activism aimed at changing the rules that circumscribe African-American women's lives. Traditionally, Black women have either been excluded from or suppressed within organizations devoted to institutional transformation (Terborg-Penn 1978, 1985; Hooks 1981; Davis 1981). Patterns of Black women's activism thus reflect less about Black women's preferred political choices and more about patterns of race, gender, and class relations pervading organizations devoted to institutional change.

Depending on historical time and place, African-American women employed a range of strategies in challenging the rules governing our subordination. In many cases Black women practiced individual protest against unfair rules and practices. When she was a law student at Howard University in the 1940s, Ruth Powell's first encounter with Jim Crow in Washington, D.C.'s drugstore cafeterias was devastating: "I sat there for about ten minutes watching the waitresses whizzing back and forth in front of me, when suddenly the awful truth dawned and I realized what was happening" (Murray 1987, 205). She left the store. She knew that "I, alone, couldn't do anything concrete to revolutionize conditions," but she also believed "I had to do something to preserve what remained of my self-respect" (p. 205). Ruth Powell's "something" evolved into a one-woman campaign. She would enter cafeterias, politely ask for service, and, when refused, sit quietly sometimes for hours at a time. During her sit-ins she would pick out a waiter and stare at him for perhaps an hour or more. "Whether I was finally served or not was unimportant," Powell explained. "What I believed was that all these little bits of agitation would go toward that vital . . . awakening process" (p. 205).

Powell's stance represents action taken to get the rules themselves changed. Black women have also protested by working through formal organizations and groups. Many African-American women's organizations actively engaged in the struggle for group survival also were active lobbyists for reforms in the legal apparatus and its accompanying cluster of everyday customs. Black women have also seen the need for principled coalitions with groups affected by similar issues. The contributions of countless Black female rank-and-file activists in civil rights, feminist, and labor movements reflect strategies designed to change the rules of the system by working within reformist organizations (Giddings 1984). During the 1970s and 1980s, even though Black women remained underrepresented in elected public office relative to their proportion of the population, Black women made greater gains than white women in election to mayoral, state legislative, and congressional office (Darcy and Hadley 1988). Still other cases involve African-American women's involvement in violent resistance against slavery and other forms of political and legal oppression (Terborg-Penn 1986).

Being one of the few groups negatively affected by multiple systems of oppression, African-American women have been in a better position to see the interrelationships among race, gender, and social class oppression. Thus the diverse strategies employed in the struggle for institutional transformation have been paralleled by a similar diversity in the types of rules Black women have challenged. Black women have had an enduring interest not just in resisting racist and sexist laws and customs, but in changing a broad segment of the rules shaping American society. As of 1980, 24 percent of Black women workers were members of labor organizations, while only 15 percent of white women workers were members (Terborg-Penn 1985). In spite of the fact that Black women do not readily identify themselves as feminists, high levels of support for feminist issues exist among African-American women (King 1988).

Although African-American women may implicitly support a humanist vision for institutional transformation, Black women's political strategies may not explicitly address this vision. Many women begin their political activism as advocates for African-Americans, the poor, or, less frequently, women. But over time Black women activists come to see the interconnection of race, class, and gender oppression and the need for broad-based political action. Rather than joining a range of organizations each of which is devoted to single-purpose issues, many Black women activists either start new organizations or work to transform the institutions in which they are situated. For example, Black women in the civil rights movement initially joined to address racial inequality but found themselves protesting gender inequality as well (Evans 1979). Faye Wattleton's astute leadership of Planned Parenthood, Gloria Scott's resourceful actions to make the Girl Scouts of America more racially and economically inclusive, and Marian Wright Edelman's judicious leadership of the Children's Defense Fund all appear to tie these women to single-issue causes that are not race-specific. But closer examination reveals that even though these women do not project themselves as being advocates for Black women, their organizational actions directly benefit Black women. Overall African-American women's active participation in labor, feminist, and civil rights movements demonstrates a commitment to a broad range of social issues.

BLACK WOMEN'S LEADERSHIP AND INSTITUTIONAL TRANSFORMATION

Black women's long-standing participation in organized political activities fosters a rethinking of the ways in which Black women conceptualize and use power. Black women's use of power seems to grow from distinctly Afrocentric feminist conceptions of how people become empowered, how power can be structured and shared in organizational settings, and how organizations would look if people were to be fully empowered within them. Examining Black women's leadership in organizations whose mission is institutional change offers a route to examining these larger questions.

African-American women have been active in movements for Black civil rights such as the abolitionist movement, the antilynching struggles in the early twentieth century, and the more recent civil rights movement in the South (Prestage 1980; Giddings 1984). While Black women in such organizations rarely forwarded an agenda designed exclusively for Black women, the types of issues they championed and the way in which they operated within these organizations suggest that they brought an Afrocentric feminist sensibility to their political activism.

Black women's organizational style within predominantly Black organizations reveals much about how Black women employ traditional sources of Black female power. The power that accrues to community othermothers and the power gained from creating and conserving culture are both used to shape agendas for Black political action. Drawing on the model of education as empowerment, Black women routinely reject models of authority based on hierarchical power relations. For example, Black activist Septima Clark disagreed with the style of leadership in the Southern Christian Leadership Conference during the civil rights movement. Ms. Clark pointed out, "you can work behind the scenes all you want. . . . But don't come forth and try to lead. That's not the kind of thing they [Black men] want" (Brown 1986, 77). Ms. Clark tried to influence the male-dominated organization: "I sent a letter to Dr. King asking him not to lead all the marches himself, but instead to develop leaders who could lead their own marches. Dr. King read that letter before the staff. It just tickled them; they just laughed" (p. 77).

African-American women like Septima Clark carried distinctive notions of leadership and empowerment into the Black civil rights struggle, ideas whereby, according to Nikki Giovanni, "the purpose of any leadership is to build more leadership. The purpose of being a spokesperson is to speak until the people gain a voice" (1988, 135). Septima Clark's explanation of why she wished to develop a broad base of community leaders illustrates how the commitment to education as an empowering tool can operate in Black women's political activism: "I thought that you develop leaders as you go along, and as you develop these people let them show forth their development by leading" (p. 77).

Black women's style of activism also reflects a belief that teaching people how to be self-reliant fosters more empowerment than teaching them how to follow. Black civil rights activist Ella Baker, a major figure in the Southern Christian Leadership Conference who worked closely with students, recounts how she nurtured the empowerment of student civil rights workers: "I never intervened between the struggles if I could avoid it. Most of the youngsters had been trained to believe in or to follow adults if they could. I felt they ought to have a chance to learn to think things through and to make the decisions" (Cantarow 1980, 87). Drawing on both the community othermother model of relationships and education as a tool of empowerment, Ms. Baker did intervene, but only if she felt that the students were in danger.

"We must strive to 'lift as we climb.' . . . We must climb in such a way as to guarantee that all our sisters, regardless of social class, and indeed all of our brothers climb with us. This must be the essential dynamic of our quest for power," counsels Angela Davis (1989, 5). The models of leadership offered by both Septima Clark and Ella Baker speak to a distinctively Black female mode of political activism captured by the motto "lift as we climb." Both women clearly could have been leaders in the traditional sense of being figureheads with formal authority. But studying their actual behavior reveals that they both wielded considerable power within their organizations which grew from their Afrocentric and feminist standpoint on social change.[4]

The strategies employed by African-American women within labor organizations reinforces this theme that traditional sources of Black women's empowerment influence Black women's organizational behavior. One intriguing case study of a sustained and eventually successful effort to organize secretaries at a hospital in a small southern city illustrates how Black women draw on prevailing Afrocentric conceptions of family and community (Sacks 1984, 1988).[5] Community and kin ties drew Black women together across the hospital's bureaucratic units. These workplace networks in turn became the basis for organizing. People in the networks shared a family idiom by celebrating one another's family and life-cycle events and referring to themselves as "family."

Certain women in these overlapping community and workplace networks became "centerwomen." The skills centerwomen gained from their centrality in their families enabled them to keep people together, ensure that obligations were fulfilled, and maintain group consensus. Thus the Black women's mothering tradition emerged in the union-organizing drive as a powerful foundation for this particular effort at institutional transformation. The drive was successful because of the existence of two equally important dimensions of leadership: that offered by spokesmen or spokespersons who engaged in direct negotiations with management, and that provided by centerwomen or centerpersons who fostered group solidarity among the workers. While men and women are capable of exercising both types, in this particular case the functions were divided by gender. Men were spokespersons and women were centerpersons.

Cheryl Gilkes's (1983b, 1988) work on Black women community leaders reinforces this notion that Black women work for institutional transformation in characteristically Afrocentric feminist ways. The 25 Black women leaders in her study used their positions as heads of social service agencies to change the rules by which those agencies operated. One agency director commented, "you will never eliminate discrimination through complaints. . . . The thing that you've got to do is to get into those institutions and work from top to bottom: how they set policies; who's setting policies; why this is the policy" (1983b, 129). Even though their agencies were funded and controlled by whites, in the same way that Black women domestic workers used their positions to deliver material goods and skills to their children, these women used their institutions to empower African-Americans. They "saw the black community as a group of relatives and other friends whose interests should be advanced and promoted at all times, under all conditions, and by almost any means" (1983b, 117).

These women's work for institutional transformation often put their jobs in jeopardy. Because the work, and not the particular job, was their focus, they moved on when organizational limits combined with turning points in their self-development. By defining their jobs as institutional transformation versus trying to fit into the existing system, they gained a degree of "spiritual independence." Acquiring a focused education by moving through jobs enabled the women to see the bigger picture obscured by working only within one setting.

By fostering African-American autonomy through their institutions, these women expanded their web of affiliations to make principled coalitions among themselves. In spite of ideological differences, the women participating in this web of community workers sat on one another's boards and generally helped to further the distinctive goals of their individual organizations. Gilkes assesses this strategic placement on agency boards:

> The affiliations are reflections of the locations and types of problems in the community. Although a community worker may have a well-articulated political ideology, her affiliations are not always a reflection of her choice between sides of an ideological debate such as integration versus separatism or radical political strategies versus traditional party politics. The women's affiliations with white-controlled institutions are a reflection of where they feel Black folks need to be in order to exert some control over their lives and futures. (Gilkes 1988, 68)

Both African-American women and men have been workers for Black community development. Although Gilkes does not take this position,

I suspect that women community workers in her study—and African-American women in general—are more likely to engage in this strategic affiliation and reject ideology as the overarching framework structuring our political activism. This does not mean that Black women lack ideology but, rather, that our experiences as othermothers, centerwomen, and community othermothers foster a distinctive form of political activism based on negotiation and a higher degree of attention to context (Gilligan 1982; Belenky et al. 1986).

Currently the changing social class structure of African-American families and communities is affecting the shape and effectiveness of this long-standing Black women's activist tradition. More than 70 percent of Black college students attend predominantly white institutions, and, unlike the community leaders in Gilkes's study, many fail to see the importance of gaining focused educations for either group survival or institutional transformation. Teaching as an arena of Black women's political activism has been correspondingly eroded by factors such as Black women's increased access to other managerial and professional careers and the suburbanization of the Black middle class. Angela Davis counsels middle-class Black women to build on the Black women's activist tradition:

> Black women scholars and professionals cannot afford to ignore the straits of our sisters who are acquainted with the immediacy of oppression in a way many of us are not. The process of empowerment cannot be simplistically defined in accordance with our own particular class interests. We must learn to lift as we climb. (1989, 9)

The humanist vision in Black feminist thought has deep historical roots in the political activism of African-American women such as Sara Brooks, anonymous slave mothers, turn-of-the-century Black women educators, countless Ruth Powells, the centerwomen in the hospital union, and the community women workers in Gilkes's study. These Black women activists generally transcended their differences in order to create a powerful Black women's activist tradition. It remains to be seen whether African-American women facing the challenges of contemporary race, class, and gender oppression will continue this tradition and create new ways to "lift as we climb."

NOTES

1. The meaning of power has long been contested in traditional academic discourse. Conceptualizations of power have included exchange theory assessments that view power

as a commodity unequally possessed by individuals competing in the marketplace, Marxist analyses that equate power with the domination inherent in the state and class struggle, analyses of the mechanisms of power as they operate in microinteractions, and feminist theorizations that view power as energy, capacity, and self-actualization. See Flammang (1983), Hartsock (1983b), and Lukes (1986) for comprehensive discussions of these and other treatments of power. Definitions of the related concepts of political activism and political resistance reflect similar conceptual diversity.

2. The Black women's activist tradition offers a new model for examining African-American political activism overall. Philosophies of Black nationalism and racial integration, ideological positions in Black social and political thought (Cruse 1967), parallel struggles for group survival and institutional transformation. These philosophies have long been presented as dichotomous opposites in African-American scholarship. But this debate suffers from the either/or dichotomous thinking pervading Western social thought. Instead, by viewing autonomy and coalition as complementary and essential parts of the same process, a Black women's activist tradition rooted in a both/and humanist vision of society offers new ways of viewing this long-standing and divisive debate.

3. James Scott (1985) suggests that this dimension of political activity can be thought of as constituting a social movement. Curiously, this is a social movement "with no formal organization, no formal leaders, no manifestos, no dues, no name, and no banner" (Scott 1985, 35). Black women's individual acts of resistance in the labor market occur in the context of a culture of resistance. Seen in the light of a supportive Black community and the knowledge that the risk to any single resister is generally reduced to the extent that the whole community is involved, Scott's analysis suggests that Black women's actions constitute a social movement.

4. Another suggested source of Black women's power within African-American communities concerns Black women's authority as spiritual leaders. Rosalyn Terborg-Penn (1986) suggests that in cases in which women lead community resistance movements, respected older women often became leaders. These women were revered generally because of "supernatural or spiritual powers, which their followers believed were strong enough to combat the oppressive forces against which their society was struggling" (1986, 190).

5. Karen Sacks's case study describes an atypical case of Black women's experiences in unions. For many years Black women have participated in and organized a variety of labor actions designed to improve working conditions, wages, and occupational mobility. But the segregation of Black women in private domestic work which left them largely outside of industry, the occupational discrimination within industry, and prejudice within the unions themselves all worked to shape Black women's behavior as unionists (Terborg-Penn 1985).

Chapter 8 ————————————————————————

THE SEXUAL POLITICS OF BLACK WOMANHOOD

Even I found it almost impossible to let her say what had happened to her as *she* perceived it . . . And why? Because once you strip away the lie that rape is pleasant, that children are not permanently damaged by sexual pain, that violence done to them is washed away by fear, silence, and time, you are left with the positive horror of the lives of thousands of children . . . who have been sexually abused and who have never been permitted their own language to tell about it.

—Alice Walker 1988, 57

In *The Color Purple* Alice Walker creates the character of Celie, a Black adolescent girl who is sexually abused by her stepfather. By writing letters to God and forming supportive relationships with other Black women, Celie finds her own voice, and her voice enables her to transcend the fear and silence of her childhood. By creating Celie and giving her the language to tell of her sexual abuse, Walker adds Celie's voice to muted yet growing discussions of the sexual politics of Black womanhood in Black feminist thought. Black feminists have investigated how rape as a specific form of sexual violence is embedded in a system of interlocking race, gender, and class oppression (Davis 1978, 1981, 1989; Hall 1983). Reproductive rights issues such as access to information on sexuality and birth control, the struggles for abortion rights, and patterns of forced sterilization have also garnered attention (Davis 1981). Black lesbian feminists have vigorously challenged the basic assumptions and mechanisms of control underlying compulsory heterosexuality and have investigated homophobia's impact on African-American women (Clarke 1983; Shockley 1983; Barbara Smith 1983; Lorde 1984).

But when it comes to other important issues concerning the sexual politics of Black womanhood, like Alice Walker, Black feminists have found it almost impossible to say what has happened to Black women. In the flood of scholarly and popular writing about Black heterosexual relationships, analyses of domestic violence against African-American women—especially those that link this form of sexual violence to existing gender ideology concerning Black masculinity and Black femininity—remain rare. Theoretical work explaining patterns of Black women's inclusion in the burgeoning international pornography industry has been similarly neglected. Perhaps the most curious omission has been the virtual silence of the Black feminist community concerning the participation of far too many Black women in prostitution. Ironically, while the image of African-American women as prostitutes has been aggressively challenged, the reality of African-American women who work as prostitutes remains unexplored.

These patterns of inclusion and neglect in Black feminist thought merit investigation. Examining the links between sexuality and power in a system of interlocking race, gender, and class oppression should reveal how important controlling Black women's sexuality has been to the effective operation of domination overall. The words of Angela Davis, Audre Lorde, Barbara Smith, and Alice Walker provide a promising foundation for a comprehensive Black feminist analysis. But Black feminist analyses of sexual politics must go beyond chronicling how sexuality has been used to oppress. Equally important is the need to reconceptualize sexuality with an eye toward empowering African-American women.

A WORKING DEFINITION OF SEXUAL POLITICS

Sexual politics examines the links between sexuality and power. In defining sexuality it is important to distinguish among sexuality and the related terms, *sex* and *gender* (Vance 1984; Andersen 1988). Sex is a biological category attached to the body—humans are born female or male. In contrast, gender is socially constructed. The sex/gender system consists of marking the categories of biological sex with socially constructed gender meanings of masculinity and femininity. Just as sex/gender systems vary from relatively egalitarian systems to sex/gender hierarchies, ideologies of sexuality attached to particular sex/gender systems exhibit similar diversity. Sexuality is socially constructed through the sex/gender system on both the personal level of individual consciousness and interpersonal relationships and the social structural level of social institutions (Foucault 1980). This multilevel sex/gender system reflects the needs of a given historical moment such that social constructions of sexuality change in tandem with changing social conditions.

African-American women inhabit a sex/gender hierarchy in which inequalities of race and social class have been sexualized. Privileged groups define their alleged sexual practices as the mythical norm and label sexual practices and groups who diverge from this norm as deviant and threatening (Lorde 1984; Vance 1984). Maintaining the mythical norm of the financially independent, white middle-class family organized around a monogamous heterosexual couple requires stigmatizing African-American families as being deviant, and a primary source of this assumed deviancy stems from allegations about Black sexuality. This sex/gender hierarchy not only operates on the social structural level but is potentially replicated within each individual. Differences in sexuality thus take on more meaning than just benign sexual variation. Each individual becomes a powerful conduit for social relations of domination whereby individual anxieties, fears, and doubts about sexuality can be annexed by larger systems of oppression (Hoch 1979; Foucault 1980, 99).

According to Cheryl Clarke, African-Americans have been profoundly affected by this sex/gender hierarchy:

> Like all Americans, black Americans live in a sexually repressive culture. And we have made all manner of compromise regarding our sexuality in order to live here. We have expended much energy trying to debunk the racist mythology which says our sexuality is depraved. Unfortunately, many of us have overcompensated and assimilated. . . . Like everyone else in America who is ambivalent in these respects, black folk have to live with the contradictions of this limited sexual system by repressing or closeting any other sexual/erotic urges, feelings, or desires. (Clarke 1983, 199)

Embedded in Clarke's statement is the theme of self-censorship inherent when a hierarchy of any kind invades interpersonal relationships among individuals and the actual consciousness of individuals themselves. Sexuality and power as domination become intertwined.

In her ground-breaking essay, "Uses of the Erotic: The Erotic as Power," Black feminist poet Audre Lorde explores this fundamental link between sexuality and power:

There are many kinds of power, used and unused, acknowledged or otherwise. The erotic is a resource within each of us that lies in a deeply female and spiritual plane, firmly rooted in the power of our unexpressed or unrecognized feeling. In order to perpetuate itself, every oppression must corrupt or distort those various sources of power within the culture of the oppressed that can provide energy for change. For women, this has meant a suppression of the erotic as a considered source of power and information in our lives. (Lorde 1984, 53)

For Lorde sexuality is a component of the larger construct of the erotic as a source of power in women. Lorde's notion is one of power as energy, as something people possess which must be annexed in order for larger systems of oppression to function.[1]

Sexuality becomes a domain of restriction and repression when this energy is tied to the larger system of race, class, and gender oppression. But Lorde's words also signal the potential for Black women's empowerment by showing sexuality and the erotic to be a domain of exploration, pleasure, and human agency. From a Black feminist standpoint sexuality encompasses the both/and nature of human existence, the potential for a sexuality that simultaneously oppresses and empowers.

One key issue for Black feminist thought is the need to examine the processes by which power as domination on the social structural level—namely, institutional structures of racism, sexism, and social class privilege—annexes this basic power of the erotic on the personal level—that is, the construct of power as energy, for its own ends.

BLACK WOMEN AND THE SEX/GENDER HIERARCHY

The social construction of Black women's sexuality is embedded in this larger, overarching sex/gender hierarchy designed to harness power as energy to the exigencies of power as race, gender, and social class domination. The discussion in Chapter 3 on slaveowner attempts to control Black women's fertility, the analysis in Chapter 4 of the significance of the controlling images of Black women in regulating Black women's sexuality and fertility, and the analysis in Chapter 6 of Black motherhood all explore efforts by the dominant group to control and exploit Black women's reproduction. Pornography, prostitution, and rape as a specific tool of sexual violence have also been key to the sexual politics of Black womanhood. Together they form three essential and interrelated components of the sex/gender hierarchy framing Black women's sexuality.

Pornography and Black Women's Bodies

For centuries the black woman has served as the primary pornographic "outlet" for white men in Europe and America. We need only think of the black women used as breeders, raped for the pleasure and profit of their owners. We need only think of the license the "master" of the slave women enjoyed. But, most telling of all, we need only study the old slave societies of the South to note the sadistic treatment—at the hands of white "gentlemen"— of "beautiful young quadroons and octoroons" who became increasingly (and were deliberately bred to become) indistinguishable from white women, and were the more highly prized as slave mistresses because of this. (Walker 1981, 42)

Alice Walker's description of the rape of enslaved African women for the "pleasure and profit of their owners" encapsulates several elements of contemporary pornography. First, Black women were used as sex objects for the pleasure of white men. This objectification of African-American women parallels the portrayal of women in pornography as sex objects whose sexuality is available for men (McNall 1983). Exploiting Black women as breeders objectified them as less than human because only animals can be bred against their will. In contemporary pornography women are objectified through being portrayed as pieces of meat, as sexual animals awaiting conquest. Second, African-American women were raped, a form of sexual violence. Violence is typically an implicit or explicit theme in pornography. Moreover, the rape of Black women linked sexuality and violence, another characteristic feature of pornography (Eisenstein 1983). Third, rape and other forms of sexual violence act to strip victims of their will to resist and make them passive and submissive to the will of the rapist. Female passivity, the fact that women have things done to them, is a theme repeated over and over in contemporary pornography (McNall 1983). Fourth, the profitability of Black women's sexual exploitation for white "gentlemen" parallels pornography's financially lucrative benefits for pornographers (Eisenstein 1983). Finally, the actual breeding of "quadroons and octoroons" not only reinforces the themes of Black women's passivity, objectification, and malleability to male control but reveals pornography's grounding in racism and sexism. The fates of both Black and white women were intertwined in this breeding process. The ideal African-American woman as a pornographic object was indistinguishable from white women and thus approximated the images of beauty, asexuality, and chastity forced on white women. But inside was a highly sexual whore, a "slave mistress" ready to cater to her owner's pleasure.[2]

Contemporary pornography consists of a series of icons or representations that focus the viewer's attention on the relationship between the portrayed individual and the general qualities ascribed to that class of individuals. Pornographic images are iconographic in that they represent realities in a manner determined by the historical position of the observers, their relationship to their own time, and to the history of the conventions which they employ (Gilman 1985). The treatment of Black women's bodies in nineteenth-century Europe and the United States may be the foundation upon which contemporary pornography as the representation of women's objectification, domination, and control is based. Icons about the sexuality of Black women's bodies emerged in these contexts. Moreover, as race/gender-specific representations, these icons have implications for the treatment of both African-American and white women in contemporary pornography.

I suggest that African-American women were not included in pornography as an afterthought but instead form a key pillar on which contemporary pornography itself rests. As Alice Walker points out, "the more ancient roots of modern pornography are to be found in the almost always pornographic treatment of black women who, from the moment they entered slavery . . . were subjected to rape as the 'logical' convergence of sex and violence. Conquest, in short" (1981, 42).

One key feature about the treatment of Black women in the nineteenth century was how their bodies were objects of display. In the antebellum American South white men did not have to look at pornographic pictures of women because they could become voyeurs of Black women on the auction block. A chilling example of this objectification of the Black female body is provided by the exhibition, in early nineteenth-century Europe, of Sarah Bartmann, the so-called Hottentot Venus. Her display formed one of the original icons for Black female sexuality. An African women, Sarah Bartmann was often exhibited at fashionable parties in Paris, generally wearing little clothing, to provide entertainment. To her audience she represented deviant sexuality. At the time European audiences thought that Africans had deviant sexual practices and searched for physiological differences, such as enlarged penises and malformed female genitalia, as indications of this deviant sexuality. Sarah Bartmann's exhibition stimulated these racist and sexist beliefs. After her death in 1815, she was dissected. Her genitalia and buttocks remain on display in Paris (Gilman 1985).

Sander Gilman explains the impact that Sarah Bartmann's exhibition had on Victorian audiences:

> It is important to note that Sarah Bartmann was exhibited not to show her genitalia—but rather to present another anomaly which the European audience . . . found riveting. This was the steatopygia, or protruding buttocks, the other physical characteristic of the Hottentot female which captured the eye of early European travelers. . . . The figure of Sarah Bartmann was reduced to her sexual parts. The audience which had paid to see her buttocks and had fantasized about the uniqueness of her genitalia when she was alive could, after her death and dissection, examine both. (1985, 213)

In this passage Gilman unwittingly describes how Bartmann was used as a pornographic object similar to how women are represented in contemporary pornography. She was reduced to her sexual parts, and these parts came to represent a dominant icon applied to Black women throughout the nineteenth century. Moreover, the fact that Sarah Bartmann was both African and a woman underscores the importance of gender in maintaining notions of racial purity. In this case Bartmann symbolized Blacks as a "race." Thus the creation of the icon applied to Black women demonstrates that notions of gender, race, and sexuality were linked in overarching structures of political domination and economic exploitation.

The process illustrated by the pornographic treatment of the bodies of enslaved African women and of women like Sarah Bartmann has developed into a full-scale industry encompassing all women objectified differently by racial/ethnic category. Contemporary portrayals of Black women in pornography represent the continuation of the historical treatment of their actual bodies. African-American women are usually depicted in a situation of bondage and slavery, typically in a submissive posture, and often with two white men. As Bell observes, "this setting reminds us of all the trappings of slavery: chains, whips, neck braces, wrist clasps" (1987, 59). White women and women of color have different pornographic images applied to them. The image of Black women in pornography is almost consistently one featuring them breaking from chains. The image of Asian women in pornography is almost consistently one of being tortured (Bell 1987, 161).

The pornographic treatment of Black women's bodies challenges the prevailing feminist assumption that since pornography primarily affects white women, racism has been grafted onto pornography. African-American women's experiences suggest that Black women were not added into a preexisting pornography, but rather that pornography itself must be reconceptualized as an example of the interlocking nature of race, gender, and class oppression. At the heart of both racism and sexism are notions of biological determinism claiming that people of African descent and women possess immutable biological characteristics marking their inferiority to elite white men (Gould 1981; Fausto-Sterling 1989; Halpin 1989). In pornography these racist and sexist beliefs are sexualized. Moreover, for African-American women pornography has not been timeless and universal but was tied to Black women's experiences with the European colonization of Africa and with American slavery. Pornography emerged within a specific system of social class relationships.

This linking of views of the body, social constructions of race and gender, and conceptualizations of sexuality that inform Black women's treatment as pornographic objects promises to have significant implications for how we assess contemporary pornography. Moreover, examining how pornography has been central to the race, gender, and class oppression of African-American women offers new routes for understanding the dynamics of power as domination.

Investigating racial patterns in pornography offers one route for such an analysis. Black women have often claimed that images of white women's sexuality were intertwined with the controlling image of the sexually denigrated Black woman: "In the United States, the fear and fascination of female sexuality was projected onto black women; the passionless lady arose in symbiosis with the primitively sexual slave" (Hall 1983, 333). Comparable linkages exist in pornography (Gardner 1980). Alice Walker provides a fictional account of a Black man's growing awareness of the different ways that African-American and white women are objectified in pornography: "What he has refused to see—because to see it would reveal yet another area in which he is unable to protect or defend black women—is that where white women are depicted in pornography as 'objects,' black women are depicted as animals. Where white women are depicted as human bodies if not beings, black women are depicted as shit" (Walker 1981, 52).

Walker's distinction between "objects" and "animals" is crucial in untangling gender, race, and class dynamics in pornography. Within the mind/body, culture/nature, male/female oppositional dichotomies in Western social thought, objects occupy an uncertain interim position. As objects white women become creations of culture—in this case, the mind of white men—using the materials of nature—in this case, uncontrolled female sexuality. In contrast, as animals Black women receive no such redeeming dose of culture and remain open to the type of exploitation visited on nature overall. Race becomes the distinguishing feature in determining the type of objectification women will encounter. Whiteness as symbolic of both civilization and culture is used to separate objects from animals.

The alleged superiority of men to women is not the only hierarchical relationship that has been linked to the putative superiority of the mind to the body. Certain "races" of people have been defined as being more bodylike, more animallike, and less godlike than others (Spelman 1982, 52). Race and gender oppression may both revolve around the same axis of distain for the body; both portray the sexuality of subordinate groups as animalistic and therefore deviant. Biological notions of race and gender prevalent in the early nineteenth century which fostered the animalistic icon of Black female sexuality were joined by the appearance of a racist biology incorporating the concept of degeneracy (Foucault 1980). Africans and women were both perceived as embodied entities, and Blacks were seen as degenerate. Fear of and distain for the body thus formed a key element in both sexist and racist thinking (Spelman 1982).

While the sexual and racial dimensions of being treated like an animal are important, the economic foundation underlying this treatment is critical. Animals can be economically exploited, worked, sold, killed, and consumed. As "mules," African-American women become susceptible to such treatment. The political economy of pornography also merits careful attention. Pornography is pivotal in mediating contradictions in changing societies (McNall 1983). It is no accident that racist biology, religious justifications for slavery and women's subordination, and other explanations for nineteenth-century racism and sexism arose during a period of profound political and economic change. Symbolic means of domination become particularly important in mediating contradictions in changing political economies. The exhibition of Sarah Bartmann and Black women on the auction block were not benign intellectual exercises—these practices defended real material and political interests. Current transformations in international capitalism require similar ideological justifications. Where does pornography fit in these current transformations? This question awaits a comprehensive Afrocentric feminist analysis.

Publicly exhibiting Black women may have been central to objectifying Black women as animals and to creating the icon of Black women as animals. Yi-Fu Tuan (1984) offers an innovative argument about similarities in efforts to control nature—especially plant life—the domestication of animals, and the domination of certain groups of humans. Tuan suggests that displaying humans alongside animals implies that such humans are more like monkeys and bears than they are like "normal" people. This same juxtaposition leads spectators to view the captive animals in a special way. Animals acquire definitions of being like humans, only more openly carnal and sexual, an aspect of animals that forms a major source of attraction for visitors to modern zoos. In discussing the popularity of monkeys in zoos, Tuan notes: "some visitors are especially attracted by the easy sexual behavior of the monkeys. Voyeurism is forbidden except when applied to subhumans" (1984, 82). Tuan's analysis suggests that the public display of Sarah Bartmann and of the countless enslaved African women on the auction blocks of the antebellum American South—especially in proximity to animals—fostered their image as animalistic.

This linking of Black women and animals is evident in nineteenth-century scientific literature. The equation of women, Blacks, and animals is revealed in the following description of an African woman published in an 1878 anthropology text:

> She had a way of pouting her lips exactly like what we have observed in the orangutan. Her movements had something abrupt and fantastical about them, reminding one of those of the ape. Her ear was like that of many apes. . . . These are animal characters. I have never seen a human head more like an ape than that of this woman. (Halpin 1989, 287)

In a climate such as this, it is not surprising that one prominent European physician even stated that Black women's "animallike sexual appetite went so far as to lead black women to copulate with apes" (Gilman 1985, 212).

The treatment of all women in contemporary pornography has strong ties to the portrayal of Black women as animals. In pornography women become nonpeople and are often represented as the sum of their fragmented body parts. Scott McNall observes:

> This fragmentation of women relates to the predominance of rear-entry position photographs. . . . All of these kinds of photographs reduce the woman to her reproductive system, and, furthermore, make her open, willing, and available—not in control. . . . The other thing rear-entry position photographs tell us about women is that they are animals. They are animals because they are the same as dogs—bitches in heat who can't control themselves. (McNall 1983, 197–98)

This linking of animals and white women within pornography becomes feasible when grounded in the earlier denigration of Black women as animals.

Developing a comprehensive analysis of the race, gender, and class dynamics of pornography offers possibilities for change. Those Black feminist intellectuals investigating sexual politics imply that the situation is much more complicated than that advanced by some prominent white feminists (see, e.g., Dworkin 1981) in which "men oppress women" because they are men. Such approaches implicitly assume biologically deterministic views of sex, gender, and sexuality and offer few possibilities for change. In contrast, Afrocentric feminist analyses routinely provide for human agency and its corresponding empowerment and for the responsiveness of social structures to human action. In the short story "Coming Apart," Alice Walker describes one Black man's growing realization that his enjoyment of pornography, whether of white women as "objects" or Black women as "animals," degraded him:

> He begins to feel sick. For he realizes that he has bought some of the advertisements about women, black and white. And further, inevitably, he has bought the advertisements about himself. In pornography the black man is portrayed as being capable of fucking anything . . . even a piece of shit. He is defined solely by the size, readiness and unselectivity of his cock. (Walker 1981, 52)

Walker conceptualizes pornography as a race/gender system that entraps everyone. But by exploring an African-American *man's* struggle for a self-defined standpoint on pornography, Walker suggests that a changed consciousness is essential to social change. If a Black man can understand how pornography affects him, then other groups emeshed in the same system are equally capable of similar shifts in consciousness and action.

Prostitution and the Commodification of Sexuality

In *To Be Young, Gifted and Black*, Lorraine Hansberry creates three characters: a young domestic worker, a chic professional, middle-aged woman, and a mother in her thirties. Each speaks a variant of the following:

> In these streets out there, any little white boy from Long Island or Westchester sees me and leans out of his car and yells—"Hey there, *hot chocolate*! Say there, Jezebel! Hey you—'Hundred Dollar Misunderstanding'! YOU! Bet you know where there's a good time tonight . . . " Follow me sometimes and see if I lie. I can be coming from eight hours on an assembly line or fourteen hours in Mrs. Halsey's kitchen. I can be all filled up that day with three hundred years of rage so that my eyes are flashing and my flesh is trembling—and the white boys in the streets, they look at me and think of sex. They look at me and that's *all* they think. . . . Baby, you could be Jesus in drag—but if you're brown they're sure you're selling! (Hansberry 1969, 98)

Like the characters in Hansberry's fiction, all Black women are affected by the widespread controlling image that African-American women are sexually promiscuous, potential prostitutes. The pervasiveness of this image is vividly recounted in Black activist lawyer Pauli Murray's description of an incident she experienced while defending two women from Spanish Harlem who had been arrested as prostitutes: "The first witness, a white man from New Jersey, testified on the details of the sexual transaction and his payment of money. When asked to identify the woman with whom he had engaged in sexual intercourse, he unhesitatingly pointed directly at me, seated beside my two clients at the defense table!" (Murray 1987, 274). Murray's clients were still convicted.

The creation of Jezebel, the image of the sexually denigrated Black woman, has been vital in sustaining a system of interlocking race, gender, and class oppression. Exploring how the image of the African-American woman as prostitute has been used by each system of oppression illustrates how sexuality links the three systems. But Black women's treatment also demonstrates how manipulating sexuality has been essential to the political economy of domination within each system and across all three.

Yi-Fu Tuan (1984) suggests that power as domination involves reducing humans to animate nature in order to exploit them economically or to treat them condescendingly as pets. Domination may be either cruel and exploitative with no affection or may be exploitative yet coexist with affection. The former produces the victim—in this case, the Black woman as "mule" whose labor has been exploited. In contrast, the combination of dominance and affection produces the pet, the individual who is subordinate but whose survival depends on the whims of the more powerful. The "beautiful young quadroons and octoroons" described by Alice Walker were bred to be pets—enslaved Black mistresses whose existence required that they retain the affection of their owners. The treatment afforded these women illustrates a process that affects all African-American women: their portrayal as actual or potential victims and pets of elite white males.[3]

African-American women simultaneously embody the coexistence of the victim and the pet, with survival often linked to the ability to be appropriately subordinate as victims or pets. Black women's experiences as unpaid and paid workers demonstrate the harsh lives victims are forced to lead. While the life of the victim is difficult, pets experience a distinctive form of exploitation. Zora Neale Hurston's 1943 essay, "The 'Pet' Negro System," speaks contemptuously of this ostensibly benign situation that combines domination with affection. Written in a Black oratorical style, Hurston notes, "Brother and Sisters, I take my text this morning from the Book of Dixie. . . . Now it says here, 'And every white man shall be allowed to pet himself a Negro. Yea, he shall take a black man unto himself to pet and cherish, and this same Negro shall be perfect in his sight' " (Walker 1979a, 156). Pets are treated as exceptions and live with the constant threat that they will no longer be "perfect in his sight," that their owners will tire of them and relegate them to the unenviable role of victim.

Prostitution represents the fusion of exploitation for an economic purpose—namely, the commodification of Black women's sexuality—with the demeaning treatment afforded pets. Sex becomes commodified not merely in the sense that it can be purchased—the dimension of economic exploitation—but also in the sense that one is dealing with a totally alienated being who is separated from and who does not control her body: the dimension of power as domination (McNall 1983). Commodified sex can then be appropriated by the powerful. When the "white boys from Long Island" look at Black women and *all* they think about is sex, they believe that they can appropriate Black women's bodies. When they yell "Bet you know where there's a good time tonight," they expect commodified sex with Black women as "animals" to be better than sex with white women as "objects." Both pornography and prostitution commodify sexuality and imply to the "white boys" that all African-American women can be bought.

Prostitution under European and American capitalism thus exists within a complex web of political and economic relationships whereby sexuality is conceptualized along intersecting axes of race and gender. Gilman's (1985) analysis of the exhibition of Sarah Bartmann as the "Hottentot Venus" suggests another intriguing connection between race, gender, and sexuality in nineteenth-century Europe—the linking of the icon of the Black woman with the icon of the white prostitute. While the Hottentot woman stood for the essence of Africans as a race, the white prostitute symbolized the sexualized woman. The prostitute represented the embodiment of sexuality and all that European society associated with it: disease as well as passion. As Gilman points out, "it is this uncleanliness, this disease, which forms the final link between two images of women, the black and the prostitute. Just as the genitalia of the Hottentot were perceived as parallel to the diseased genitalia of the prostitute, so to the power of the idea of corruption links both images" (1985, 237). These connections between the icons of Black women and white prostitutes demonstrate how race, gender, and the social class structure of the European political economy interlock.

In the American antebellum South both of these images were fused in the forced prostitution of enslaved African women. The prostitution of Black women allowed white women to be the opposite; Black "whores" make white "virgins" possible. This race/gender nexus fostered a situation whereby white men could then differentiate between the sexualized woman-as-body who is dominated and "screwed" and the asexual woman-as-pure-spirit who is idealized and brought home to mother (Hoch 1979, 70). The sexually denigrated woman, whether she was made a victim through her rape or a pet through her seduction, could be used as the yardstick against which the cult of true womanhood was measured. Moreover, this entire situation was profitable.

Rape and Sexual Violence

Force was important in creating African-American women's centrality to American images of the sexualized woman and in shaping their experiences with both pornography and prostitution. Black women did not willingly submit to their exhibition on southern auction blocks—they were forced to do so. Enslaved African women could not choose whether to work—they were beaten and often killed if they refused. Black domestics who resisted the sexual advances of their employers often found themselves looking for work where none was to be found. Both the reality and the threat of violence have acted as a form of social control for African-American women.

Rape has been one fundamental tool of sexual violence directed against African-American women. Challenging the pervasiveness of Black women's rape and sexual extortion by white men has long formed a prominent theme in Black women's writings. Autobiographies such as Maya Angelou's *I Know Why the Caged Bird Sings* (1970) and Harriet Jacobs's "The Perils of a Slave Woman's Life" (1860/1987) from *Incidents in the Life of a Slave Girl* record examples of actual and threatened sexual assault. The effects of rape on African-American women is a prominent theme in Black women's fiction. Gayl Jones's *Corregidora* (1975) and Rosa Guy's *A Measure of Time* (1983) both explore interracial rape of Black women. Toni Morrison's *The Bluest Eye* (1970), Alice Walker's *The Color Purple* (1982), and Gloria Naylor's *The Women of Brewster Place* (1980) all examine rape within African-American families and communities. Elizabeth Clark-Lewis's (1985) study of domestic workers found that mothers, aunts, and community othermothers warned young Black women about the threat of rape. One respondent in Clark-Lewis's study, an 87-year-old North Carolina Black domestic worker, remembers, "nobody was sent out before you was told to be careful of the white man or his sons" (Clark-Lewis 1985, 15).

Rape and other acts of overt violence that Black women have experienced, such as physical assault during slavery, domestic abuse, incest, and sexual extortion, accompany Black women's subordination in a system of race, class, and gender oppression. These violent acts are the visible dimensions of a more generalized, routinized system of oppression. Violence against Black women tends to be legitimated and therefore condoned while the same acts visited on other groups may remain nonlegitimated and nonexcusable. Certain forms of violence may garner the backing and control of the state while others remain uncontrolled (Edwards 1987). Specific acts of sexual violence visited on African-American women reflect a broader process by which violence is socially constructed in a race- and gender-specific manner. Thus Black women, Black men, and white women experience distinctive forms of sexual violence. As Angela Davis points out, "it would be a mistake to regard the institutionalized pattern of rape during slavery as an expression of white men's sexual urges. . . . Rape was a weapon of domination, a weapon of repression, whose covert goal was to extinguish slave women's will to resist, and in the process, to demoralize their men" (1981, 23).

Angela Davis's work (1978, 1981, 1989) illustrates this effort to conceptualize sexual violence against African-American women as part of a system of interlocking race, gender, and class oppression. Davis suggests that sexual violence has been central to the economic and political subordination of African-Americans overall. But while Black men and women were both victims of sexual violence, the specific forms they encountered were gender specific.

Depicting African-American men as sexually charged beasts who desired white women created the myth of the Black rapist.[4] Lynching emerged as the specific form of sexual violence visited on Black men, with the myth of the Black rapist as its ideological justification. The significance of this myth is that it "has been methodically conjured up when recurrent waves of violence and terror against the black community required a convincing explanation" (Davis 1978, 25). Black women experienced a parallel form of race- and gender-specific sexual violence. Treating African-American women as pornographic objects and portraying them as sexualized animals, as prostitutes, created the controlling image of Jezebel. Rape became the specific act of sexual violence forced on Black women, with the myth of the Black prostitute as its ideological justification.

Lynching and rape, two race/gender-specific forms of sexual violence, merged with their ideological justifications of the rapist and prostitute in order to provide an effective system of social control over African-Americans. Davis asserts that the controlling image of Black men as rapists has always "strengthened its inseparable companion: the image of the black woman as chronically promiscuous. And with good reason, for once the notion is accepted that black men harbor irresistable, animal-like sexual urges, the entire race is invested with bestiality" (1978, 27). A race of "animals" can be treated as such—as victims or pets. "The mythical rapist implies the mythical whore—and a race of rapists and whores deserves punishment and nothing more" (Davis 1978, 28).

Some suggestive generalizations exist concerning the connection between the social constructions of the rapist and the prostitute and the tenets of racist biology. Tuan (1984) notes that humans practice certain biological procedures on plants and animals to ensure their suitability as pets. For animals the goal of domestication is manageability and control, a state that can be accomplished through selective breeding or, for some male animals, by castration. A similar process may have affected the historical treatment of African-Americans. Since dominant groups have generally refrained from trying to breed humans in the same way that they breed animals, the pervasiveness of rape and lynching suggests that these practices may have contributed to mechanisms of population control. While not widespread, in some slave settings selective breeding and, if that failed, rape were used to produce slaves of a certain genetic heritage. In an 1858 slave narrative, James Roberts recounts the plantation of Maryland planter Calvin Smith, a man who kept 50–60 "head of women" for reproductive purposes. Only whites were permitted access to these women in order to ensure that 20–25 racially mixed children were born annually. Roberts also tells of a second planter who competed with Smith in breeding mulattos, a group that at that time brought higher prices, the "same as men strive to raise the most stock of any kind, cows, sheep, horses, etc." (Weisbord 1975, 27). For Black men, lynching was frequently accompanied by castration. Again, the parallels to techniques used to domesticate animals, or at least serve as a warning to those Black men who remained alive, is striking.

Black women continue to deal with this legacy of the sexual violence visited on African-Americans generally and with our history as collective rape victims. One effect lies in the treatment of rape victims. Such women are twice victimized, first by the actual rape, in this case the collective rape under slavery. But they are victimized again by family members, community residents, and social institutions such as criminal justice systems which somehow believe that rape victims are responsible for their own victimization. Even though current statistics indicate that Black women are more likely to be victimized than white women, Black women are less likely to report their rapes, less likely to have their cases come to trial, less likely to have their trials result in convictions, and, most disturbing, less likely to seek counseling and other support services. Existing evidence suggests that African-American women are aware of their lack of protection and that they resist rapists more than other groups (Bart and O'Brien 1985).

Another significant effect of this legacy of sexual violence concerns Black women's absence from antirape movements. Angela Davis argues, "if black women are conspicuously absent from the ranks of the anti-rape movement today, it is, in large part, their way of protesting the movement's posture of indifference toward the frame-up rape charge as an incitement to racist aggression" (1978, 25). But this absence fosters Black women's silence concerning a troubling issue: the fact that most Black women are raped by Black men. While the historical legacy of the triad of pornography, prostitution, and the institutionalized rape of Black women may have created the larger social context within which all African-Americans reside, the unfortunate current reality is that many Black men have internalized the controlling images of the sex/gender hierarchy and condone either Black women's rape by other Black men or their own behavior as rapists. Far too many African-American women live with the untenable position of putting up with abusive Black men in defense of an elusive Black unity.

The historical legacy of Black women's treatment in pornography, prostitution, and rape forms the institutional backdrop for a range of interpersonal relationships that Black women currently have with Black men, whites, and one another. Without principled coalitions with other groups, African-American women may not be able to effect lasting change on the social structural level of social institutions. But the first step to forming such coalitions is examining exactly how these institutions harness power as energy for their own use by invading both relationships among individuals and individual consciousness itself. Thus understanding the contemporary dynamics of the sexual politics of Black womanhood in order to empower African-American women requires investigating how social structural factors infuse the private domain of Black women's relationships.

NOTES

1. French philosopher Michel Foucault makes a similar point: "I believe that the political significance of the problem of sex is due to the fact that sex is located at the point of intersection of the discipline of the body and the control of the population" (1980, 125). The erotic is something felt, a power than is embodied. Controlling sexuality harnesses that power for the needs of larger, hierarchical systems by controlling the body and hence the population.

2. Offering a similar argument about the relationship between race and masculinity, Paul Hoch (1979) suggests that the ideal white man is a hero who upholds honor. But inside lurks a "Black beast" of violence and sexuality, traits that the white hero deflects onto men of color.

3. Any group can be made into pets. Consider Tuan's (1984) discussion of the role that young Black boys played as exotic ornaments for wealthy white women in the 1500s to the early 1800s in England. Unlike other male servants, the boys were the favorite attendants of noble ladies and gained entry into their mistresses' drawing rooms, bedchambers, and theater boxes. Boys were often given fancy collars with padlocks to wear. "As they did with their pet dogs and monkeys, the ladies grew genuinely fond of their black boys" (p. 142). In addition, Nancy White's analysis in Chapter 5 of the differences between how white and Black women are treated by white men uses this victim/pet metaphor (Gwaltney 1980, 148).

4. See Hoch's (1979) discussion of the roots of the white hero, black beast myth in Eurocentric thought. Hoch contends that white masculinity is based on the interracial competition for women. To become a "man," the white, godlike hero must prove himself victorious over the dark "beast" and win possession of the "white goddess." Through numerous examples Hoch suggests that this explanatory myth underlies Western myth, poetry, and literature. One example describing how Black men were depicted during the witch hunts is revealing. Hoch notes, "the Devil was often depicted as a lascivious black male with cloven hoofs, a tail, and a huge penis capable of super-masculine exertion—an archetypal leering "black beast from below" (1979, 44).

Chapter 9

SEXUAL POLITICS AND BLACK WOMEN'S RELATIONSHIPS

In Toni Morrison's *Beloved* (1987), Sethe tells her friend Paul D how she felt after escaping from slavery:

> It was a kind of selfishness I never knew nothing about before. It felt good. Good and right. I was big, Paul D, and deep and wide and when I stretched out my arms all my children could get in between. I was *that* wide. Look like I loved em more after I got here. Or maybe I couldn't love em proper in Kentucky because they wasn't mine to love. But when I got here, when I jumped down off that wagon—there wasn't nobody in the world I couldn't love if I wanted to. You know what I mean? (Morrison 1987, 162)

By distorting Sethe's ability to love her children "proper," slavery annexed Sethe's power as energy for its own ends. Her words touch a deep chord in Paul D, for he too remembers how slavery felt. His mental response to Sethe expresses the mechanisms used by systems of domination such as slavery in harnessing potential sources of power in a subordinated group:

> So you protected yourself and loved small. Picked the tiniest stars out of the sky to own; lay down with head twisted in order to see the loved one

over the rim of the trench before you slept. Stole shy glances at her between the trees at chain-up. Grass blades, salamanders, spiders, woodpeckers, beetles, a kingdom of ants. Anything bigger wouldn't do. A woman, a child, a brother—a big love like that would split you wide open in Alfred, Georgia. He knew exactly what she meant: to get to a place where you could love anything you chose—not to need permission for desire—well, now, *that* was freedom. (Morrison 1987, 162)

Sethe and Paul D's words suggest that in order to perpetuate itself, slavery corrupts and distorts those sources of power within the culture of the oppressed which provide energy for change. To them, freedom from slavery meant not only the absence of capricious masters and endless work but regaining the power to "love anything you chose." Both Sethe and Paul D understood how slavery inhibited their ability to have "a big love," whether for children, for friends, or for each other. Both saw that systems of oppression function by controlling the "permission for desire"—in other words, by harnessing the energy of fully human relationships to the exigencies of domination.

African-American women's experiences with pornography, prostitution, and rape demonstrate how sexuality is socially constructed within the sex/gender hierarchy on the social structural level of social institutions. Equally important is how the sex/gender hierarchy pervades Black women's interpersonal relationships and infuses the consciousness of Black women and those closest to us. When people "protect themselves and love small" by seeing certain groups of people as worthy of love and deeming others less deserving, potential sources of power as energy that can flow from love relationships are attenuated. But when people reject the world as it is constructed by dominant groups, the power as energy that can flow from a range of love relationships becomes possible.

Political economies of domination such as slavery and the ideologies that justify them aim to thwart the power as energy available to subordinate groups. The sex/gender hierarchy and the sexual politics that Black women encounter within it represent a powerful system of repression because they intrude on people's daily lives at the point of consciousness. Exactly how have ideologies of domination, like the sexual politics of Black womanhood, infused relationships Black women have with people around us? More important, how might an increased understanding of these relationships fostered by an Afrocentric feminist analysis empower African-American women?

BLACK MEN AND THE LOVE AND TROUBLE TRADITION

In her ground-breaking essay, "On the Issue of Roles," Toni Cade Bambara remarks, "now it doesn't take any particular expertise to observe that one of the most characteristic features of our community is the antagonism between our men and our women" (Bambara 1970a, 106). Exploring the tensions between African-American men and women has been a long-standing theme in Black feminist thought. In an 1833 speech, Maria Stewart boldly challenged what she saw as Black men's lackluster response to racism: "Talk, without effort, is nothing; you are abundantly capable, gentlemen, of making yourselves men of distinction; and this gross neglect, on your part, causes my blood to boil within me" (Richardson 1987, 58). Ma Rainey, Bessie Smith, and other classic Black women blues singers offer rich advice to Black women on how to deal with unfaithful and unreliable men (Harrison 1978, 1988; Lieb 1981; Russell 1982). More recently, Black women's troubles with Black men have generated anger and, from that anger, self-reflection: "We have been and are angry sometimes," suggests Bonnie Daniels, "not for what men have done, but for what we've allowed ourselves to become, again and again in my past, in my mother's past, in my centuries of womanhood passed over, for the 'sake' of men, whose manhood we've helped undermine" (1979, 62).

Another long-standing theme in Black feminist thought is the great love Black women feel for Black men. African-American slave narratives contain countless examples of newly emancipated slaves who spent years trying to locate their lost loved ones (Gutman 1976). Love poems written to Black men characterize much of Black women's poetry (Stetson 1981). Black women's music is similarly replete with love songs. Whether the playful voice of Alberta Hunter proclaiming that her "man is a handy man," the mournful cries of Billie Holiday singing "My Man," the sadness Nina Simone evokes in "I Loves You Porgy" at being forced to leave her man, or the powerful voice of Jennifer Holliday, who cries out, "you're gonna love me," Black vocalists identify Black women's relationships with Black men as a source of strength, support, and sustenance (Harrison 1978, 1988; Russell 1982). Black activist Fannie Lou Hamer succinctly captures what a good relationship between a Black woman and man can be: "You know, I'm not hung up on this about liberating myself from the black man, I'm not going to try that thing. I got a black husband, six feet three, two hundred and forty pounds, with a 14 shoe, that I don't *want* to be liberated from" (Lerner 1972, 612).

African-American women have long commented on this "love and trouble" tradition in Black women's relationships with Black men. Novelist

Gayl Jones explains: "The relationships between the men and the women I'm dealing with are blues relationships. So they're out of a tradition of 'love and trouble.' . . . Blues talks about the simultaneity of good and bad, as feeling, as something felt. . . . Blues acknowledges all different kinds of feelings at once" (Harper 1979, 360). Both the tensions between African-American women and men and the strong attachment that we feel for one another represent the both/and conceptual stance in Black feminist thought.

Understanding this love and trouble tradition requires assessing the influence of Eurocentric gender ideology—particularly its emphasis on oppositional dichotomous sex roles—on the work and family experiences of African-Americans. Definitions of appropriate gender behavior for Black women, Black men, white women, and white men not only affect social institutions such as schools and labor markets, they also simultaneously shape daily interactions among and within each group. Analyses claiming that African-Americans would be "just like whites" if offered comparable opportunities implicitly support the prevailing sex/gender hierarchy and offer the allegedly "normal" gender ideology of white male and female sex roles as alternatives for putatively "deviant" Afrocentric ones. Similarly, those proclaiming that Black men experience more severe oppression than Black women and that Black women must unquestioningly support Black male sexism rarely challenge the overarching gender ideology that confines both whites and Blacks (see, e.g., Staples 1979). As Audre Lorde queries, "if society ascribes roles to black men which they are not allowed to fulfill, is it black women who must bend and alter our lives to compensate, or is it society that needs changing?" (1984, 61). Bonnie Daniels provides an answer: "I've learned . . . that being less than what I am capable of being to boost someone else's ego *does not help either of us* for real" (1979, 61).

Black women intellectuals directly challenge not only that portion of Eurocentric gender ideology applied to African-Americans—for example, the controlling images of mammy, the matriarch, the welfare mother, and Jezebel—but often base this rejection on a more general critique of Eurocentric gender ideology itself. Sojourner Truth's 1851 query, "I could work as much and eat as much as a man—when I could get it—and bear the lash as well! And ain't I a woman?" confronts the premises of the cult of true womanhood that "real" women were fragile and ornamental. Toni Cade Bambara contends that Eurocentric sex roles are not only troublesome for African-Americans but damaging: "I have always, I think, opposed the stereotypical definitions of 'masculine' and 'feminine,' . . . because I always found the either/or implicit in those definitions antithetical to what I was all about—and what revolution for self is all about—the whole person" (Bambara 1970a, 101). Black activist Frances Beale echoes Bambara by identifying the negative effects that sexism within the Black community had on Black political activism in the 1960s:

> Unfortunately, there seems to be some confusion in the Movement today as to who has been oppressing whom. Since the advent of Black power, the Black male has exerted a more prominent leadership role in our struggle for justice in this country. He sees the system for what it really is for the most part, but where he rejects its values and mores on many issues, when it comes to women, he seems to take his guidelines from the pages of the *Ladies' Home Journal*. (Beale 1970, 92)

While some African-American women criticize Eurocentric gender ideology, even fewer have directly challenged Black men who accept externally defined notions of both Black and white masculinity (Sizemore 1973; Wallace 1978). The blues tradition provides the most consistent and long-standing text of Black women who demand that Black men reject stereotypical sex roles and "change their ways." Songs often encourage Black men to define new types of relationships. In "Do Right Woman—Do Right Man," when Aretha Franklin (1967) sings that a woman is only human and is not a plaything but is flesh and blood just like a man, she echoes Sojourner Truth's claim that women and men are equally human. Aretha sings about knowing that she's living in a "man's world" but she encourages her man not to "prove" that he's a man by using or abusing her. As long as she and her man are together, she wants him to show some "respect" for her. Her position is clear—if he wants a "do right, all night woman," he's got to be a "do right, all night man." Aretha challenges African-American men to reject Eurocentric gender ideology that posits "it's a man's world" in order to be a "do right man." By showing Black women respect and being an "all night" man—one who is faithful, financially reliable, and sexually expressive—Black men can have a relationship with a "do right woman."[1]

BLACK WOMEN AND ABUSE

The importance of developing a comprehensive analysis of Black hetero-sexual relationships cannot be overstated. Much of the antagonism African-American women and men feel may stem from an unstated resentment toward Eurocentric gender ideology and against one another as enforcers of the dichotomous sex roles inherent in that ideology. Eurocentric gender ideology objectifies both sexes so that when Black men see Black women as nothing more than mammies, matriarchs, or Jezebels, or even if they insist on placing African-American women on the same queenly pedestal reserved for white women, they objectify not only Black women but their own sexuality (Gardner 1980).

Some African-American men feel they cannot be men unless they dominate a Black woman. Alice Walker's *The Color Purple* portrays Mister, a Black man who abuses his wife Celie. Invoking the both/and conceptual orientation of an Afrocentric feminist standpoint, Alice Walker offers one explanation for the coexistence of love and trouble in African-American communities generally, and in Black men specifically:

> At the root of the denial of easily observable and heavily documented sexist brutality in the black community—the assertion that black men don't act like Mister, and if they do, they're justified by the pressure they're under as black men in a white society—is our deep, painful refusal to accept the fact that we are not only descendants of slaves, but we are also the descendants of slave *owners*. And that just as we have had to struggle to rid ourselves of slavish behaviors we must as ruthlessly eradicate any desire to be mistress or "master." (1989, 80)

Those Black men who wish to become "master" by fulfilling traditional definitions of masculinity—both Eurocentric and white-defined for African-Americans—and who are blocked from doing so can become dangerous to those closest to them (Asbury 1987).

The emerging efforts by some Black feminists to assess that danger by analyzing Black women's experiences as victims of physical and emotional abuse stem from this effort to rearticulate Black heterosexual relationships (E. White 1985). Black feminist analyses are characterized by careful attention to how the system of race, gender, and class oppression shapes the context in which African-Americans construct gender ideology. Angela Davis contends, "we cannot grasp the true nature of sexual assault without situating it within its larger sociopolitical context" (1989, 37). Author Gayl Jones concurs: "It's important for me to clarify . . . relationships in *situation*, rather than to have some theory of the way men are with women" (Harper 1979, 356). In Toni Morrison's *The Bluest Eye* (1970), Pecola Breedlove is a study in emotional abuse. Morrison portrays the internalized oppression that can affect a child who experiences daily assaults on her sense of self. Pecola's family is the immediate source of her pain, but Morrison also exposes the role of the larger community in condoning Pecola's victimization. In her choreopoem *For Colored Girls Who Have Considered Suicide*, Ntozake Shange (1975) creates the character Beau

Willie Brown, a man who abuses his lover, Crystal, and who kills their two young children. Rather than blaming Beau Willie Brown as the source of Crystal's oppression, Shange considers how the situation of "no air"—in this case, the lack of opportunities for both individuals—stifles the humanity of *both* Crystal and Beau Willie Brown.

Investigating the problems caused by abusive Black men often exposes Black women intellectuals to criticism. Alice Walker's treatment of male violence in works such as *The Third Life of Grange Copeland* (1970) and *The Color Purple* (1982) attracted censure. Even though Ntozake Shange's choreopoem is about Black women, one criticism leveled at her work is its purportedly negative portrayal of Black men (Staples 1979). Particularly troubling to some critics is the depiction of Beau Willie Brown. In an interview Claudia Tate asked Ntozake Shange, "why did you have to tell about Beau Willie Brown?" In this question Tate invokes the bond of family secrecy that often pervades dysfunctional families because she wants to know why Shange violated the African-American community's collective family "secret." Shange's answer is revealing: "I refuse to be a part of this conspiracy of silence. I will not do it. So that's why I wrote about Beau Willie Brown. I'm tired of living lies" (Tate 1983, 158–59).

This "conspiracy of silence" about Black men's physical and emotional abuse of Black women is part of a larger system of legitimated, routinized violence (Benjamin 1983; Richie 1985). Because of its everyday nature, some women do not perceive of themselves or those around them as victims. Sara Brooks's husband first assaulted her when she was pregnant, once threw her out of a window, and often called her his "Goddam knock box." In spite of his excessive violence, she considered his behavior routine: "If I tried to talk to him he'd hit me so hard with his hands till I'd see stars. Slap me, and what he slap me for, I don't know. . . . My husband would slap me and then go off to his woman's house. That's the way life was" (Simonsen 1986, 162). Ostensibly positive images of Black women make some women more likely to accept domestic violence as routine (E. White 1985; Coley and Beckett 1988). Many African-American women have had to exhibit independence and self-reliance to ensure their own survival and that of their loved ones. But this image of the self-reliant Black woman can be troublesome for women in violent relationships. When an abused woman like Sara Brooks believes that "strength and independence are expected of her, she may be more reluctant to call attention to her situation, feeling that she should be able to handle it on her own; she may deny the seriousness of her situation" (Asbury 1987, 101).

Abused women, particularly those bearing the invisible scars of emotional abuse, are often silenced by the image of the "superstrong" Black woman

(Richie 1985; Coley and Beckett 1988). But according to Audre Lorde, sexual violence against Black women is "a disease striking the heart of Black nationhood, and silence will not make it disappear" (1984, 120). To Lorde, such violence is exacerbated by racism and powerlessness such that "violence against Black women and children often becomes a standard within our communities, one by which manliness can be measured. But these woman-hating acts are rarely discussed as crimes against Black women" (p. 120). By making the pain the victims feel visible, Black feminist intellectuals like Alice Walker, Audre Lorde, and Ntozake Shange challenge the alleged "rationality" of this particular system of control and rearticulate it as violence.

An Afrocentric feminist analysis of abuse generally, and domestic violence in particular, must avoid excusing abuse as an inevitable consequence of the racism Black men experience (Richie 1985). Instead we need a holistic analysis of how race, gender, and class oppression frame the gender ideology internalized by both African-American women and men. By deconstructing violence as a seemingly inevitable outcome of racism and sexism, other alternatives become possible.

A good part of the foundation for such an analysis exists. One of the best Black feminist analyses of domestic violence is found is Zora Neale Hurston's *Their Eyes Were Watching God* (1937). In the following passage Hurston recounts how Tea Cake responded to a threat that another man would win the affections of Janie:

> Before the week was over he had whipped Janie. Not because her behavior justified his jealousy, but it relieved that awful fear inside him. Being able to whip her reassured him in possession. "Tea Cake, you sho is a lucky man," Sop-de-Bottom told him. "Uh person can see every place you hit her. Ah bet she never raised her hand tuh hit yuh back, neither. Take some uh dese ol' rusty black women and dey would fight yuh all night long and next day nobody couldn't tell you ever hit 'em. . . . Lawd! wouldn't Ah love tuh whip uh tender woman lak Janie! Ah bet she don't even holler. She jus' cries, eh Tea Cake?" (Hurston 1937, 121)

Hurston uses the love and trouble tradition to lay the foundation for a Black feminist analysis of domestic violence. Tea Cake and Sop-de-Bottom see women as commodities, property that they can whip to "reassure their possession." Janie is not a person; she is objectified as something owned by Tea Cake. Even if a man loves a woman, as is clearly the case of Tea Cake and Janie, the threat of competition from another male is enough to develop an "awful fear" that Janie will choose another man and thus deem him less manly than his competitors. Whipping Janie reassured Tea Cake that she was his. The conversation between the two men is also revealing. Images of color and beauty pervade their conversation. Sop-de-Bottom is envious because he can "see every place" that Tea Cake hit her and that she was passive and did not resist like the rest of the "rusty black women." Tea Cake and Sop-de-Bottom have accepted Eurocentric sex roles of masculinity and femininity and have used force to maintain them. Furthermore, Janie's uncommitted transgression was the potential to become unfaithful, the possibility to be sexually promiscuous, to become a whore.[2] Finally, the domestic violence occurs in an intimate relationship where love is present. This incident shows the process by which power as domination—in this case gender oppression structured through Eurocentric gender ideology and class oppression reflected in the objectification and commodification of Janie—has managed to annex the basic power of the erotic in Janie and Tea Cake's relationship. Tea Cake does not want to beat Janie, but he does because he *feels*, not thinks, he must.[3] Their relationship represents the linking of sexuality and power, the potential for domination through domestic violence, and the potential for using the erotic, their love for each other, as a catalyst for change.

RELATIONSHIPS WITH WHITES

"White men use different forms of enforcing oppression of white women and of women of Color," argues Chicana scholar Aida Hurtado. "As a consequence, these groups of women have different political responses and skills, and at times these differences cause the two groups to clash" (1989, 843). For Black women the historical relationship with white men has been one of rejection: white men have exploited, objectified, and rejected African-American women. Because white male power is largely predicated on Black female subordination, few delusions of sharing that power and enjoying the privileges attached to white male power have existed among Black women. In contrast, white women have been offered a share of white male power, but only if they agree to be subordinate. "Sometimes I really feel more sorrier for the white woman than I feel for ourselves because she been caught up in this thing, caught up feeling very special," observes Fannie Lou Hamer (Lerner 1972, 610). Thus "white women, as a group, are subordinated through seduction, women of Color, as a group, through rejection" (Hurtado 1989, 844).

This historical legacy of rejection and seduction frames relationships among Black and white women. Black women often express anger and bitterness against white women for their history of excusing the transgressions of their sons, husbands, and fathers. In her diary a slaveholder described white women's widespread predilection to ignore white men's actions:

> Under slavery, we live surrounded by prostitutes. . . . Who thinks any worse of a negro or mulatto woman for being a thing we can't name? God forgive us, but ours is a monstrous system. . . . Like the patriarchs of old, our men live all in one house with their wives and their concubines; and the mulattoes one sees in every family partly resemble the white children. Any lady is ready to tell you who is the father of all the mulatto children in everybody's household but her own. Those, she seems to think drop from the clouds. (Lerner 1972, 51)

If white women under slavery could ignore actions of this magnitude, grappling with the subtleties of contemporary racism must present even more of a challenge for many white women.

For many African-American women, far too few white women are willing to acknowledge—let alone challenge—the actions of white men because they have benefited from them. Fannie Lou Hamer analyzes white women's culpability in Black women's subordination: "You've been caught up in this thing because, you know, you worked my grandmother, and after that you worked my mother, and then finally you got hold of me. And you really thought . . . you thought that you was *more* because you was a woman, and especially a white woman, you had this kind of angel feeling that you were untouchable" (Lerner 1972, 610).

White women's inability to acknowledge their own racism, especially how it privileges them, is another outcome of the differential relationship that white and Black women have to white male power. "I think whites are carefully taught not to recognize white privilege," argues white feminist scholar Peggy McIntosh, "just as males are taught not to recognize male privilege" (1988, 1). McIntosh describes her own struggles with learning to see how she had been privileged: "I have come to see white privilege as an invisible package of unearned assets which I can count on cashing in each day, but about which I was 'meant' to remain oblivious" (p. 1).

One manifestation of white women's privilege is the seeming naiveté many white women have concerning interracial relationships with Black men. In *Dessa Rose*, Nathan, a Black slave, and Rufel, a white woman on whose land they all live, have sexual relations. Even though Dessa, a Black woman, is not romantically attracted to Nathan, she deeply resents his behavior:

> White folks had taken everything in the world from me except my baby and my life and they had tried to take them. And to see him, who had helped to save me, had friended with me through so much of it, laying up,

> wallowing in what had hurt me so—I didn't feel that nothing I could say
> would tell him what that pain was like. And I didn't feel like it was on me
> to splain why he shouldn't be messing with no white woman; I thought it
> was on him to say why he was doing it. (Williams 1986, 186)

Like many African-American women, Dessa sees Black male admiration
for white women as a rejection of her and as an acceptance of Eurocentric
gender ideology and aesthetics. She asks, "Had he really wanted me to be
like Mistress, I wondered, like Miz Ruint, that doughy skin and slippery
hair? Was *that* what they wanted?" (Williams 1986, 199).

Relationships among Black and white women are framed by the web
of sexual politics that seduce white women with an artificial sense of specialness and vest them with the power to sustain that illusion. When white
women come to accept Fannie Lou Hamer's analysis of the interlocking
nature of race, class, and gender oppression, groundwork might be laid
for better relationships:

> In the past, I don't care how poor this white woman was, in the South she
> still felt like she was more than us. In the North, I don't care how poor or
> how rich this white woman has been, she still felt like she was more than
> us. But coming to the realization of the thing, her freedom is shackled in
> chains to mine, and she realizes for the first time that she is not free until
> I am free. (Lerner 1972, 611)

The relationships among Black women and white men have long been
constrained by the legacy of Black women's sexual abuse by white men
and the unresolved tensions this creates. Traditionally, freedom for Black
women has meant freedom *from* white men, not the freedom to choose
white men as lovers and friends. Black women who have willingly chosen
white male friends and lovers have been severely chastized in African-
American communities for selling out the "race," or they are accused of
being like prostitutes, demeaning themselves by willingly using white men
for their own financial or social gain.

The pervasiveness of this legacy of sexual politics can infect the relationships of Black women and white men far removed from their daily
American expressions. In Andrea Lee's novel *Sarah Phillips* (1984),
Sarah, a middle-class, light-skinned woman who "came out of college
equipped with an unfocused snobbery, vague literary aspirations, and a
lively appetite for white boys" (p. 4), moves to France, never intending
to return to the United States. In Paris she lives with her white lover,
Henri, and his two friends. After the following exchange among Roger
and Henri, Sarah realizes how sexual politics intrude on even the most
basic of relationships. Roger states:

"Sarah, ma vielle, you're certainly pretty enough, but why don't you put your hair up properly? Or cut it off? You have the look of a savage!" Henri giggled and grabbed my frizzy ponytail. "She *is* a savage!" he exclaimed, with the delighted air of a child making a discovery. "A savage from the shores of the Mississippi." (Lee 1984, 11)

The playful dialogue soon turned ugly. Henri continues:

"Did you ever wonder, Roger, old, boy," he said in a casual, intimate tone, "why our beautiful Sarah is such a mixture of races, why she has pale skin but hair that's as kinky as that of a Haitian? Well, I'll tell you. Her mother was an Irishwoman, and her father was a monkey." (p. 11)

Images of bestiality linking Black sexuality with animals and degeneracy pervade Henri's words. Henri's attraction to Sarah occurs in a context in which her pale skin signals her closeness to a white woman's beauty but her "look of a savage" resulting from her "kinky hair" links her to Eurocentric notions of unrestrained Black sexuality. All of this spills out in the foregoing exchange. Even though Sarah cooly observes that she "wasn't upset by the racism of what Henri had said," because "nasty remarks about race and class were part of our special brand of humor," she realizes that no matter how much she wants to cut off ties with the "griefs, embarrassments, and constraints of a country, a family," she cannot do so. Sarah Phillips realizes that she is a member of a community infused with sexual politics.

In spite of the powerful restrictions imposed by the sex/gender hierarchy on interpersonal relationships, many African-American women refuse to "protect themselves and love small," and manage to form close, loving relationships with whites. But given the legacy of the sexual politics of Black womanhood, for large numbers of African-Americans, fully human relationships with whites remain out of reach.

HOMOPHOBIA AND BLACK LESBIANS

One of the most important challenges from and to Black feminist thought has come through the voices of Black lesbians. One major contribution by Black lesbian theorists and activists has been to illuminate homophobia and the toll it takes on African-American women. "The oppression that affects Black gay people, female and male, is pervasive, constant, and not abstract. Some of us die from it," argues Barbara Smith (1983, xlvii). By making the effects of homophobia on Black lesbians visible, Black lesbians have furthered theoretical analyses of the links between sexuality and power.

One theme raised by Black lesbians concerns the extent of homophobia in African-American communities. Cheryl Clarke explains that homophobia among African-Americans is "largely reflective of the homophobic culture in which we live" (1983, 197). For Black lesbians homophobia represents a form of oppression that affects their lives with the same intensity as does race, class, and gender oppression. "What I think many heterosexual Black people don't know, and don't want to know," observes Barbara Smith, "is the toll homophobia takes on a daily basis. Too many pretend that lesbian and gay oppression is an inconsequential matter, not a real oppression" (1983, xlvi). African-Americans have tried to ignore homophobia generally and have avoided serious analysis of homophobia within African-American communities.[4] And yet, counsels Cheryl Clarke, African-Americans cannot "rationalize the disease of homophobia among black people as the white man's fault, for to do so is to absolve ourselves of our responsibility to transform ourselves" (1983, 197).

Black feminist writers, especially Black feminist lesbian writers, have begun this transformation by investigating Black lesbian relationships in Black women's literature. Ann Allen Shockley's 1974 novel, *Loving Her*, provides the first book-length depiction of a Black lesbian as a central character. The 1980s saw increased attention to Black lesbian relationships. Black feminist critic Barbara Christian (1985) points out that while Black women writers have always written about Black women's friendships, their writing in the 1980s explores relationships between women who "find other women sexually attractive and gratifying" (p. 189). Using this working definition of lesbianism, Christian proceeds to examine contributions made by four books in examining the "buried lives" of Black lesbians: Audre Lorde's *Zami, A New Spelling of My Name* (1982), Gloria Naylor's *The Women of Brewster Place* (1980), Ntozake Shange's *Sassafrass, Cypress and Indigo* (1982), and Alice Walker's *The Color Purple* (1982).

In spite of the catalyst of Black women's writings, achieving transformation within African-American communities concerning homophobia and Black lesbians has been difficult. Especially troubling to Black lesbians has been the reluctance on the part of Black heterosexual women to examine their own homophobia. "I am more than a little tired of Black women who say they are political, who say they are feminists, who rely on Black lesbians' friendships, insights, commitment, and work, but who, when it comes down to the crunch and the time to be accountable, turn their backs," deplores Barbara Smith (1983, xlvii).

Why have African-American women been strangely silent on the issue of Black lesbianism? Barbara Smith suggests one compelling reason: "Heterosexual privilege is usually the only privilege that Black women have. None of us have racial or sexual privilege, almost none of us have class privilege, maintaining 'straightness' is our last resort" (1982b, 171). In the same way that white feminists identify with their victimization as women yet ignore the privilege that racism grants them, and that Black men decry racism yet see sexism as being less objectionable, African-American women may perceive their own race and gender oppression yet victimize someone else by invoking the benefits of heterosexual privilege. Barbara Smith raises a critical point that can best be seen through the outsider-within standpoint available to Black lesbians—namely, that within a system of interlocking race, gender, class, and sexual oppression, there are few pure oppressors or victims.

Another reason Black women have been silenced about Black lesbian relationships concerns the traditional treatment in Eurocentric thought of the lesbian as the ultimate Other. Black lesbians are not white, male, or heterosexual and generally are not affluent. As such they represent the antithesis of Audre Lorde's "mythical norm" and become the standard by which other groups measure their own so-called normality. The sex/gender hierarchy functions smoothly only if sexual nonconformity is kept invisible. "By being sexually independent of men, lesbians, by their very existence, call into question society's definition of woman at its deepest level," observes Barbara Christian (1985, 199). Visible Black lesbians challenge the mythical norm that the best people are white, male, rich, and heterosexual. In doing so lesbians generate anxiety, discomfort, and a challenge to the dominant group's control of power and sexuality on the interpersonal level (Vance 1984).

Interestingly, there has been a curious linking of the image of the lesbian with that of the prostitute and with images of Black women as the embodiment of the Black "race." Christian notes that Black women writers broadened the physical image of lesbians: "The stereotypical body type of a black lesbian was that she looked mannish; . . . she was not so much a woman as much as she was a defective man, a description that has sometimes been applied to any Negroid-looking or uppity-acting black woman" (1985, 191). Note Christian's analysis of the links among gender roles, race, and sexuality. Lesbianism, an allegedly deviant sexual practice, becomes linked to biological markers of race and looking "mannish."

Another perspective on the links among gender, race, and sexuality is provided in Sander Gilman's work on images of Black women and prostitutes in nineteenth-century Europe. Gilman describes how European scientists thought that Black women and prostitutes possessed physical abnormalities that set them apart from "normal" women. Note Gilman's observations about how aging prostitutes were portrayed in European science and art: "What is most striking is that as the prostitute ages, she begins to appear more and more mannish . . . here, the link is between two further models of sexual deviancy, the prostitute and the lesbian. Both are seen as possessing the physical signs which set them apart from the normal" (1985, 226). Gilman's work suggests that the pornographic images of Black women as sexually animalistic, the role of prostitutes in maintaining dualistic conceptions of good woman/bad woman based on a comparable chastity/promiscuity duality, and the depiction of lesbians as a challenge to the woman/man dichotomy all depend on notions of deviant sexuality for sustenance. All of these social constructions of sexual deviance stem from comparable biologically deterministic roots, and all become central to the functioning of the overarching structure of race, gender, and class oppression.

African-American women inhabit this conceptual terrain and have not been immune to its assumptions. For Black women who have already been labeled the Other by virtue of our race and gender, the threat of being labeled a lesbian can have a chilling effect on Black women's ideas and on our relationships with one another. In speculating about why so many competent Black women writers and reviewers have avoided examining lesbianism, Ann Allen Shockley suggests that "the fear of being labeled a Lesbian, whether they were one or not" (1983, 84), has been a major deterrent. June Jordan contends that the male bias in the Black intellectual community has used the notion of Black lesbians as the ultimate Other in discrediting Black feminism: "Evidently, feminism was being translated into lesbianism, into something interchangeable with lesbianism, and the taboo on feminism, within the Black intellectual community, had long been exceeded in its orthodox severity only by the taboo on the subject of the lesbian" (1981, 140). To Jordan the Black intellectual community has done a disservice to African-Americans because "the phenomena of self-directed Black women or the phenomena of Black women loving other women have hardly been uncommon, let alone unbelievable, events to Black people not privy to theoretical strife about correct and incorrect Black experience" (1981, 140).

Black women's silence about homophobia and the treatment of Black lesbians reflects another, equally important dimension of Eurocentric masculinist thought. "I think the reason that Black women are so homophobic," suggests Barbara Smith, "is that attraction-repulsion thing. They have to speak out vociferously against lesbianism because if they don't they may have to deal with their own deep feelings for women" (Smith and Smith 1981, 124). Shockley agrees: "most black women feared and abhorred Lesbians more than rape—perhaps because of the fear bred from their deep inward potentiality for Lesbianism" (1974, 31–32). In the same sense that men who accept Eurocentric notions of masculinity fear and deny the dimensions of themselves that they associate with femininity—for example, interpreting male expressiveness as being weak and unmanly (Hoch 1979)—Black women may suppress their own strong feelings for other Black women for fear of being stigmatized as lesbians. Similarly, in the way that male domination of women embodies men's fears about their own masculinity, Black heterosexual women's treatment of Black lesbians reflects fears that all African-American women are essentially the same. Yet, as Audre Lorde points out, "in the same way that the existence of the self-defined Black woman is no threat to the self-defined Black man, the Black lesbian is an emotional threat only to those Black women whose feelings of kinship and love for other Black women are problematic in some way" (1984, 49).

LOVE AND EMPOWERMENT

"In order to perpetuate itself, every oppression must corrupt or distort those various sources of power within the culture of the oppressed that can provide energy for change" (Lorde 1984, 53). The ability of social institutions such as pornography, prostitution, and rape to infuse the private domain of Black women's love relationships with Black men, with whites, and with one another typifies this process. The parallels between distortions of deep human feelings in racial oppression and of the distortions of the erotic in gender oppression are striking. Analysts of the interpersonal dynamics of racism point out that whites fear in Blacks those qualities they project onto Blacks that they most fear in themselves. By labeling Blacks as sexually animalistic and by dominating Blacks, whites in actuality aim to repress these dimensions of their own inner being (Hoch 1979). When men dominate women and accuse them of being sexually passive, the act of domination, from pressured sexual intercourse to rape, reduces male anxiety about male impotence, the ultimate sexual passivity (Hoch 1979). Similarly, the suppression of gays and lesbians symbolizes the repression of strong feelings for members of one's own gender, feelings this culture has sexualized and stigmatized in the overarching sex/gender hierarchy. All of these emotions—the fact that whites know that Blacks are human, the fact that men love women, and the fact that women have deep feelings for one another—must be distorted on the emotional level of the erotic in order for oppressive systems to endure. Sexuality and power on the personal level become wedded to the sex/gender hierarchy on the social structural level in order to ensure the smooth operation of race, gender, and class oppression.

Recognizing that corrupting and distorting basic feelings human beings have for one another lies at the heart of multiple systems of oppression opens up new possibilities for transformation and change. June Jordan (1981) explores this connection between embracing feeling and human empowerment: "As I think about anyone or any thing—whether history or literature or my father or political organizations or a poem or a film—as I seek to evaluate the potentiality, the life-supportive commitment/possibilities of anyone or any thing, the decisive question is, always, *where is the love?*" (p. 141).

Jordan's question touches a deep nerve in African-American social and ethical thought. In her work *Black Womanist Ethics*, Katie G. Cannon (1988) suggests that love, community, and justice are deeply intertwined in African-American ethics. Cannon examines the work of two prominent Black male theorists—Howard Thurman and Martin Luther King, Jr.—and concludes that their ideas represent core values from which Black women draw strength. According to Thurman, love is the basis of community, and community is the arena for moral agency. Only love of self, love between individuals, and love of God can shape, empower, and sustain social change. Martin Luther King, Jr., gives greater significance in his ethics to the relationship of love and justice, suggesting that love is active, dynamic, determined, and generates the motive and drive for justice. For both Thurman and King, everything moves toward community and the expression of love within the context of community. It is this version of love and community, argues Cannon, that stimulates a distinctive Black womanist ethics.

For June Jordan love begins with self-love and self-respect, actions that propel African-American women toward the self-determination and political activism essential for social justice. By grappling with this simple yet profound question, "where is the love?" Black women resist multiple types of oppression. This question encourages all groups embedded in systems of domination to move toward a place where, as Toni Morrison's Paul D expresses it, "you could love anything you chose—not to need permission for desire—well, now, *that* was freedom" (1987, 162).

NOTES

1. Black women's efforts to encourage Black men to rethink their gender ideology have encountered often serious opposition. Black literary critic Calvin Hernton describes how this antagonistic posture by some Black men operates in Black literature:

> Too often Black men have a philosophy of manhood that relegates women to the back burner. Therefore it is perceived as an offense for black women to struggle on their own, let alone achieve something independently. Thus, no matter how original, beautiful, and formidable the works of black women writers might be,

black men become "offended" if such works bear the slightest criticism of them, or if the women receive recognition from other women, especially from the white literary establishment. They do not behave as though something of value has been added to the annals of black literature. Rather, they behave as though something has been subtracted, not only from the literature, but from the entire race, and specifically, from *them*. (Hernton 1985, 6)

2. Margo St. James offers an interesting connection between domestic violence and prostitution: "I feel that the stigmatizing, the whore stigma, is what legitimizes violence, even in the home, because when the husband slugs his wife, he precedes the abuse with, 'You slut!' 'You whore!'" (Bell 1987, 130).

3. Michel Foucault refers to this phenomenon as a "network or circuit of bio-power, or somato-power, which acts as the formative matrix of sexuality itself" (1980, 186). To Foucault, "power relations can materially penetrate the body in depth, without depending even on the mediation of the subject's own representations. If power takes hold on the body, this isn't through its having first to be interiorized in people's consciousness" (p. 186). This particular dimension of power as domination is extremely effective precisely because it is felt and not conceptualized.

4. The degree and shape of homophobia within African-American communities needs to be determined. Cheryl Clarke suggests that the Black intellectual community is more homophobic than the larger Black community: "Since no one has bothered to study the black community's attitudes on . . . homosexuality . . . it is not accurate to attribute homophobia to the mass of black people" (1983, 205). Clarke contends that a history of racial oppression has made African-Americans more empathetic, but "as it stands now, the black political community seems bereft of that humanity" (p. 206).

Part Three ———————————

BLACK FEMINISM AND EPISTEMOLOGY

Chapter 10

TOWARD AN AFROCENTRIC FEMINIST EPISTEMOLOGY

> A small girl and her mother passed a statue depicting a European man who had barehandedly subdued a ferocious lion. The little girl stopped, looked puzzled and asked, "Mama, something's wrong with that statue. Everybody knows that a man can't whip a lion." "But darling," her mother replied, "you must remember that the man made the statue."
>
> —As told by Katie G. Cannon

Black feminist thought, like all specialized thought, reflects the interests and standpoint of its creators. Tracing the origin and diffusion of any body of specialized thought reveals its affinity to the power of the group that created it (Mannheim 1936). Because elite white men and their representatives control structures of knowledge validation, white male interests pervade the thematic content of traditional scholarship. As a result, Black women's experiences with work, family, motherhood, political activism, and sexual politics have been routinely distorted in or excluded from traditional academic discourse.

Black feminist thought as specialized thought reflects the thematic content of African-American women's experiences. But because Black women have had to struggle against white male interpretations of the world in order to express a self-defined standpoint, Black feminist thought can best be viewed as subjugated knowledge. The suppression of Black women's efforts for self-definition in traditional sites of knowledge production has led African-American women to use alternative sites such as music, literature, daily conversations, and everyday behavior as important locations for articulating the core themes of a Black feminist consciousness.

Investigating the subjugated knowledge of subordinate groups—in this case a Black women's standpoint and Black feminist thought—requires more ingenuity than that needed to examine the standpoints and thought of dominant groups. I found my training as a social scientist inadequate to the task of studying the subjugated knowledge of a Black women's standpoint. This is because subordinate groups have long had to use alternative ways to create independent self-definitions and self-valuations and to rearticulate them through our own specialists. Like other subordinate groups, African-American women have not only developed a distinctive Black women's standpoint, but have done so by using alternative ways of producing and validating knowledge.

Epistemology is the study of the philosophical problems in concepts of knowledge and truth. The techniques I use in this volume to rearticulate a Black women's standpoint and to further Black feminist thought may appear to violate some of the basic epistemological assumptions of my training as a social scientist. In choosing the core themes in Black feminist thought that merited investigation, I consulted established bodies of academic research. But I also searched my own experiences and those of African-American women I know for themes we thought were important. My use of language signals a different relationship to my material than that which currently prevails in social science literature. For example, I often use the pronoun "our" instead of "their" when referring to African-American women, a choice that embeds me in the group I am studying instead of distancing me from it. In addition, I occasionally place my own concrete experiences in the text. To support my analysis, I cite few statistics and instead rely on the voices of Black women from all walks of life. These conscious epistemological choices signal my attempts not only to explore the thematic content of Black feminist thought but to do so in a way that does not violate its basic epistemological framework.

One key epistemological concern facing Black women intellectuals is the question of what constitutes adequate justifications that a given knowledge claim, such as a fact or theory, is true. In producing the specialized knowledge of Black feminist thought, Black women intellectuals often encounter two distinct epistemologies: one representing elite white male interests and the other expressing Afrocentric feminist concerns. Epistemological choices about who to trust, what to believe, and why something is true are not benign academic issues. Instead, these concerns tap the fundamental question of which versions of truth will prevail and shape thought and action.

THE EUROCENTRIC, MASCULINIST KNOWLEDGE VALIDATION PROCESS

Institutions, paradigms, and other elements of the knowledge validation procedure controlled by elite white men constitute the Eurocentric masculinist knowledge validation process. The purpose of this process is to represent a white male standpoint. Although it reflects powerful white males interest, various dimensions of the process are not necessarily managed by white men themselves. Scholars, publishers, and other experts represent specific interests and credentialing processes, and their knowledge claims must satisfy the political and epistemological criteria of the contexts in which they reside (Kuhn 1962; Mulkay 1979).

Two political criteria influence the knowledge validation process. First, knowledge claims are evaluated by a community of experts whose members represent the standpoints of the groups from which they originate. Within the Eurocentric masculinist process this means that a scholar making a knowledge claim must convince a scholarly community controlled by white men that a given claim is justified. Second, each community of experts must maintain its credibility as defined by the larger group in which it is situated and from which it draws its basic, taken-for-granted knowledge. This means that scholarly communities that challenge basic beliefs held in the culture at large will be deemed less credible than those which support popular perspectives.

When white men control the knowledge validation process, both political criteria can work to suppress Black feminist thought. Given that the general culture shaping the taken-for-granted knowledge of the community of experts is permeated by widespread notions of Black and female inferiority, new knowledge claims that seem to violate these fundamental assumptions are likely to be viewed as anomalies (Kuhn 1962). Moreover, specialized thought challenging notions of Black and female inferiority is unlikely to be generated from within a white-male-controlled academic community because both the kinds of questions that could be asked and the explanations that would be found satisfying would necessarily reflect a basic lack of familiarity with Black women's reality.

The experiences of African-American women scholars illustrate how individuals who wish to rearticulate a Black women's standpoint through Black feminist thought can be suppressed by a white-male-controlled knowledge validation process. Exclusion from basic literacy, quality educational experiences, and faculty and administrative positions has limited Black women's access to influential academic positions (Zinn et al. 1986). While Black women can produce knowledge claims that contest those advanced by the white male community, this community does not grant that Black women scholars have competing knowledge claims based in another knowledge validation process. As a consequence, any credentials controlled by white male academicians can be denied to Black women producing Black feminist thought on the grounds that it is not credible research.

Black women with academic credentials who seek to exert the authority that our status grants us to propose new knowledge claims about African-American women face pressures to use our authority to help legitimate a system that devalues and excludes the majority of Black women. When an outsider group—in this case, African-American women—recognizes that the insider group—namely, white men—requires special privileges from the larger society, a special problem arises of keeping the outsiders out and at the same time having them acknowledge the legitimacy of this procedure. Accepting a few "safe" outsiders addresses this legitimation problem (Berger and Luckmann 1966). One way of excluding the majority of Black women from the knowledge validation process is to permit a few Black women to acquire positions of authority in institutions that legitimate knowledge, and to encourage us to work within the taken-for-granted assumptions of Black female inferiority shared by the scholarly community and by the culture at large. Those Black women who accept these assumptions are likely to be rewarded by their institutions, often at significant personal cost. Those challenging the assumptions run the risk of being ostracized.

African-American women academicians who persist in trying to rearticulate a Black women's standpoint also face potential rejection of our knowledge claims on epistemological grounds. Just as the material realities of the powerful and the dominated produce separate standpoints, each group may also have distinctive epistemologies or theories of knowledge. Black women scholars may know that something is true but be unwilling or unable to legitimate our claims using Eurocentric, masculinist criteria for consistency with substantiated knowledge and criteria for methodological adequacy. For any body of knowledge, new knowledge claims must be consistent with an existing body of knowledge that the group controlling the interpretive context accepts as true. The methods used to validate knowledge claims must also be acceptable to the group controlling the knowledge validation process.

The criteria for the methodological adequacy of positivism illustrate the epistemological standards that Black women scholars would have to satisfy in legitimating Black feminist thought using a Eurocentric masculinist epistemology. While I describe Eurocentric masculinist approaches as a single process, many schools of thought or paradigms are subsumed under this one process. Moreover, my focus on positivism should be interpreted neither to mean that all dimensions of positivism are inherently problematic for Black women nor that nonpositivist frameworks are better. For example, most traditional frameworks that women of color internationally regard as oppressive to women are not positivist, and Eurocentric feminist critiques of positivism may have less political importance for women of color, especially those in traditional societies than they have for white feminists (Narayan 1989).

Positivist approaches aim to create scientific descriptions of reality by producing objective generalizations. Because researchers have widely differing values, experiences, and emotions, genuine science is thought to be unattainable unless all human characteristics except rationality are eliminated from the research process. By following strict methodological rules, scientists aim to distance themselves from the values, vested interests, and emotions generated by their class, race, sex, or unique situation. By decontextualizing themselves, they allegedly become detached observers and manipulators of nature (Jaggar 1983; Harding 1986). Moreover, this researcher decontextualization is paralleled by comparable efforts to remove the objects of study from their contexts. The result of this entire process is often the separation of information from meaning (Fausto-Sterling 1989).

Several requirements typify positivist methodological approaches. First, research methods generally require a distancing of the researcher from her or his "object" of study by defining the researcher as a "subject" with full human subjectivity and by objectifying the "object" of study (Keller 1985; Asante 1987; Hooks 1989). A second requirement is the absence of emotions from the research process (Hochschild 1975; Jaggar 1983). Third, ethics and values are deemed inappropriate in the research process, either as the reason for scientific inquiry or as part of the research process itself (Richards 1980; Haan et al. 1983). Finally, adversarial debates, whether written or oral, become the preferred method of ascertaining truth: the arguments that can withstand the greatest assault and survive intact become the strongest truths (Moulton 1983).

Such criteria ask African-American women to objectify ourselves, devalue our emotional life, displace our motivations for furthering knowledge about Black women, and confront in an adversarial relationship those with more social, economic and professional power. It therefore seems unlikely that Black women would use a positivist epistemological stance in rearticulating a Black women's standpoint. Black women are more likely to choose an alternative epistemology for assessing knowledge claims, one using different standards that are consistent with Black women's criteria for substantiated knowledge and with our criteria for methodological adequacy. If such an epistemology exists, what are its contours? Moreover, what is its role in the production of Black feminist thought?

THE CONTOURS OF AN AFROCENTRIC FEMINIST EPISTEMOLOGY

Africanist analyses of the Black experience generally agree on the fundamental elements of an Afrocentric standpoint (Okanlawon 1972). Despite varying histories, Black societies reflect elements of a core African value system that existed prior to and independently of racial oppression (Jahn 1961; Mbiti 1969; Diop 1974; Zahan 1979; Sobel 1979; Richards 1980, 1990; Asante 1987; Myers 1988). Moreover, as a result of colonialism, imperialism, slavery, apartheid, and other systems of racial domination, Black people share a common experience of oppression. These two factors foster shared Afrocentric values that permeate the family structure, religious institutions, culture, and community life of Blacks in varying parts of Africa, the Caribbean, South America, and North America (Walton 1971; Gayle 1971; Smitherman 1977; Shimkin et al. 1978; Walker 1980; Sudarkasa 1981b; Thompson 1983; Mitchell and Lewter 1986; Asante 1987; Brown 1989). This Afrocentric consciousness permeates the shared history of people of African descent through the framework of a distinctive Afrocentric epistemology (Turner 1984).

Feminist scholars advance a similar argument by asserting that women share a history of gender oppression, primarily through sex/gender hierarchies (Eisenstein 1983; Hartsock 1983b; Andersen 1988). These experiences transcend divisions among women created by race, social class, religion, sexual orientation, and ethnicity and form the basis of a women's standpoint with a corresponding feminist consciousness and epistemology (Rosaldo 1974; D. Smith 1987; Hartsock 1983a; Jaggar 1983).

Because Black women have access to both the Afrocentric and the feminist standpoints, an alternative epistemology used to rearticulate a Black women's standpoint should reflect elements of both traditions. The search for the distinguishing features of an alternative epistemology used by African-American women reveals that values and ideas Africanist scholars identify as characteristically "Black" often bear remarkable resemblance to similar ideas claimed by feminist scholars as characteristically "female."[1] This similarity suggests that the material conditions of race, class, and gender oppression can vary dramatically and yet generate some uniformity in the epistemologies of subordinate groups. Thus the significance of an Afrocentric feminist epistemology may lie in how such an epistemology enriches our understanding of how subordinate groups create knowledge that fosters resistance.

The parallels between the two conceptual schemes raise a question: Is the worldview of women of African descent more intensely infused with the overlapping feminine/Afrocentric standpoints than is the case for either African-American men or white women? While an Afrocentric feminist epistemology reflects elements of epistemologies used by African-Americans and women as groups, it also paradoxically demonstrates features that may be unique to Black women. On certain dimensions Black women may more closely resemble Black men; on others, white women; and on still others Black women may stand apart from both groups. Black women's both/and conceptual orientation, the act of being simultaneously a member of a group and yet standing apart from it, forms an integral part of Black women's consciousness. Black women negotiate these contradictions, a situation Bonnie Thornton Dill (1979) labels the "dialectics of Black womanhood," by using this both/and conceptual orientation.

Rather than emphasizing how a Black women's standpoint and its accompanying epistemology are different from those in Afrocentric and feminist analyses, I use Black women's experiences to examine points of contact between the two. Viewing an Afrocentric feminist epistemology in this way challenges additive analyses of oppression claiming that Black women have a more accurate view of oppression than do other groups. Such approaches suggest that oppression can be quantified and compared and that adding layers of oppression produces a potentially clearer standpoint (Spelman 1982). One implication of standpoint approaches is that the more subordinated the group, the purer the vision of the oppressed group. This is an outcome of the origins of standpoint approaches in Marxist social theory, itself an analysis of social structure rooted in Western either/or dichotomous thinking. Ironically, by quantifying and ranking human oppressions, standpoint theorists invoke criteria for methodological adequacy characteristic of positivism. Although it is tempting to claim that Black women are more oppressed than everyone else and therefore have the best standpoint from which to understand the mechanisms, processes, and effects of oppression, this simply may not be the case.

Like a Black women's standpoint, an Afrocentric feminist epistemology is rooted in the everyday experiences of African-American women. In spite of diversity that exists among women, what are the dimensions of an Afrocentric feminist epistemology?

CONCRETE EXPERIENCE AS A CRITERION OF MEANING

"My aunt used to say, 'A heap see, but a few know,' " remembers Carolyn Chase, a 31-year-old inner-city Black woman (Gwaltney 1980, 83). This saying depicts two types of knowing—knowledge and wisdom—and taps the first dimension of an Afrocentric feminist epistemology. Living life as Black women requires wisdom because knowledge about the dynamics of race, gender, and class oppression has been essential to Black women's survival. African-American women give such wisdom high credence in assessing knowledge.

Allusions to these two types of knowing pervade the words of a range of African-American women. Zilpha Elaw, a preacher of the mid-1800s, explains the tenacity of racism: "The pride of a white skin is a bauble of great value with many in some parts of the United States, who readily sacrifice their intelligence to their prejudices, and possess more knowledge than wisdom" (Andrews 1986, 85). In describing differences separating African-American and white women, Nancy White invokes a similar rule: "When you come right down to it, white women just *think* they are free. Black women *know* they ain't free" (Gwaltney 1980, 147). Geneva Smitherman, a college professor specializing in African-American linguistics, suggests that "from a black perspective, written documents are limited in what they can teach about life and survival in the world. Blacks are quick to ridicule 'educated fools,' . . . they have 'book learning' but no 'mother wit,' knowledge, but not wisdom" (Smitherman 1977, 76). Mabel Lincoln eloquently summarizes the distinction between knowledge and wisdom: "To black people like me, a fool is funny—you know, people who love to break bad, people you can't tell anything to, folks that would take a shotgun to a roach" (Gwaltney 1980, 68).

African-American women need wisdom to know how to deal with the "educated fools" who would "take a shotgun to a roach." As members of a subordinate group, Black women cannot afford to be fools of any type, for our objectification as the Other denies us the protections that white skin, maleness, and wealth confer. This distinction between knowledge and wisdom, and the use of experience as the cutting edge dividing them, has been key to Black women's survival. In the context of race, gender, and class oppression, the distinction is essential. Knowledge without wisdom is adequate for the powerful, but wisdom is essential to the survival of the subordinate.

For most African-American women those individuals who have lived through the experiences about which they claim to be experts are more believable and credible than those who have merely read or thought about such experiences. Thus concrete experience as a criterion for credibility frequently is invoked by Black women when making knowledge claims. For instance, Hannah Nelson describes the importance personal experience has for her: "Our speech is most directly personal, and every black person assumes that every other black person has a right to a personal opinion. In speaking of grave matters, your personal experience is considered very good evidence. With us, distant statistics are certainly not as important as the actual experience of a sober person" (Gwaltney 1980, 7). Similarly, Ruth Shays uses her concrete experiences to challenge the idea that formal education is the only route to knowledge: "I am the kind of person who doesn't have a lot of education, but both my mother and my father had good common sense. Now, I think that's all you need. I might not know how to use thirty-four words where three would do, but that does not mean that I don't know what I'm talking about. . . . I know what I'm talking about because I'm talking about myself. I'm talking about what I have lived" (Gwaltney 1980, 27, 33). Implicit in Ms. Shays's self-assessment is a critique of the type of knowledge that obscures the truth, the "thirty-four words" that cover up a truth that can be expressed in three.

Even after substantial mastery of white masculinist epistemologies, many Black women scholars invoke our own concrete experiences and those of other African-American women in selecting topics for investigation and methodologies used. For example, Elsa Barkley Brown (1986) subtitles her essay on Black women's history, "how my mother taught me to be an historian in spite of my academic training." Similarly, Joyce Ladner (1972) maintains that growing up as a Black woman in the South gave her special insights in conducting her study of Black adolescent women. Lorraine Hansberry alludes to the potential epistemological significance of valuing the concrete: "In certain peculiar ways, we have been conditioned to think not small—but tiny. And the thing, I think, which has strangled us most is the tendency to turn away from the world in search of the universe. That is chaos in science—can it be anything else in art?" (1969, 134).

Experience as a criterion of meaning with practical images as its symbolic vehicles is a fundamental epistemological tenet in African-American thought systems (Mitchell and Lewter 1986). "Look at my arm!" Sojourner Truth proclaimed: "I have ploughed, and planted, and gathered into barns, and no man could head me! And ain't I a woman?" (Loewenberg and Bogin 1976, 235). By invoking concrete practical images from her own life to symbolize new meanings, Truth deconstructed the prevailing notions of woman. Stories, narratives, and Bible principles are selected for their applicability to the lived experiences of African-Americans and become symbolic representations of a whole wealth of experience. Bible tales are often told for the wisdom they express about everyday life, so their interpretation involves no need for scientific historical verification. The narrative method requires that the story be told, not torn apart in analysis, and trusted as core belief, not "admired as science" (Mitchell and Lewter 1986, 8).

June Jordan's essay about her mother's suicide illustrates the multiple levels of meaning that can occur when concrete experiences are used as a criterion of meaning. Jordan describes her mother, a women who literally died trying to stand up, and the effect her mother's death had on her own work:

> I think all of this is really about women and work. Certainly this is all about me as a woman and my life work. I mean I am not sure my mother's suicide was something extraordinary. Perhaps most women must deal with a similar inheritance, the legacy of a woman whose death you cannot possibly pinpoint because she died so many, many times and because, even before she became your mother, the life of that woman was taken. . . . I came too late to help my mother to her feet. By way of everlasting thanks to all of the women who have helped me to stay alive I am working never to be late again. (Jordan 1985, 26)

While Jordan has knowledge about the concrete act of her mother's death, she also strives for wisdom concerning the meaning of that death.

Some feminist scholars offer a similar claim that women as a group are more likely than men to use concrete knowledge in assessing knowledge claims. For example, a substantial number of the 135 women in a study of women's cognitive development were "connected knowers" and were drawn to the sort of knowledge that emerges from first-hand observation (Belenky et al. 1986). Such women felt that because knowledge comes from experience, the best way of understanding another person's ideas was to develop empathy and share the experiences that led the person to form those ideas.

In valuing the concrete, African-American women invoke not only an Afrocentric tradition but a women's tradition as well. Some feminist theorists suggest that women are socialized in complex relational nexuses where contextual rules versus abstract principles govern behavior (Chodorow 1978; Gilligan 1982). This socialization process is thought to stimulate characteristic ways of knowing (Hartsock 1983a; Belenky et al. 1986). These theorists suggest that women are more likely to experience two modes of knowing: one located in the body and the space it occupies and the other passing beyond it. Through their child-rearing and nurturing activities, women mediate these two modes and use the concrete experiences of their daily lives to assess more abstract knowledge claims (D. Smith 1987).

Although valuing the concrete may be more representative of women than men, social class differences among women may generate differential expression of this women's value. One study of working-class women's ways of knowing found that both white and African-American women rely on common sense and intuition (Luttrell 1989). These forms of knowledge allow for subjectivity between the knower and the known, rest in the women themselves (not in higher authorities), and are experienced directly in the world (not through abstractions).

Amanda King, a young African-American mother, describes how she used the concrete to assess the abstract and points out how difficult mediating these two modes of knowing can be:

> The leaders of the ROC [a labor union] lost their jobs too, but it just seemed like they were used to losing their jobs. . . . This was like a lifelong thing for them, to get out there and protest. They were like, what do you call them—intellectuals. . . . You got the ones that go to the university that are supposed to make all the speeches, they're the ones that are supposed to lead, you know, put this little revolution together, and then you got the little ones . . . that go to the factory everyday, they be the ones that have to fight. I had a child and I thought I don't have the time to be running around with these people. . . . I mean I understand some of that stuff they were talking about, like the bourgeoisie, the rich and the poor and all that, but I had surviving on my mind for me and my kid. (Byerly 1986, 198)

For Ms. King abstract ideals of class solidarity were mediated by the concrete experience of motherhood and the connectedness it involved.

In traditional African-American communities Black women find considerable institutional support for valuing concrete experience. Black women's centrality in families, churches, and other community organizations allows us to share our concrete knowledge of what it takes to be self-defined Black women with younger, less experienced sisters. "Sisterhood is not new to Black women," asserts Bonnie Thornton Dill, but "while Black women have fostered and encouraged sisterhood, we have not used it as the anvil to forge our political identities" (1983, 134). Though not expressed in explicitly political terms, this relationship of sisterhood among Black women can be seen as a model for a whole series of relationships African-American women have with one another (Gilkes 1985; Giddings 1988).

Given that Black churches and families are both woman-centered, Afrocentric institutions, African-American women traditionally have found considerable institutional support for this dimension of an Afrocentric feminist epistemology. While white women may value the concrete, it is questionable whether white families—particularly middle-class nuclear ones—and white community institutions provide comparable types of support. Similarly, while Black men are supported by Afrocentric institutions, they cannot participate in Black women's sisterhood. In terms of Black women's relationships with one another, African-American women may find it easier than others to recognize connectedness as a primary way of knowing, simply because we are encouraged to do so by a Black women's tradition of sisterhood.

THE USE OF DIALOGUE IN ASSESSING KNOWLEDGE CLAIMS

"Dialogue implies talk between two subjects, not the speech of subject and object. It is a humanizing speech, one that challenges and resists domination," asserts Bell Hooks (1989, 131). For Black women new knowledge claims are rarely worked out in isolation from other individuals and are usually developed through dialogues with other members of a community. A primary epistemological assumption underlying the use of dialogue in assessing knowledge claims is that connectedness rather than separation is an essential component of the knowledge validation process (Belenky et al. 1986, 18).

This belief in connectedness and the use of dialogue as one of its criteria for methodological adequacy has Afrocentric roots. In contrast to Western, either/or dichotomous thought, the traditional African worldview is holistic and seeks harmony. "One must understand that to become human, to realize the promise of becoming human, is the only important task of the person," posits Molefi Asante (1987, 185). People become more human and empowered only in the context of a community, and only when they "become seekers of the type of connections, interactions, and meetings that lead to harmony" (p. 185). The power of the word generally (Jahn 1961), and dialogues specifically, allows this to happen.

Not to be confused with adversarial debate, the use of dialogue has deep roots in an African-based oral tradition and in African-American culture (Sidran 1971; Smitherman 1977; Kochman 1981; Stanback 1985). Ruth Shays describes the importance of dialogue in the knowledge validation process of enslaved African-Americans:

> They would find a lie if it took them a year. . . . The foreparents found
> the truth because they listened and they made people tell their part
> many times. Most often you can hear a lie. . . . Those old people was
> everywhere and knew the truth of many disputes. They believed that a
> liar should suffer the pain of his lies, and they had all kinds of ways of
> bringing liars to judgement. (Gwaltney 1980, 32)

The widespread use of the call-and-response discourse mode among
African-Americans illustrates the importance placed on dialogue. Composed of spontaneous verbal and nonverbal interaction between speaker
and listener in which all of the speaker's statements, or "calls," are
punctuated by expressions, or "responses," from the listener, this Black
discourse mode pervades African-American culture. The fundamental
requirement of this interactive network is active participation of all
individuals (Smitherman 1977, 108). For ideas to be tested and validated,
everyone in the group must participate. To refuse to join in, especially
if one really disagrees with what has been said, is seen as "cheating"
(Kochman 1981, 28).

June Jordan's analysis of Black English points to the significance of
this dimension of an alternative epistemology:

> Our language is a system constructed by people constantly needing to
> insist that we exist. . . . Our language devolves from a culture that abhors
> all abstraction, or anything tending to obscure or delete the fact of the
> human being who is here and now/the truth of the person who is speaking
> or listening. Consequently, *there is no passive voice construction possible
> in Black English*. For example, you cannot say, "Black English is being
> eliminated." You must say, instead, "White people eliminating Black
> English." The assumption of the presence of life governs all of Black
> English . . . every sentence assumes the living and active participation
> of at least two human beings, the speaker and the listener. (Jordan
> 1985, 129)

Many Black women intellectuals invoke the relationships and connectedness provided by use of dialogue. When asked why she chose the
themes she did, novelist Gayl Jones replied: "I was . . . interested . . . in
oral traditions of storytelling—Afro-American and others, in which there
is always the consciousness and importance of the hearer" (Tate 1983,
91). In describing the difference in the way male and female writers
select significant events and relationships, Jones points out that "with
many women writers, relationships within family, community, between
men and women, and among women—from slave narratives by black
women writers on—are treated as complex and significant relationships,

whereas with many men the significant relationships are those that involve confrontations—relationships outside the family and community" (in Tate 1983, 92). Alice Walker's reaction to Zora Neale Hurston's book, *Mules and Men*, is another example of the use of dialogue in assessing knowledge claims. In *Mules and Men* Hurston chose not to become a detached observer of the stories and folktales she collected but instead, through extensive dialogues with the people in the communities she studied, placed herself in the center of her analysis. Using a similar process, Walker tests the truth of Hurston's knowledge claims:

> When I read *Mules and Men* I was delighted. Here was this perfect book! The "perfection" of which I immediately tested on my relatives, who are such typical Black Americans they are useful for every sort of political, cultural, or economic survey. Very regular people from the South, rapidly forgetting their Southern cultural inheritance in the suburbs and ghettos of Boston and New York, they sat around reading the book themselves, listening to me read the book, listening to each other read the book, and a kind of paradise was regained. (Walker 1977, xii)

Black women's centrality in families and community organizations provides African-American women with a high degree of support for invoking dialogue as a dimension of an Afrocentric feminist epistemology. However, when African-American women use dialogues in assessing knowledge claims, we might be invoking a particularly female way of knowing as well. Feminist scholars contend that men and women are socialized to seek different types of autonomy—the former based on separation, the latter seeking connectedness—and that this variation in types of autonomy parallels the characteristic differences between male and female ways of knowing (Chodorow 1978; Keller 1983; Belenky et al. 1986). For instance, in contrast to the visual metaphors (such as equating knowledge with illumination, knowing with seeing, and truth with light) that scientists and philosophers typically use, women tend to ground their epistemological premises in metaphors suggesting finding a voice, speaking, and listening (Belenky et al. 1986). The words of the Black woman who struggled for her education at Medgar Evers College resonate with the importance placed on voice: "I was basically a shy and reserved person prior to the struggle at Medgar, but I found my voice—and I used it! Now, I will never lose my voice again!" (Nicola-McLaughlin and Chandler 1988, 195).

While significant differences exist between Black women's family experiences and those of middle-class white women, African-American women clearly are affected by general cultural norms prescribing certain familial roles for women. Thus in terms of the role of dialogue in an Afrocentric feminist epistemology, Black women may again experience a convergence of the values of the African-American community and women's experiences.

THE ETHIC OF CARING

"Ole white preachers used to talk wid dey tongues widdout sayin' nothin', but Jesus told us slaves to talk wid our hearts" (Webber 1978, 127). These words of an ex-slave suggest that ideas cannot be divorced from the individuals who create and share them. This theme of talking with the heart taps the ethic of caring, another dimension of an alternative epistemology used by African-American women. Just as the ex-slave used the wisdom in his heart to reject the ideas of the preachers who talked "wid dey tongues widdout sayin' nothin'," the ethic of caring suggests that personal expressiveness, emotions, and empathy are central to the knowledge validation process.

One of three interrelated components comprising the ethic of caring is the emphasis placed on individual uniqueness. Rooted in a tradition of African humanism, each individual is thought to be a unique expression of a common spirit, power, or energy inherent in all life.[2] When Alice Walker "never doubted her powers of judgment because her mother assumed they were sound," she invokes the sense of individual uniqueness taught to her by her mother (Washington 1984, 145). The polyrhythms in African-American music, in which no one main beat subordinates the others, is paralleled by the theme of individual expression in Black women's quilting. Black women quilters place strong color and patterns next to one another and see the individual differences not as detracting from each piece but as enriching the whole quilt (Brown 1989). This belief in individual uniqueness is illustrated by the value placed on personal expressiveness in African-American communities (Smitherman 1977; Kochman 1981; Mitchell and Lewter 1986). Johnetta Ray, an inner-city resident, describes this Afrocentric emphasis on individual uniqueness: "No matter how hard we try, I don't think black people will ever develop much of a herd instinct. We are profound individualists with a passion for self-expression" (Gwaltney 1980, 228).

A second component of the ethic of caring concerns the appropriateness of emotions in dialogues. Emotion indicates that a speaker believes in the validity of an argument. Consider Ntozake Shange's description of one of the goals of her work: "Our [Western] society allows people to be absolutely neurotic and totally out of touch with their feelings and everyone else's feelings, and yet be very respectable. This, to me, is a travesty. . . . I'm trying to change the idea of seeing emotions and intellect as distinct faculties" (Tate 1983, 156). The Black women's blues tradition's history of personal expressiveness heals this either/or dichotomous rift separating emotion and intellect. For example, in her rendition of "Strange Fruit," Billie Holiday's lyrics blend seamlessly with the emotion of her delivery to render a trenchant social commentary on southern lynching. Without emotion, Aretha Franklin's (1967) cry for "respect" would be virtually meaningless.

A third component of the ethic of caring involves developing the capacity for empathy. Harriet Jones, a 16-year-old Black woman, explains to her interviewer why she chose to open up to him: "Some things in my life are so hard for me to bear, and it makes me feel better to know that you feel sorry about those things and would change them if you could" (Gwaltney 1980, 11). Without her belief in his empathy, she found it difficult to talk. Black women writers often explore the growth of empathy as part of an ethic of caring. For example, the growing respect that the Black slave woman Dessa and the white woman Rufel gain for one another in Sherley Anne Williams's *Dessa Rose* stems from their increased understanding of each other's positions. After watching Rufel fight off the advances of a white man, Dessa lay awake thinking: "The white woman was subject to the same ravisment as me; this the thought that kept me awake. I hadn't knowed white mens could use a white woman like that, just take her by force same as they could with us" (1986, 220). As a result of her new-found empathy, Dessa observed, "it was like we had a secret between us" (p. 220).

These components of the ethic of caring—the value placed on individual expressiveness, the appropriateness of emotions, and the capacity for empathy—pervade African-American culture. One of the best examples of the interactive nature of the importance of dialogue and the ethic of caring in assessing knowledge claims occurs in the use of the call-and-response discourse mode in traditional Black church services. In such services both the minister and the congregation routinely use voice rhythm and vocal inflection to convey meaning. The sound of what is being said is just as important as the words themselves in what is, in a sense, a dialogue of reason and emotion. As a result it is nearly impossible to filter out the strictly linguistic-cognitive abstract meaning from the sociocultural psychoemotive meaning (Smitherman 1977, 135, 137). While the ideas presented by a speaker must have validity (i.e., agree with the general body of knowledge shared by the Black congregation), the group also appraises the way knowledge claims are presented.

There is growing evidence that the ethic of caring may be part of women's experience as well (Noddings 1984). Certain dimensions of women's ways of knowing bear striking resemblance to Afrocentric expressions of the ethic of caring. Belenky et al. (1986) point out that two contrasting epistemological orientations characterize knowing: one an epistemology of separation based on impersonal procedures for establishing truth and the other, an epistemology of connection in which truth emerges through care. While these ways of knowing are not gender specific, disproportionate numbers of women rely on connected knowing.

The emphasis placed on expressiveness and emotion in African-American communities bears marked resemblance to feminist perspectives on the importance of personality in connected knowing. Separate knowers try to subtract the personality of an individual from his or her ideas because they see personality as biasing those ideas. In contrast, connected knowers see personality as adding to an individual's ideas and feel that the personality of each group member enriches a group's understanding. The significance of individual uniqueness, personal expressiveness, and empathy in African-American communities thus resembles the importance that some feminist analyses place on women's "inner voice" (Belenky et al. 1986).

The convergence of Afrocentric and feminist values in the ethic of caring seems particularly acute. White women may have access to a women's tradition valuing emotion and expressiveness, but few Eurocentric institutions except the family validate this way of knowing. In contrast, Black women have long had the support of the Black church, an institution with deep roots in the African past and a philosophy that accepts and encourages expressiveness and an ethic of caring. Black men share in this Afrocentric tradition. But they must resolve the contradictions that confront them in searching for Afrocentric models of masculinity in the face of abstract, unemotional notions of masculinity imposed on them (Hoch 1979). The differences among race/gender groups thus hinge on differences in their access to institutional supports valuing one type of knowing over another. Although Black women may be denigrated within white-male-controlled academic institutions, other institutions, such as Black families and churches, which encourage the expression of Black female power seem to do so, in part, by way of their support for an Afrocentric feminist epistemology.

THE ETHIC OF PERSONAL ACCOUNTABILITY

An ethic of personal accountability is the final dimension of an alternative epistemology. Not only must individuals develop their knowledge claims through dialogue and present them in a style proving their concern for their ideas, but people are expected to be accountable for their knowledge claims. Zilpha Elaw's description of slavery reflects this notion that every idea has an owner and that the owner's identity matters: "Oh, the abominations of slavery! . . . Every case of slavery, however lenient its inflictions and mitigated its atrocities, indicates an oppressor, the oppressed, and oppression" (Andrews 1986, 98). For Elaw abstract definitions of slavery mesh with the concrete identities of its perpetrators and its victims. African-Americans consider it essential for individuals to have personal positions on issues and assume full responsibility for arguing their validity (Kochman 1981).

Assessments of an individual's knowledge claims simultaneously evaluate an individual's character, values, and ethics. African-Americans reject the Eurocentric, masculinist belief that probing into an individual's personal viewpoint is outside the boundaries of discussion. Rather, all views expressed and actions taken are thought to derive from a central set of core beliefs that cannot be other than personal (Kochman 1981, 23). "Does Aretha really *believe* that Black women should get 'respect,' or is she just mouthing the words?" is a valid question in an Afrocentric feminist epistemology. Knowledge claims made by individuals respected for their moral and ethical connections to their ideas will carry more weight than those offered by less respected figures.

An example drawn from an undergraduate course composed entirely of Black women which I taught might help to clarify the uniqueness of this portion of the knowledge validation process. During one class discussion I asked the students to evaluate a prominent Black male scholar's analysis of Black feminism. Instead of severing the scholar from his context in order to dissect the rationality of his thesis, my students demanded facts about the author's personal biography. They were especially interested in concrete details of his life, such as his relationships with Black women, his marital status, and his social class background. By requesting data on dimensions of his personal life routinely excluded in positivist approaches to knowledge validation, they invoked concrete experience as a criterion of meaning. They used this information to assess whether he really cared about his topic and drew on this ethic of caring in advancing their knowledge claims about his work. Furthermore, they refused to evaluate the rationality of his written ideas without some indication of his personal credibility as an ethical human being. The entire exchange could only have occurred as a dialogue among members of a class that had established a solid enough community to employ an alternative epistemology in assessing knowledge claims.

The ethic of personal accountability is clearly an Afrocentric value, but is it feminist as well? While limited by its attention to middle-class, white women, Carol Gilligan's (1982) work suggests that there is a female model for moral development whereby women are more inclined to link morality to responsibility, relationships, and the ability to maintain social ties. If this is the case, then African-American women again experience a convergence of values from Afrocentric and female institutions.

The use of an Afrocentric feminist epistemology in traditional Black church services illustrates the interactive nature of all four dimensions and also serves as a metaphor for the distinguishing features of an Afrocentric feminist way of knowing. The services represent more than dialogues between the rationality used in examining biblical texts and stories and the emotion inherent in the use of reason for this purpose. The rationale for such dialogues involves the task of examining concrete experiences for the presence of an ethic of caring. Neither emotion nor ethics is subordinated to reason. Instead, emotion, ethics, and reason are used as interconnected, essential components in assessing knowledge claims. In an Afrocentric feminist epistemology, values lie at the heart of the knowledge validation process such that inquiry always has an ethical aim.

Alternative knowledge claims in and of themselves are rarely threatening to conventional knowledge. Such claims are routinely ignored, discredited, or simply absorbed and marginalized in existing paradigms. Much more threatening is the challenge that alternative epistemologies offer to the basic process used by the powerful to legitimate their knowledge claims. If the epistemology used to validate knowledge comes into question, then all prior knowledge claims validated under the dominant model become suspect. An alternative epistemology challenges all certified knowledge and opens up the question of whether what has been taken to be true can stand the test of alternative ways of validating truth. The existence of a self-defined Black women's standpoint using an Afrocentric feminist epistemology calls into question the content of what currently passes as truth and simultaneously challenges the process of arriving at that truth.

NOTES

1. In critiques of the Eurocentric, masculinist knowledge validation process, what Africanist scholars label "white" and "Eurocentric" feminist scholars describe as "male-dominated" and "masculinist." Although he does not emphasize its patriarchal and racist features, Morris Berman's *The Reenchantment of the World* (1981) provides an important discussion of Western thought. Afrocentric analyses of this same process can be found in Asante (1987) and Richards (1980, 1990). For feminist analyses see Hartsock (1983a, 1983b) and Harding (1986), especially Chapter Seven, "Other 'Others' and Fractured Identities: Issues for Epistemologists," pp. 163–96.

2. In discussing the West African Sacred Cosmos, Mechal Sobel notes that *Nyam*, a root word in many West African languages, connotes an enduring spirit, power, or energy possessed by all life. Despite the pervasiveness of this important concept in African humanism (see Jahn 1961, for example), its definition remains elusive. Sobel observes, "every individual analyzing the various Sacred Cosmos of West Africans has recognized the reality of this force, but no one has yet adequately translated this concept into Western terms" (1979, 13). For a comprehensive discussion of African spirituality, see Richards (1990).

Chapter 11 ———————————————

KNOWLEDGE, CONSCIOUSNESS, AND THE POLITICS OF EMPOWERMENT

Black feminist thought demonstrates Black women's emerging power as agents of knowledge. By portraying African-American women as self-defined, self-reliant individuals confronting race, gender, and class oppression, Afrocentric feminist thought speaks to the importance that knowledge plays in empowering oppressed people. One distinguishing feature of Black feminist thought is its insistence that both the changed consciousness of individuals and the social transformation of political and economic institutions constitute essential ingredients for social change. New knowledge is important for both dimensions of change.

Knowledge is a vitally important part of the social relations of domination and resistance. By objectifying African-American women and recasting our experiences to serve the interests of elite white men, much of the Eurocentric masculinist worldview fosters Black women's subordination. But placing Black women's experiences at the center of analysis offers fresh insights on the prevailing concepts, paradigms, and epistemologies of this worldview and on its feminist and Afrocentric critiques. Viewing the world through a both/and conceptual lens of the simultaneity of race, class, and gender oppression and of the need for a humanist vision of community creates new possibilities for an empowering Afrocentric feminist knowledge. Many Black feminist intellectuals have long thought about the world in this way because this is the way we experience the world.

Afrocentric feminist thought offers two significant contributions toward furthering our understanding of the important connections among knowledge, consciousness, and the politics of empowerment. First, Black feminist thought fosters a fundamental paradigmatic shift in how we think about oppression. By embracing a paradigm of race, class, and gender as interlocking systems of oppression, Black feminist thought reconceptualizes the social relations of domination and resistance. Second, Black feminist thought addresses ongoing epistemological debates in feminist theory and in the sociology of knowledge concerning ways of assessing "truth." Offering subordinate groups new knowledge about their own experiences can be empowering. But revealing new ways of knowing that allow subordinate groups to define their own reality has far greater implications.

PARADIGMATIC SHIFTS: DOMINATION AND RESISTANCE

Reconceptualizing Race, Class, and Gender as Interlocking Systems of Oppression

"What *I* really feel is radical is trying to make coalitions with people who are different from you," maintains Barbara Smith. "I feel it is radical to be dealing with race and sex and class and sexual identity all at one time. I think *that* is really radical because it has never been done before" (Smith and Smith 1981, 126). Black feminist thought fosters a fundamental paradigmatic shift that rejects additive approaches to oppression. Instead of starting with gender and then adding in other variables such as age, sexual orientation, race, social class, and religion, Black feminist thought sees these distinctive systems of oppression as being part of one overarching structure of domination (Smith 1983; Steady 1987; Hooks 1989). Viewing relations of domination for Black women for any given sociohistorical context as being structured via a system of interlocking race, class, and gender oppression expands the focus of analysis from merely describing the similarities and differences distinguishing these systems of oppression and focuses greater attention on how they interconnect. Assuming that each system needs the others in order to function creates a distinct theoretical stance that stimulates the rethinking of basic social science concepts.

Afrocentric feminist notions of family reflect this reconceptualization process. Black women's experiences as bloodmothers, othermothers, and community othermothers reveal that the mythical norm of a heterosexual, married couple, nuclear family with a nonworking spouse and a husband earning a "family wage" is far from being natural, universal, and preferred but instead is deeply embedded in specific race and class formations (Sudarkasa 1981b; Oppong 1982; Dill 1988b; Mullings 1986b). Placing African-American women in the center of analysis not only reveals much-needed information about Black women's experiences but also questions Eurocentric masculinist perspectives on family.

Black women's experiences and the Afrocentric feminist thought rearticulating them also challenge prevailing definitions of community. Black women's actions in the struggle for group survival suggest a vision of community that stands in opposition to that extant in the dominant culture (Gilkes 1980, 1983b, 1988). The definition of community implicit in the market model sees community as arbitrary and fragile, structured fundamentally by competition and domination (Hartsock 1983b). In contrast, Afrocentric models of community stress connections, caring, and personal accountability (Turner 1984; Asante 1987; Myers 1988). As cultural workers, African-American women have rejected the generalized ideology of domination advanced by the dominant group in order to conserve Afrocentric conceptualizations of community (Radford-Hill 1986; Reagon 1987). Denied access to the podium, Black women have been unable to spend time theorizing about alternative conceptualizations of community. Instead, through daily actions African-American women have *created* alternative communities that empower (Gilkes 1985).

This vision of community sustained by African-American women in conjunction with African-American men addresses the larger issue of reconceptualizing power. The type of Black women's power discussed here does resemble feminist theories of power which emphasize energy and community. However, in contrast to this body of literature whose celebration of women's power is often accompanied by a lack of attention to the importance of power as domination, Black women's experiences as mothers, community othermothers, educators, church leaders, labor union centerwomen, and community leaders seem to suggest that power as energy can be fostered by creative acts of resistance (Bush 1986; Terborg-Penn 1986).

The spheres of influence created and sustained by African-American women are not meant solely to provide a respite from oppressive situations or a retreat from their effects. Rather, these Black female spheres of influence constitute potential sanctuaries where individual Black women and men are nurtured in order to confront oppressive social institutions. Power from this perspective is a creative power used for the good of the community, whether that community is conceptualized as one's family, church community, or the next generation of the community's children.

By making the community stronger, African-American women become empowered, and that same community can serve as a source of support when Black women encounter race, gender, and class oppression.

Rethinking Black women's activism uncovers a new vision of Black women's empowerment that is distinct from existing models of power as domination. Black women have not conceptualized our quest for empowerment as one of replacing elite white male authorities with ourselves as benevolent Black female ones. Instead, African-American women have overtly rejected theories of power based on domination in order to embrace an alternative vision of power based on a humanist vision of self-actualization, self-definition, and self-determination (Lorde 1984; Steady 1987; Davis 1989; Hooks 1989).

It is important to develop analyses of contemporary social phenomena that explore the connections among race, class, and gender oppression and use new reconceptualizations of family, community, and power in doing so. Such analyses must retain the creative tension between the specificity needed to study the workings of race, class, and gender in Black women's lives and generalizations about these systems created by cross-cultural and transhistorical research.

Approaches that assume that race, gender, and class are interconnected have immediate practical applications. For example, African-American women continue to be inadequately protected by Title VII of the Civil Rights Act of 1964 (Scarborough 1989). The primary purpose of the statute is to eradicate all aspects of discrimination. But judicial treatment of Black women's employment discrimination claims has encouraged Black women to identify race *or* sex as the so-called primary discrimination. "To resolve the inequities that confront Black women," counsels Scarborough, "the courts must first correctly conceptualize them as 'Black women,' a distinct class protected by Title VII" (p. 1474). Such a shift, from protected categories to protected classes of people whose Title VII claims might be based on more than two discriminations, would work to alter the entire basis of current antidiscrimination efforts.

Reconceptualizing phenomena such as the rapid growth of female-headed households in African-American communities would also benefit from a race-, class-, and gender-inclusive analysis. Case studies of Black women heading households must be attentive to racially segmented local labor markets and community patterns, to changes in local political economies specific to a given city or region, and to established racial and gender ideology for a given location. This approach would go far to deconstruct Eurocentric, masculinist analyses that implicitly rely on controlling images of the matriarch or the welfare mother as guiding conceptual premises. This level of specificity could lead to generalizations about how race, class, and gender as interlocking phenomena produce an increase in female-headed households in national and international contexts. Revised definitions of family and community refocus attention on cross-cultural patterns of this household structure (Blumberg and Garcia 1977), especially those stimulated by changes in the international division of labor (Steady 1981; Burnham 1985; Simms and Malveaux 1986), and offer new visions of race- and class-inclusive analyses of Black women's gender experiences. Black feminist thought that rearticulates experiences such as these fosters an enhanced theoretical understanding of how race, gender, and class oppression are part of a single, historically created system.

The Matrix of Domination

Additive models of oppression are firmly rooted in the either/or dichotomous thinking of Eurocentric, masculinist thought. One must be either Black or white in such thought systems—persons of ambiguous racial and ethnic identity constantly battle with questions such as "what are you, anyway?" This emphasis on quantification and categorization occurs in conjunction with the belief that either/or categories must be ranked. The search for certainty of this sort requires that one side of a dichotomy be privileged while its other is denigrated. Privilege becomes defined in relation to its other.

Replacing additive models of oppression with interlocking ones creates possibilities for new paradigms. The significance of seeing race, class, and gender as interlocking systems of oppression is that such an approach fosters a paradigmatic shift of thinking inclusively about other oppressions, such as age, sexual orientation, religion, and ethnicity. Race, class, and gender represent the three systems of oppression that most heavily affect African-American women. But these systems and the economic, political, and ideological conditions that support them may not be the most fundamental oppressions, and they certainly affect many more groups than Black women. Other people of color, Jews, the poor, white women, and gays and lesbians have all had similar ideological justifications offered for their subordination. All categories of humans labeled Others have been equated to one another, to animals, and to nature (Halpin 1989).

Placing African-American women and other excluded groups in the center of analysis opens up possibilities for a both/and conceptual stance, one in which all groups possess varying amounts of penalty and privilege in one historically created system. In this system, for example, white women are penalized by their gender but privileged by their race. Depending on the context, an individual may be an oppressor, a member of an oppressed group, or simultaneously oppressor and oppressed.

Adhering to a both/and conceptual stance does not mean that race, class, and gender oppression are interchangeable. For example, whereas race, class, and gender oppression operate on the social structural level of institutions, gender oppression seems better able to annex the basic power of the erotic and intrude in personal relationships via family dynamics and within individual consciousness. This may be because racial oppression has fostered historically concrete communities among African-Americans and other racial/ethnic groups. These communities have stimulated cultures of resistance (Caulfield 1974; Scott 1985). While these communities segregate Blacks from whites, they simultaneously provide counter-institutional buffers that subordinate groups such as African-Americans use to resist the ideas and institutions of dominant groups. Social class may be similarly structured. Traditionally conceptualized as a relationship of *individual* employees to their employers, social class might be better viewed as a relationship of *communities* to capitalist political economies (Sacks 1989). Moreover, significant overlap exists between racial and social class oppression when viewing them through the collective lens of family and community. Existing community structures provide a primary line of resistance against racial and class oppression. But because gender cross-cuts these structures, it finds fewer comparable institutional bases to foster resistance.

Embracing a both/and conceptual stance moves us from additive, separate systems approaches to oppression and toward what I now see as the more fundamental issue of the social relations of domination. Race, class, and gender constitute axes of oppression that characterize Black women's experiences within a more generalized matrix of domination. Other groups may encounter different dimensions of the matrix, such as sexual orientation, religion, and age, but the overarching relationship is one of domination and the types of activism it generates.

Bell Hooks labels this matrix a "politic of domination" and describes how it operates along interlocking axes of race, class, and gender oppression. This politic of domination

> refers to the ideological ground that they share, which is a belief in domination, and a belief in the notions of superior and inferior, which are components of all of those systems. For me it's like a house, they share the foundation, but the foundation is the ideological beliefs around which notions of domination are constructed. (Hooks 1989, 175)

Johnella Butler claims that new methodologies growing from this new paradigm would be "non-hierarchical" and would "refuse primacy to either race, class, gender, or ethnicity, demanding instead a recognition of their matrix-like interaction" (1989, 16). Race, class, and gender may not be the most fundamental or important systems of oppression, but they have most profoundly affected African-American women. One significant dimension of Black feminist thought is its potential to reveal insights about the social relations of domination organized along other axes such as religion, ethnicity, sexual orientation, and age. Investigating Black women's particular experiences thus promises to reveal much about the more universal process of domination.

Multiple Levels of Domination

In addition to being structured along axes such as race, gender, and social class, the matrix of domination is structured on several levels. People experience and resist oppression on three levels: the level of personal biography; the group or community level of the cultural context created by race, class, and gender; and the systemic level of social institutions. Black feminist thought emphasizes all three levels as sites of domination and as potential sites of resistance.

Each individual has a unique personal biography made up of concrete experiences, values, motivations, and emotions. No two individuals occupy the same social space; thus no two biographies are identical. Human ties can be freeing and empowering, as is the case with Black women's heterosexual love relationships or in the power of motherhood in African-American families and communities. Human ties can also be confining and oppressive. Situations of domestic violence and abuse or cases in which controlling images foster Black women's internalized oppression represent domination on the personal level. The same situation can look quite different depending on the consciousness one brings to interpret it.

This level of individual consciousness is a fundamental area where new knowledge can generate change. Traditional accounts assume that power as domination operates from the top down by forcing and controlling unwilling victims to bend to the will of more powerful superiors. But these accounts fail to account for questions concerning why, for example, women stay with abusive men even with ample opportunity to leave or why slaves did not kill their owners more often. The willingness of the victim to collude in her or his own victimization becomes lost. They also fail to account for sustained resistance by victims, even when chances for victory appear remote. By emphasizing the power of self-definition and the necessity of a free mind, Black feminist thought speaks to the importance African-American women thinkers place on consciousness as a sphere of freedom. Black women intellectuals realize that domination operates not only by structuring power from the top down but by simultaneously annexing the power as energy of those on the bottom for its own ends. In their efforts to rearticulate the standpoint of African-American women as a group, Black feminist thinkers offer individual African-American women the conceptual tools to resist oppression.

The cultural context formed by those experiences and ideas that are shared with other members of a group or community which give meaning to individual biographies constitutes a second level at which domination is experienced and resisted. Each individual biography is rooted in several overlapping cultural contexts—for example, groups defined by race, social class, age, gender, religion, and sexual orientation. The cultural component contributes, among other things, the concepts used in thinking and acting, group validation of an individual's interpretation of concepts, the "thought models" used in the acquisition of knowledge, and standards used to evaluate individual thought and behavior (Mannheim 1936). The most cohesive cultural contexts are those with identifiable histories, geographic locations, and social institutions. For Black women African-American communities have provided the location for an Afrocentric group perspective to endure.

Subjugated knowledges, such as a Black women's culture of resistance, develop in cultural contexts controlled by oppressed groups. Dominant groups aim to replace subjugated knowledge with their own specialized thought because they realize that gaining control over this dimension of subordinate groups' lives simplifies control (Woodson 1933; Fanon 1963). While efforts to influence this dimension of an oppressed group's experiences can be partially successful, this level is more difficult to control than dominant groups would have us believe. For example, adhering to externally derived standards of beauty leads many African-American women to dislike their skin color or hair texture. Similarly, internalizing Eurocentric gender ideology leads some Black men to abuse Black women. These are cases of the successful infusion of the dominant group's specialized thought into the everyday cultural context of African-Americans. But the long-standing existence of a Black women's culture of resistance as expressed through Black women's relationships with one another, the Black women's blues tradition, and the voices of contemporary African-American women writers all attest to the difficulty of eliminating the cultural context as a fundamental site of resistance.

Domination is also experienced and resisted on the third level of social institutions controlled by the dominant group: namely, schools, churches, the media, and other formal organizations. These institutions expose individuals to the specialized thought representing the dominant group's standpoint and interests. While such institutions offer the promise of both literacy and other skills that can be used for individual empowerment and social transformation, they simultaneously require docility and passivity. Such institutions would have us believe that the theorizing of elites constitutes the whole of theory. The existence of African-American women thinkers such as Maria Stewart, Sojourner Truth, Zora Neale Hurston, and Fannie Lou Hamer who, though excluded from and/or marginalized within such institutions, continued to produce theory effectively opposes this hegemonic view. Moreover, the more recent resurgence of Black feminist thought within these institutions, the case of the outpouring of contemporary Black feminist thought in history and literature, directly challenges the Eurocentric masculinist thought pervading these institutions.

Resisting the Matrix of Domination

Domination operates by seducing, pressuring, or forcing African-American women and members of subordinated groups to replace individual and cultural ways of knowing with the dominant group's specialized thought. As a result, suggests Audre Lorde, "the true focus of revolutionary change is never merely the oppressive situations which we seek to escape, but that piece of the oppressor which is planted deep within each of us" (1984, 123). Or as Toni Cade Bambara succinctly states, "revolution begins with the self, in the self" (1970a, 109).

Lorde and Bambara's suppositions raise an important issue for Black feminist intellectuals and for all scholars and activists working for social change. Although most individuals have little difficulty identifying their own victimization within some major system of oppression—whether it be by race, social class, religion, physical ability, sexual orientation, ethnicity, age or gender—they typically fail to see how their thoughts and actions uphold someone else's subordination. Thus white feminists routinely point with confidence to their oppression as women but resist seeing how much their white skin privileges them. African-Americans who possess eloquent analyses of racism often persist in viewing poor white women as symbols of white power. The radical left fares little better. "If only people of color and women could see their true class interests," they argue, "class solidarity would eliminate racism and sexism." In essence, each group identifies the oppression with which it feels most comfortable as being fundamental and classifies all others as being of lesser importance. Oppression is filled with such contradictions because these approaches fail to recognize that a matrix of domination contains few pure victims or oppressors. Each individual derives varying amounts of penalty and privilege from the multiple systems of oppression which frame everyone's lives.

A broader focus stresses the interlocking nature of oppressions that are structured on multiple levels, from the individual to the social structural, and which are part of a larger matrix of domination. Adhering to this inclusive model provides the conceptual space needed for each individual to see that she or he is *both* a member of multiple dominant groups *and* a member of multiple subordinate groups. Shifting the analysis to investigating how the matrix of domination is structured along certain axes—race, gender, and class being the axes of investigation for African-American women—reveals that different systems of oppression may rely in varying degrees on systemic versus interpersonal mechanisms of domination.

Empowerment involves rejecting the dimensions of knowledge, whether personal, cultural, or institutional, that perpetuate objectification and dehumanization. African-American women and other individuals in subordinate groups become empowered when we understand and use those dimensions of our individual, group, and disciplinary ways of knowing that foster our humanity as fully human subjects. This is the case when Black women value our self-definitions, participate in a Black women's activist tradition, invoke an Afrocentric feminist epistemology as central to our worldview, and view the skills gained in schools as part of a focused education for Black community development. C. Wright Mills (1959) identifies this holistic epistemology as the "sociological imagination" and identifies its task and its promise as a way of knowing that enables individuals to grasp the relations between history and biography within society. Using one's standpoint to engage the sociological imagination can empower the individual. "My fullest concentration of energy is available to me," Audre Lorde maintains, "only when I integrate all the parts of who I am, openly, allowing power from particular sources of my living to flow back and forth freely through all my different selves, without the restriction of externally imposed definition" (1984, 120–21).

EPISTEMOLOGICAL SHIFTS: DIALOGUE, EMPATHY, AND TRUTH

Black Women as Agents of Knowledge

Living life as an African-American woman is a necessary prerequisite for producing Black feminist thought because within Black women's communities thought is validated and produced with reference to a particular set of historical, material, and epistemological conditions. African-American women who adhere to the idea that claims about Black women must be substantiated by Black women's sense of our own experiences and who anchor our knowledge claims in an Afrocentric feminist epistemology have produced a rich tradition of Black feminist thought.

Traditionally such women were blues singers, poets, autobiographers, storytellers, and orators validated by everyday Black women as experts on a Black women's standpoint. Only a few unusual African-American feminist scholars have been able to defy Eurocentric masculinist epistemologies and explicitly embrace an Afrocentric feminist epistemology. Consider Alice Walker's description of Zora Neale Hurston:

> In my mind, Zora Neale Hurston, Billie Holiday, and Bessie Smith form a sort of unholy trinity. Zora *belongs* in the tradition of black women singers, rather than among "the literati." . . . Like Billie and Bessie she followed her own road, believed in her own gods, pursued her own dreams, and refused to separate herself from "common" people. (Walker 1977, xvii–xviii)

Zora Neale Hurston is an exception for prior to 1950, few African-American women earned advanced degrees and most of those who did complied with Eurocentric masculinist epistemologies. Although these women worked on behalf of Black women, they did so within the confines of pervasive race and gender oppression. Black women scholars were in a position to see the exclusion of African-American women from scholarly discourse, and the thematic content of their work often reflected their interest in examining a Black women's standpoint. However, their tenuous status in academic institutions led them to adhere to Eurocentric masculinist epistemologies so that their work would be accepted as scholarly. As a result, while they produced Black feminist thought, those African-American women most likely to gain academic credentials were often least likely to produce Black feminist thought that used an Afrocentric feminist epistemology.

An ongoing tension exists for Black women as agents of knowledge, a tension rooted in the sometimes conflicting demands of Afrocentricity and feminism. Those Black women who are feminists are critical of how Black culture and many of its traditions oppress women. For example, the strong pronatal beliefs in African-American communities that foster early motherhood among adolescent girls, the lack of self-actualization that can accompany the double-day of paid employment and work in the home, and the emotional and physical abuse that many Black women experience from their fathers, lovers, and husbands all reflect practices opposed by African-American women who are feminists. But these same women may have a parallel desire as members of an oppressed racial group to affirm the value of that same culture and traditions (Narayan 1989). Thus strong Black mothers appear in Black women's literature, Black women's economic contributions to families is lauded, and a curious silence exists concerning domestic abuse.

As more African-American women earn advanced degrees, the range of Black feminist scholarship is expanding. Increasing numbers of African-American women scholars are explicitly choosing to ground their work in Black women's experiences, and, by doing so, they implicitly adhere to an Afrocentric feminist epistemology. Rather than being restrained by their both/and status of marginality, these women make creative use of their outsider-within status and produce innovative Afrocentric feminist thought. The difficulties these women face lie less in demonstrating that they have mastered white male epistemologies than in resisting the hegemonic nature of these patterns of thought in order to see, value, and use existing alternative Afrocentric feminist ways of knowing.

In establishing the legitimacy of their knowledge claims, Black women scholars who want to develop Afrocentric feminist thought may encounter the often conflicting standards of three key groups. First, Black feminist thought must be validated by ordinary African-American women who, in the words of Hannah Nelson, grow to womanhood "in a world where the saner you are, the madder you are made to appear" (Gwaltney 1980, 7). To be credible in the eyes of this group, scholars must be personal advocates for their material, be accountable for the consequences of their work, have lived or experienced their material in some fashion, and be willing to engage in dialogues about their findings with ordinary, everyday people. Second, Black feminist thought also must be accepted by the community of Black women scholars. These scholars place varying amounts of importance on rearticulating a Black women's standpoint using an Afrocentric feminist epistemology. Third, Afrocentric feminist thought within academia must be prepared to confront Eurocentric masculinist political and epistemological requirements.

The dilemma facing Black women scholars engaged in creating Black feminist thought is that a knowledge claim that meets the criteria of adequacy for one group and thus is judged to be an acceptable knowledge claim may not be translatable into the terms of a different group. Using the example of Black English, June Jordan illustrates the difficulty of moving among epistemologies:

> You cannot "translate" instances of Standard English preoccupied with abstraction or with nothing/nobody evidently alive into Black English. That would warp the language into uses antithetical to the guiding perspective

of its community of users. Rather you must first change those Standard English sentences, themselves, into ideas consistent with the person-centered assumptions of Black English. (Jordan 1985, 130)

Although both worldviews share a common vocabulary, the ideas themselves defy direct translation.

For Black women who are agents of knowledge, the marginality that accompanies outsider-within status can be the source of both frustration and creativity. In an attempt to minimize the differences between the cultural context of African-American communities and the expectations of social institutions, some women dichotomize their behavior and become two different people. Over time, the strain of doing this can be enormous. Others reject their cultural context and work against their own best interests by enforcing the dominant group's specialized thought. Still others manage to inhabit both contexts but do so critically, using their outsider-within perspectives as a source of insights and ideas. But while outsiders within can make substantial contributions as agents of knowledge, they rarely do so without substantial personal cost. "Eventually it comes to you," observes Lorraine Hansberry, "the thing that makes you exceptional, if you are at all, is inevitably that which must also make you lonely" (1969, 148).

Once Black feminist scholars face the notion that, on certain dimensions of a Black women's standpoint, it may be fruitless to try and translate ideas from an Afrocentric feminist epistemology into a Eurocentric masculinist framework, then other choices emerge. Rather than trying to uncover universal knowledge claims that can withstand the translation from one epistemology to another (initially, at least), Black women intellectuals might find efforts to rearticulate a Black women's standpoint especially fruitful. Rearticulating a Black women's standpoint refashions the concrete and reveals the more universal human dimensions of Black women's everyday lives. "I date all my work," notes Nikki Giovanni, "because I think poetry, or any writing, is but a reflection of the moment. The universal comes from the particular" (1988, 57). Bell Hooks maintains, "my goal as a feminist thinker and theorist is to take that abstraction and articulate it in a language that renders it accessible—not less complex or rigorous—but simply more accessible" (1989, 39). The complexity exists; interpreting it remains the unfulfilled challenge for Black women intellectuals.

Situated Knowledge, Subjugated Knowledge, and Partial Perspectives

"My life seems to be an increasing revelation of the intimate face of universal struggle," claims June Jordan:

> You begin with your family and the kids on the block, and next you open your eyes to what you call your people and that leads you into land reform into Black English into Angola leads you back to your own bed where you lie by yourself, wondering if you deserve to be peaceful, or trusted or desired or left to the freedom of your own unfaltering heart. And the scale shrinks to the size of a skull: your own interior cage. (Jordan 1981, xi)

Lorraine Hansberry expresses a similar idea: "I believe that one of the most sound ideas in dramatic writing is that in order to create the universal, you must pay very great attention to the specific. Universality, I think, emerges from the truthful identity of what is" (1969, 128). Jordan and Hansberry's insights that universal struggle and truth may wear a particularistic, intimate face suggest a new epistemological stance concerning how we negotiate competing knowledge claims and identify "truth."

The context in which African-American women's ideas are nurtured or suppressed matters. Understanding the content and epistemology of Black women's ideas as specialized knowledge requires attending to the context from which those ideas emerge. While produced by individuals, Black feminist thought as situated knowledge is embedded in the communities in which African-American women find ourselves (Haraway 1988).

A Black women's standpoint and those of other oppressed groups is not only embedded in a context but exists in a situation characterized by domination. Because Black women's ideas have been suppressed, this suppression has stimulated African-American women to create knowledge that empowers people to resist domination. Thus Afrocentric feminist thought represents a subjugated knowledge (Foucault 1980). A Black women's standpoint may provide a preferred stance from which to view the matrix of domination because, in principle, Black feminist thought as specialized thought is less likely than the specialized knowledge produced by dominant groups to deny the connection between ideas and the vested interests of their creators. However, Black feminist thought as subjugated knowledge is not exempt from critical analysis, because subjugation is not grounds for an epistemology (Haraway 1988).

Despite African-American women's potential power to reveal new insights about the matrix of domination, a Black women's standpoint is only one angle of vision. Thus Black feminist thought represents a partial perspective. The overarching matrix of domination houses multiple groups, each with varying experiences with penalty and privilege that produce corresponding partial perspectives, situated knowledges, and, for clearly identifiable subordinate groups, subjugated knowledges. No one group has a clear angle of vision. No one group possesses the theory or methodology that allows it to discover the absolute "truth" or, worse yet, proclaim its theories and methodologies as the universal norm evaluating other groups' experiences. Given that groups are unequal in power in making themselves heard, dominant groups have a vested interest in suppressing the knowledge produced by subordinate groups. Given the existence of multiple and competing knowledge claims to "truth" produced by groups with partial perspectives, what epistemological approach offers the most promise?

Dialogue and Empathy

Western social and political thought contains two alternative approaches to ascertaining "truth." The first, reflected in positivist science, has long claimed that absolute truths exist and that the task of scholarship is to develop objective, unbiased tools of science to measure these truths. But Afrocentric, feminist, and other bodies of critical theory have unmasked the concepts and epistemology of this version of science as representing the vested interests of elite white men and therefore as being less valid when applied to experiences of other groups and, more recently, to white male recounting of their own exploits. Earlier versions of standpoint theories, themselves rooted in a Marxist positivism, essentially reversed positivist science's assumptions concerning whose truth would prevail. These approaches suggest that the oppressed allegedly have a clearer view of "truth" than their oppressors because they lack the blinders created by the dominant group's ideology. But this version of standpoint theory basically duplicates the positivist belief in one "true" interpretation of reality and, like positivist science, comes with its own set of problems.

Relativism, the second approach, has been forwarded as the antithesis of and inevitable outcome of rejecting a positivist science. From a relativist perspective all groups produce specialized thought and each group's thought is equally valid. No group can claim to have a better interpretation of the "truth" than another. In a sense, relativism represents the opposite of scientific ideologies of objectivity. As epistemological stances, both positivist science and relativism minimize the importance of specific location in influencing a group's knowledge claims, the power inequities among groups that produce subjugated knowledges, and the strengths and limitations of partial perspective (Haraway 1988).

The existence of Black feminist thought suggests another alternative to the ostensibly objective norms of science and to relativism's claims that groups with competing knowledge claims are equal. In this volume I placed Black women's subjectivity in the center of analysis and examined the interdependence of the everyday, taken-for-granted knowledge shared by African-American women as a group, the more specialized knowledge produced by Black women intellectuals, and the social conditions shaping both types of thought. This approach allowed me to describe the creative tension linking how sociological conditions influenced a Black women's standpoint and how the power of the ideas themselves gave many African-American women the strength to shape those same sociological conditions. I approached Afrocentric feminist thought as situated in a context of domination and not as a system of ideas divorced from political and economic reality. Moreover, I presented Black feminist thought as subjugated knowledge in that African-American women have long struggled to find alternative locations and techniques for articulating our own standpoint. In brief, I examined the situated, subjugated standpoint of African-American women in order to understand Black feminist thought as a partial perspective on domination.

This approach to Afrocentric feminist thought allows African-American women to bring a Black women's standpoint to larger epistemological dialogues concerning the nature of the matrix of domination. Eventually such dialogues may get us to a point at which, claims Elsa Barkley Brown, "all people can learn to center in another experience, validate it, and judge it by its own standards without need of comparison or need to adopt that framework as their own" (1989, 922). In such dialogues, "one has no need to 'decenter' anyone in order to center someone else; one has only to constantly, appropriately, 'pivot the center' " (p. 922).

Those ideas that are validated as true by African-American women, African-American men, Latina lesbians, Asian-American women, Puerto Rican men, and other groups with distinctive standpoints, with each group using the epistemological approaches growing from its unique standpoint, thus become the most "objective" truths. Each group speaks from its own standpoint and shares its own partial, situated knowledge. But because each group perceives its own truth as partial, its knowledge is unfinished. Each group becomes better able to consider other groups' standpoints without relinquishing the uniqueness of its own standpoint or suppressing other groups' partial perspectives. "What is always needed in the appreciation of art, or life," maintains Alice Walker, "is the larger perspective. Connections made, or at least attempted, where none existed before, the straining to encompass in one's glance at the varied world the common thread, the unifying theme through immense diversity" (1983, 5). Partiality and not universality is the condition of being heard; individuals and groups forwarding knowledge claims without owning their position are deemed less credible than those who do.

Dialogue is critical to the success of this epistemological approach, the type of dialogue long extant in the Afrocentric call-and-response tradition whereby power dynamics are fluid, everyone has a voice, but everyone must listen and respond to other voices in order to be allowed to remain in the community. Sharing a common cause fosters dialogue and encourages groups to transcend their differences.

Existing power inequities among groups must be addressed before an alternative epistemology such as that described by Elsa Barkley Brown or Alice Walker can be utilized. The presence of subjugated knowledges means that groups are not equal in making their standpoints known to themselves and others. "Decentering" the dominant group is essential, and relinquishing privilege of this magnitude is unlikely to occur without struggle. But still the vision exists, one encompassing "coming to believe in the possibility of a variety of experiences, a variety of ways of understanding the world, a variety of frameworks of operation, without imposing consciously or unconsciously a notion of the norm" (Brown 1989, 921).

THE POLITICS OF EMPOWERMENT

African-American women have been victimized by race, gender, and class oppression. But portraying Black women solely as passive, unfortunate recipients of racial and sexual abuse stifles notions that Black women can actively work to change our circumstances and bring about changes in our lives. Similarly, presenting African-American women solely as heroic figures who easily engage in resisting oppression on all fronts minimizes the very real costs of oppression and can foster the perception that Black women need no help because we can "take it."

Black feminist thought's emphasis on the ongoing interplay between Black women's oppression and Black women's activism presents the matrix of domination as responsive to human agency. Such thought views the world as a dynamic place where the goal is not merely to survive or to fit in or to cope; rather, it becomes a place where we feel ownership and accountability. The existence of Afrocentric feminist thought suggests that there is always choice, and power to act, no matter how bleak the situation may appear to be. Viewing the world as one in the making raises the issue of individual responsibility for bringing about change. It also shows that while individual empowerment is key, only collective action can effectively generate lasting social transformation of political and economic institutions.

In 1831 Maria Stewart asked, "How long shall the fair daughters of Africa be compelled to bury their minds and talents beneath a load of iron pots and kettles?" (Richardson 1987, 38). Stewart's response speaks eloquently to the connections between knowledge, consciousness, and the politics of empowerment:

Until union, knowledge and love begin to flow among us. How long shall a mean set of men flatter us with their smiles, and enrich themselves with our hard earnings; their wives' fingers sparkling with rings, and they themselves laughing at our folly? Until we begin to promote and patronize each other. . . . Do you ask, what can we do? Unite and build a store of your own. . . . Do you ask where is the money? We have spent more than enough for nonsense, to do what building we should want. (Richardson 1987, 38).

REFERENCES

Albers, Patricia C. 1985. "Autonomy and Dependency in the Lives of Dakota Women: A Study in Historical Change." *Review of Radical Political Economics* 17(3): 109–34.

Alcoff, Linda. 1988. "Cultural Feminism versus Post-Structuralism: The Identity Crisis in Feminist Theory." *Signs* 13(3): 405–36.

Andersen, Margaret. 1987. *Denying Difference: The Continuing Basis for the Exclusion of Race and Gender in the Curriculum.* Curriculum Integration Publication 4. Memphis, TN: Center for Research on Women, Memphis State University.

———. 1988. *Thinking about Women: Sociological Perspectives on Sex and Gender.* 2d ed. New York: Macmillan.

Andolsen, Barbara Hilkert. 1986. *"Daughters of Jefferson, Daughters of Bootblacks": Racism and American Feminism.* Macon, GA: Mercer University Press.

Andrews, William L. 1986. *Sisters of the Spirit: Three Black Women's Autobiographies of the Nineteenth Century.* Bloomington: Indiana University Press.

Angelou, Maya. 1969. *I Know Why the Caged Bird Sings.* New York: Bantam.

Asante, Kariamu W. 1990. "Commonalities in African Dance: An Aesthetic Foundation." In *African Culture: The Rhythms of Unity*, edited by Molefi Asante and Kariamu W. Asante, 71–82. Trenton, NJ: Africa World Press.

Asante, Molefi Kete. 1987. *The Afrocentric Idea.* Philadelphia: Temple University Press.

Asbury, Jo-Ellen. 1987. "African-American Women in Violent Relationships: An Exploration of Cultural Differences." In *Violence in the Black Family: Correlates and Consequences*, edited by Robert L. Hampton, 89–105. Lexington, MA: Lexington Books.

Aschenbrenner, Joyce. 1975. *Lifelines, Black Families in Chicago.* Prospect Heights, IL: Waveland Press.

(Bambara), Toni Cade. 1970a. "On the Issue of Roles." In *The Black Woman: An Anthology*, edited by Toni Cade (Bambara), 101–10. New York: Signet.

239

————, ed. 1970b. *The Black Woman: An Anthology*. New York: Signet.

————. 1980. *The Salt Eaters*. New York: Vintage.

————. 1981. *Gorilla, My Love*. New York: Vintage.

Baran, Paul, and Paul Sweezy. 1966. *Monopoly Capital*. New York: Monthly Review Press.

Barnett, Evelyn Brooks. 1978. "Nannie Burroughs and the Education of Black Women." In *The Afro-American Woman: Struggles and Images*, edited by Sharon Harley and Rosalyn Terborg-Penn, 97–108. Port Washington, NY: Kennikat Press.

Bart, Pauline B., and Patricia H. O'Brien. 1985. "Ethnicity and Rape Avoidance: Jews, White Catholics and Blacks." In *Stopping Rape: Successful Survival Strategies*, edited by Pauline B. Bart and Patricia H. O'Brien, 70–92. New York: Pergamon Press.

Bash, Harry H. 1979. *Sociology, Race and Ethnicity*. New York: Gordon and Breach.

Beale, Frances. 1970. "Double Jeopardy: To Be Black and Female." In *The Black Woman: An Anthology*, edited by Toni Cade (Bambara), 90–100. New York: Signet.

Belenky, Mary Field, Blythe McVicker Clinchy, Nancy Rule Goldberger, and Jill Mattuck Tarule. 1986. *Women's Ways of Knowing*. New York: Basic Books.

Bell, Laurie, ed. 1987. *Good Girls/Bad Girls: Feminists and Sex Trade Workers Face to Face*. Toronto: Seal Press.

Bellah, Robert N. 1983. "The Ethical Aims of Social Inquiry." In *Social Science as Moral Inquiry*, edited by Norma Haan, Robert Bellah, Paul Rabinow, and William Sullivan, 360–81. New York: Columbia University Press.

Benhabib, Seyla, and Drucilla Cornell. 1987. "Introduction: Beyond the Politics of Gender." In *Feminism as Critique*, edited by Seyla Benhabib and Drucilla Cornell, 1–15. Minneapolis: University of Minnesota Press.

Benjamin, Jessica. 1983. "Master and Slave: The Fantasy of Erotic Domination." In *Powers of Desire: The Politics of Sexuality*, edited by Ann Snitow, Christine Stansell, and Sharon Thompson, 280–99. New York: Monthly Review Press.

Berger, Peter L. and Thomas Luckmann. 1966. *The Social Construction of Reality*. New York: Doubleday.

Berman, Morris. 1981. *The Reenchantment of the World*. New York: Bantam.

Bethel, Elizabeth Rauh. 1981. *Promiseland: A Century of Life in a Negro Community*. Philadelphia: Temple University Press.

Billie Holiday Anthology/Lady Sings the Blues. 1976. Ojai, CA: Creative Concepts Publishing.

Billingsley, Andrew. 1968. *Black Families in White America*. Englewood Cliffs, NJ: Prentice-Hall.

Blumberg, Rae Lesser, and Maria Pilar Garcia. 1977. "The Political Economy of the Mother-Child Family: A Cross-Societal View." In *Beyond the Nuclear Family Model: Cross Cultural Perspectives*, edited by Luis Lenero-Otero, 99–163. Beverly Hills, CA: Sage.

Bonner, Marita O. 1987. "On Being Young—A Woman—and Colored." In *Frye Street and Environs: The Collected Works of Marita Bonner*, edited by Joyce Flynn and Joyce Occomy Stricklin, 3–8. Boston: Beacon.

Bookman, Ann, and Sandra Morgen, eds. 1988. *Women and the Politics of Empowerment*. Philadelphia: Temple University Press.

Braverman, Harry. 1974. *Labor and Monopoly Capital*. New York: Monthly Review Press.

Brewer, Rose. 1988. "Black Women in Poverty: Some Comments on Female-Headed Families." *Signs* 13(2): 331–39.

Brittan, Arthur, and Mary Maynard. 1984. *Sexism, Racism and Oppression*. New York: Basil Blackwell.

Brooks, Evelyn. 1983. "The Feminist Theology of the Black Baptist Church, 1880–1900." In *Class, Race and Sex: The Dynamics of Control*, edited by Amy Swerdlow and Hanna Lessinger, 31–59. Boston: G. K. Hall.

Brooks, Gwendolyn. 1953. *Maud Martha*. Boston: Atlantic Press.

———. 1972. *Report from Part One: The Autobiography of Gwendolyn Brooks*. Detroit: Broadside Press.

Brown, Cynthia Stokes, ed. 1986. *Ready from Within: Septima Clark and the Civil Rights Movement*. Navarro, CA: Wild Trees Press.

Brown, Elsa Barkley. 1986. *Hearing Our Mothers' Lives*. Atlanta: Fifteenth Anniversary of African-American and African Studies, Emory University. (unpublished)

———. 1989. "African-American Women's Quilting: A Framework for Conceptualizing and Teaching African-American Women's History." *Signs* 14(4): 921–29.

Brown-Collins, Alice, and Deborah Ridley Sussewell. 1986. "The Afro-American Women's Emerging Selves." *Journal of Black Psychology* 13(1): 1–11.

Burnham, Linda. 1985. "Has Poverty Been Feminized in Black America?" *Black Scholar* 16(2): 14–24.

Burnham, Margaret A. 1987. "An Impossible Marriage: Slave Law and Family Law." *Law and Inequality* 5: 187–225.

Bush, Barbara. 1986. " 'The Family Tree is Not Cut': Women and Cultural Resistance in Slave Family Life in the British Caribbean." In *In Resistance, Studies in African, Caribbean and Afro-American History*, edited by Gary Y. Okhiro, 117–132. Amherst: University of Massachusetts Press.

Butler, Johnella. 1989. "Difficult Dialogues." *The Women's Review of Books* 6(5): 16.

Byerly, Victoria. 1986. *Hard Times Cotton Mills Girls*. Ithaca, NY: Cornell University Press.

Campbell, Loretta. 1983. "Reinventing Our Image: Eleven Black Women Filmmakers." *Heresies* 4(4): 58–62.

Campbell, Bebe Moore. 1989. *Sweet Summer: Growing Up with and without My Dad*. New York: Putnam.

Cannon, Katie G. 1985. "The Emergence of a Black Feminist Consciousness." In *Feminist Interpretations of the Bible*, edited by Letty M. Russell, 30–40. Philadelphia: Westminster Press.

———. 1988. *Black Womanist Ethics*. Atlanta: Scholars Press.

Cantarow, Ellen. 1980. *Moving the Mountain: Women Working for Social Change*. Old Westbury, NY: Feminist Press.

Carby, Hazel. 1987. *Reconstructing Womanhood: The Emergence of the Afro-American Woman Novelist*. New York: Oxford.

Caulfield, Mina Davis. 1974. "Imperialism, the Family, and Cultures of Resistance." *Socialist Review* 4(2): 67–85.

"Children of the Underclass." 1989. *Newsweek* September 11, 16–27.

Childs, John Brown. 1984. "Afro-American Intellectuals and the People's Culture." *Theory and Society* 13(1): 69–90.

Chisholm, Shirley. 1970. *Unbought and Unbossed*. New York: Avon.

Chodorow, Nancy. 1974. "Family Structure and Feminine Personality." In *Woman, Culture, and Society*, edited by Michelle Zimbalist Rosaldo and Louise Lamphere, 43–66. Stanford: Stanford University Press.

———. 1978. *The Reproduction of Mothering*. Berkeley: University of California Press.

———, and Susan Contratto. 1982. "The Fantasy of the Perfect Mother." In *Rethinking the Family: Some Feminist Questions*, edited by Barrie Thorne and Marilyn Yalom, 54–75. New York: Longman.

Christian, Barbara. 1985. *Black Feminist Criticism, Perspectives on Black Women Writers*. New York: Pergamon.

———. 1989. "But Who Do You Really Belong to—Black Studies or Women's Studies?" *Women's Studies* 17(1–2): 17–23.

Clark, Reginald M. 1983. *Family Life and School Achievement: Why Poor Black Children Succeed or Fail*. Chicago: University of Chicago Press.

Clarke, Cheryl. 1983. "The Failure to Transform: Homophobia in the Black Community." In *Home Girls: A Black Feminist Anthology*, edited by Barbara Smith, 197–208. New York: Kitchen Table Press.

———, Jewell L. Gomez, Evelyn Hammonds, Bonnie Johnson, and Linda Powell. 1983. "Conversations and Questions: Black Women on Black Women Writers." *Conditions: Nine* 3 (3): 88–137.

Clarke, Edith. 1966. *My Mother Who Fathered Me*. 2d ed. London: Allen and Unwin.

Clark-Lewis, Elizabeth. 1985. *"This Work Had a' End": The Transition from Live-In to Day Work*. Southern Women: The Intersection of Race, Class and Gender. Working Paper #2. Memphis, TN: Center for Research on Women, Memphis State University.

Claude, Judy. 1986. "Poverty Patterns for Black Men and Women." *Black Scholar* 17(5): 20–23.

Coleman, Willi. 1987. "Closets and Keepsakes." *Sage: A Scholarly Journal on Black Women* 4(2): 34–35.

Coley, Soraya M., and Joyce O. Beckett. 1988. "Black Battered Women: Practice Issues." *Social Casework* 69(8): 483–90.

Collier, Jane, Michelle Z. Rosaldo, and Sylvia Yanagisko. 1982. "Is There a Family? New Anthropological Views." In *Rethinking the Family: Some Feminist Questions*, edited by Barrie Thorne and Marilyn Yalom, 25–39. New York: Longman.

Collins, Patricia Hill. 1986a. "The Afro-American Work Family Nexus: An Exploratory Analysis." *Western Journal of Black Studies* 10(3): 148–58.

———. 1968b. "Learning from the Outsider Within: The Sociological Significance of Black Feminist Thought." *Social Problems* 33(6): 14–32.

———. 1987. "The Meaning of Motherhood in Black Culture and Black Mother/Daughter Relationships." *Sage: A Scholarly Journal on Black Women* 4(2): 4–11.

———. 1989. "A Comparison of Two Works on Black Family Life." *Signs* 14(4): 875–84.

Color. 1983. Produced and directed by Warrington Hudlin, written and coproduced by Denise Oliver. New York: Black Filmaker's Foundation.

The Combahee River Collective. 1982. "A Black Feminist Statement." In *But Some of Us Are Brave*, edited by Gloria T. Hull, Patricia Bell Scott, and Barbara Smith, 13–22. Old Westbury, NY: Feminist Press.

Cone, James H. 1972. *The Spirituals and the Blues: An Interpretation*. New York: Seabury Press.

Cooper, Anna Julia. 1892. *A Voice from the South; By a Black Woman of the South*. Xenia, OH: Aldine Printing House.

Cox, Oliver. 1948. *Caste, Class and Race*. New York: Modern Reader Paperback.

Cross, Tia, Freada Klein, Barbara Smith, and Beverly Smith. 1982. "Face-to-Face, Day-to-Day—Racism CR." In *But Some of Us Are Brave*, edited by Gloria T. Hull, Patricia Bell Scott, and Barbara Smith, 52–56. Old Westbury, NY: Feminist Press.

Cruse, Harold. 1967. *The Crisis of the Negro Intellectual*. New York: William Morrow.

Dance, Daryl. 1979. "Black Eve or Madonna? A Study of the Antithetical Views of the Mother in Black American Literature." In *Sturdy Black Bridges: Visions of Black Women in Literature*, edited by Roseann Bell, Bettye Parker, and Beverly Guy-Sheftall, 123–32. Garden City, NY: Anchor.

Daniels, Bonnie. 1979. "For Colored Girls . . . A Catharsis." *Black Scholar* 10(8–9): 61–62.

Darcy, R. and Charles D. Hadley. 1988. "Black Women in Politics: The Puzzle of Success." *Social Science Quarterly* 69(3): 629–45.

Davis, Angela Y. 1978. "Rape, Racism and the Capitalist Setting." *Black Scholar* 9(7): 24–30.

————. 1981. *Women, Race and Class*. New York: Random House.

————. 1989. *Women, Culture, and Politics*. New York: Random House.

Davis, George, and Glegg Watson. 1985. *Black Life in Corporate America*. New York: Anchor.

de Lauretis, Teresa. 1986. "Feminist Studies/Critical Studies: Issues, Terms, and Contexts." In *Feminist Studies/Critical Studies*, edited by Teresa de Lauretis, 1–19. Bloomington: Indiana University Press.

Dill, Bonnie Thornton. 1979. "The Dialectics of Black Womanhood." *Signs* 4(3): 543–55.

————. 1980. " 'The Means to Put My Children Through': Child-Rearing Goals and Strategies among Black Female Domestic Servants." In *The Black Woman*, edited by La Frances Rodgers-Rose, 107–23. Beverly Hills, CA: Sage.

————. 1983. "Race, Class, and Gender: Prospects for an All-Inclusive Sisterhood." *Feminist Studies* 9(1): 131–50.

————. 1988a. " 'Making Your Job Good Yourself': Domestic Service and the Construction of Personal Dignity." In *Women and the Politics of Empowerment*, edited by Ann Bookman and Sandra Morgen, 33–52. Philadelphia: Temple University Press.

————. 1988b. "Our Mothers' Grief: Racial Ethnic Women and the Maintenance of Families." *Journal of Family History* 13(4): 415–31.

Diop, Cheikh. 1974. *The African Origin of Civilization: Myth or Reality*. New York: L. Hill.

Dodson, Jualynne E., and Cheryl Townsend Gilkes. 1987. "Something Within: Social Change and Collective Endurance in the Sacred World of Black Christian Women." In *Women and Religion in America, Volume 3: 1900–1968*, edited by Rosemary Reuther and R. Keller, 80–130. New York: Harper and Row.

Dougherty, Molly C. 1978. *Becoming a Woman in Rural Black Culture*. New York: Holt, Rinehart and Winston.

DuBois, William E. B. 1969. *The Negro American Family*. New York: Negro Universities Press.

Dumas, Rhetaugh Graves. 1980. "Dilemmas of Black Females in Leadership." In *The Black Woman*, edited by La Frances Rodgers-Rose, 203–15. Beverly Hills, CA: Sage.

Duster, Alfreda M., ed. 1970. *Crusade for Justice: The Autobiography of Ida B. Wells*. Chicago: University of Chicago Press.

Dworkin, Andrea. 1981. *Pornography: Men Possessing Women*. New York: Perigee.

Edwards, Ann. 1987. "Male Violence in Feminist Theory: An Analysis of the Changing Conceptions of Sex/Gender Violence and Male Dominance." In *Women, Violence and Social Control*, edited by Jalna Hanmer and Mary Maynard, 13–29. Atlantic Highlands, NJ: Humanities Press.

Eisenstein, Hester. 1983. *Contemporary Feminist Thought*. Boston: G. K. Hall.

Evans, Mari, ed. 1984. *Black Women Writers (1950–1980)*. Garden City, NY: Anchor.

Evans, Sara. 1979. *Personal Politics*. New York: Vintage.

Fanon, Franz. 1963. *The Wretched of the Earth*. New York: Grove Press.

Farley, Reynolds. 1984. *Blacks and Whites: Narrowing the Gap?* Cambridge, MA: Harvard University Press.

Fausto-Sterling, Anne. 1989. "Life in the XY Corral." *Women's Studies International Forum* 12(3): 319–31.

Fields, Mamie Garvin, and Karen Fields. 1983. *Lemon Swamp and Other Places: A Carolina Memoir*. New York: Free Press.

Flammang, Janet A. 1983. "Feminist Theory: The Question of Power." In *Current Perspectives in Social Theory, Volume 4*, edited by Scott G. McNall, 37–84. Greenwich, CT: JAI Press.

Flax, Jane. 1978. "The Conflict between Nurturance and Autonomy in Mother-Daughter Relationships and within Feminism." *Feminist Studies* 4(2): 171–89.

Fortes, Meyer. 1950. "Kinship and Marriage among the Ashanti." In *African Systems of Kinship and Marriage*, edited by A. R. Radcliffe-Brown and Daryll Forde, 252–84. New York: Oxford University Press.

Foucault, Michel. 1980. *Power/Knowledge: Selected Interviews and Other Writings 1972–1977*, edited by Colin Gordon. New York: Pantheon.

Fox-Genovese, Elizabeth. 1986. "Strategies and Forms of Resistance: Focus on Slave Women in the United States." In *In Resistance, Studies in African, Caribbean and Afro-American History*, edited by Gary Y. Okhiro, 143–65. Amherst: University of Massachusetts Press.

Franklin, Aretha. 1967. *I Never Loved a Man the Way I Love You*. Atlantic Recording Corp.

Frazier, E. Franklin. 1948. *The Negro Family in the United States*. New York: Dryden Press.

Friere, Paulo. 1970. *The Pedagogy of the Oppressed*. New York: Herder and Herder.

Fusfield, Daniel R., and Timothy Bates. 1984. *The Political Economy of the Urban Ghetto*. Carbondale: Southern Illinois University Press.

Gardner, Tracey A. 1980. "Racism and Pornography in the Women's Movement." In *Take Back the Night: Women on Pornography*, edited by Laura Lederer, 105–14. New York: William Morrow.

Gayle, Addison, ed. 1971. *The Black Aesthetic*. Garden City, NY: Doubleday.

Giddings, Paula. 1984. *When and Where I Enter . . . The Impact of Black Women on Race and Sex in America*. New York: William Morrow.

———. 1988. *In Search of Sisterhood: Delta Sigma Theta and the Challenge of the Black Sorority Movement*. New York: William Morrow.

Gilkes, Cheryl Townsend. 1980. " 'Holding Back the Ocean with a Broom': Black Women and Community Work." In *The Black Woman*, edited by La Frances Rodgers-Rose, 217–32. Beverly Hills, CA: Sage.

———. 1982. "Successful Rebellious Professionals: The Black Woman's Professional Identity and Community Commitment." *Psychology of Women Quarterly* 6(3): 289–311.

———. 1983a. "From Slavery to Social Welfare: Racism and the Control of Black Women." In *Class, Race, and Sex: The Dynamics of Control*, edited by Amy Swerdlow and Hanna Lessinger, 288–300. Boston: G. K. Hall.

———. 1983b. "Going Up for the Oppressed: The Career Mobility of Black Women Community Workers." *Journal of Social Issues* 39(3): 115–39.

———. 1985. " 'Together and in Harness': Women's Traditions in the Sanctified Church." *Signs* 10(4): 678–99.

———. 1988. "Building in Many Places: Multiple Commitments and Ideologies in Black Women's Community Work." In *Women and the Politics of Empowerment*, edited by Ann Bookman and Sandra Morgen, 53–76. Philadelphia: Temple University Press.

Gilligan, Carol. 1982. *In a Different Voice*. Cambridge, MA: Harvard University Press.

Gilman, Sander L. 1985. "Black Bodies, White Bodies: Toward an Iconography of Female

Sexuality in Late Nineteenth-Century Art, Medicine, and Literature." *Critical Inquiry* 12(1): 205–43.

Giovanni, Nikki. 1971. *Gemini*. New York: Penguin.

———. 1988 *Sacred Cows . . . and Other Edibles*. New York: Quill/William Morrow.

Glenn, Evelyn Nakano. 1985. "Racial Ethnic Women's Labor: The Intersection of Race, Gender and Class Oppression." *Review of Radical Political Economics* 17(3): 86–108.

Golden, Marita. 1983. *Migrations of the Heart*. New York: Ballantine.

Gordon, David M., Richard Edwards, and Michael Reich. 1982. *Segmented Work, Divided Workers*. New York: Cambridge University Press.

Gould, Stephen Jay. 1981. *The Mismeasure of Man*. New York: W. W. Norton.

Gramsci, Antonio. 1971. *Selections from the Prison Notebooks*. London: Lawrence and Wishart.

Grant, Jacquelyn. 1982. "Black Women and the Church." In *But Some of Us Are Brave*, edited by Gloria T. Hull, Patricia Bell Scott, and Barbara Smith, 141–52. Old Westbury, NY: Feminist Press.

Gutman, Herbert. 1976. *The Black Family in Slavery and Freedom, 1750–1925*. New York: Random House.

Guy, Rosa. 1983. *A Measure of Time*. New York: Bantam.

Guy-Sheftall, Beverly. 1986. "Remembering Sojourner Truth: On Black Feminism." *Catalyst* (Fall): 54–57.

Gwaltney, John Langston. 1980. *Drylongso, A Self-Portrait of Black America*. New York: Vintage.

Haan, Norma, Robert Bellah, Paul Rabinow, and William Sullivan, eds. 1983. *Social Science as Moral Inquiry*. New York: Columbia University Press.

Hale, Janice. 1980. "The Black Woman and Child Rearing." In *The Black Woman*, edited by La Frances Rodgers-Rose, 79–88. Beverly Hills, CA: Sage.

Hall, Jacqueline Dowd. 1983. "The Mind that Burns in Each Body: Women, Rape, and Racial Violence." In *Powers of Desire: The Politics of Sexuality*, edited by Ann Snitow, Christine Stansell, and Sharon Thompson, 329–49. New York: Monthly Review Press.

Halpin, Zuleyma Tang. 1989. "Scientific Objectivity and the Concept of 'The Other.'" *Women's Studies International Forum* 12(3): 285–94.

Hansberry, Lorraine. 1959. *A Raisin in the Sun*. New York: Signet.

———. 1969. *To Be Young, Gifted and Black*. New York: Signet.

Haraway, Donna. 1988. "Situated Knowledges: The Science Question in Feminism and the Privilege of Partial Perspective." *Feminist Studies* 14(3): 575–99.

Harding, Sandra. 1986. *The Science Question in Feminism*. Ithaca, NY: Cornell University Press.

Harley, Sharon. 1978. "Anna Julia Cooper: A Voice for Black Women." In *The Afro-American Woman: Struggles and Images*, edited by Sharon Harley and Rosalyn Terborg-Penn, 87–96. Port Washington, NY: Kennikat Press.

———. 1982. "Beyond the Classroom: The Organizational Lives of Black Female Educators in the District of Columbia, 1890–1930." *Journal of Negro Education* 51(3): 254–65.

———, and Rosalyn Terborg-Penn, eds. 1978. *The Afro-American Woman: Struggles and Images*. Port Washington, NY: Kennikat Press.

Harper, Michael S. 1979. "Gayl Jones: An Interview." In *Chant of Saints: A Gathering of Afro-American Literature, Art, and Scholarship*, edited by Michael S. Harper and Robert B. Stepto, 352–75. Urbana: University of Illinois Press.

Harris, Trudier. 1981. "Three Black Women Writers and Humanism: A Folk Perspective." In *Black American Literature and Humanism*, edited by R. Baxter Miller, 50–74. Lexington: University of Kentucky Press.

————. 1982. *From Mammies to Militants: Domestics in Black American Literature*. Philadelphia: Temple University Press.

————. 1988. *Transcending Guilt: The Creation of a New Universe in the Works of Toni Cade Bambara, Alice Walker, and Toni Morrison*. Cincinnati: Women's Studies Program, University of Cincinnati Colloquium.

Harrison, Daphne Duval. 1978. "Black Women in the Blues Tradition." In *The Afro-American Woman: Struggles and Images*, edited by Sharon Harley and Rosalyn Terborg-Penn, 58–73. Port Washington, NY: Kennikat Press.

————. 1988. *Black Pearls: Blues Queens of the 1920s*. New Brunswick, NJ: Rutgers University Press.

Hartsock, Nancy M. 1983a. "The Feminist Standpoint: Developing the Ground for a Specifically Feminist Historical Materialism." In *Discovering Reality*, edited by Sandra Harding and Merrill B. Hintikka, 283–310. Boston: D. Reidel.

————. 1983b. *Money, Sex and Power*. Boston: Northeastern University Press.

Hernton, Calvin. 1985. "The Sexual Mountain and Black Women Writers." *Black Scholar* 16(4): 2–11.

Herskovits, Melville J. [1941] 1958. *The Myth of the Negro Past*. Boston: Beacon.

Higginbotham, Elizabeth. 1983. "Laid Bare by the System: Work and Survival for Black and Hispanic Women." In *Class, Race, and Sex: The Dynamics of Control*, edited by Amy Smerdlow and Hanna Lessinger, 200–215. Boston: G. K. Hall.

————. 1985. "Race and Class Barriers to Black Women's College Attendance." *Journal of Ethnic Studies* 13(1): 89–107.

————, and Sarah Watts. 1988. "The New Scholarship on Afro-American Women." *Women's Studies Quarterly* 16(1–2): 12–21.

Higginbotham, Evelyn Brooks. 1989. "Beyond the Sound of Silence: Afro-American Women in History." *Gender and History* 1(1): 50–67.

Hine, Darlene Clark. 1989. "Rape and the Inner Lives of Black Women in the Middle West: Preliminary Thoughts on the Culture of Dissemblance." *Signs* 14(4): 912–20.

————, and Kate Wittenstein. 1981. "Female Slave Resistance: The Economics of Sex." In *The Black Woman Cross-Culturally*, edited by Filomina Chioma Steady, 289–300. Cambridge, MA: Schenkman.

Hoch, Paul. 1979. *White Hero Black Beast: Racism, Sexism and the Mask of Masculinity*. London: Pluto Press.

Hochschild, Arlie Russell. 1975. "The Sociology of Feeling and Emotion: Selected Possibilities." In *Another Voice: Feminist Perspectives on Social Life and Social Science*, edited by Marcia Millman and Rosabeth Kanter, 280–307. Garden City, NY: Anchor.

Hogan, Lloyd. 1984. *Principles of Black Political Economy*. Boston: Routledge & Kegan Paul.

Hooks, Bell. 1981. *Ain't I a Woman: Black Women and Feminism*. Boston: South End Press.

————. 1984. *From Margin to Center*. Boston: South End Press.

————. 1989. *Talking Back: Thinking Feminist, Thinking Black*. Boston: South End Press.

Hull, Gloria T., ed. 1984. *Give Us Each Day: The Diary of Alice Dunbar-Nelson*. New York: W. W. Norton.

————, Patricia Bell Scott, and Barbara Smith, eds. 1982. *But Some of Us Are Brave*. Old Westbury, NY: Feminist Press.

————, and Barbara Smith. 1982. "The Politics of Black Women's Studies." In *But Some of Us Are Brave*, edited by Gloria T. Hull, Patricia Bell Scott, and Barbara Smith, xvii–xxxiv. Old Westbury, NY: Feminist Press.

Hurston, Zora Neale. [1937] 1969. *Their Eyes Were Watching God*. Greenwich, CT: Fawcett.

Hurtado, Aida. 1989. "Relating to Privilege: Seduction and Rejection in the Subordination of White Women and Women of Color." *Signs* 14(4): 833–55.

Irele, Abiola. 1983. "Introduction." In *African Philosophy, Myth and Reality*, by Paulin J. Houtondji, 7–32. Bloomington: Indiana University Press.

Jackson, Irene V. 1981. "Black Women and Music: From Africa to the New World." In *The Black Woman Cross-Culturally*, edited by Filomina Chioma Steady, 383–401. Cambridge, MA: Schenkman.

Jackson, Mahalia. 1985. "Singing of Good Tidings and Freedom." In *Afro-American Religious History*, edited by Milton C. Sernett, 446–57. Durham, NC: Duke University Press.

Jacobs, Harriet. [1860] 1987. "The Perils of a Slave Woman's Life." In *Invented Lives: Narratives of Black Women 1860–1960*, edited by Mary Helen Washington, 16–67. Garden City, NY: Anchor.

Jaggar, Alison M. 1983. *Feminist Politics and Human Nature*. Totawa, NJ: Rowman & Allanheld.

Jahn, Janheinz. 1961. *Muntu: An Outline of Neo-African Culture*. London: Faber and Faber.

Johnson, Charles S. [1934] 1979. *Shadow of the Plantation*. Chicago: University of Chicago Press.

Johnson, Leanor Boulin. 1981. "Perspectives on Black Family Empirical Research: 1965–1978." In *Black Families*, edited by Harriette Pipes McAdoo, 87–102. Beverly Hills, CA: Sage.

Jones, Gayl. 1975. *Corregidora*. New York: Bantam.

———. 1976. *Eva's Man*. Boston: Beacon.

Jones, Jacqueline. 1985. *Labor of Love, Labor of Sorrow: Black Women, Work, and the Family from Slavery to the Present*. New York: Basic Books.

Jordan, June. 1981. *Civil Wars*. Boston: Beacon.

———. 1985. *On Call*. Boston: South End Press.

Joseph, Gloria. 1981. "Black Mothers and Daughters: Their Roles and Functions in American Society." In *Common Differences*, edited by Gloria Joseph and Jill Lewis, 75–126. Garden City, NY: Anchor.

———. 1984. "Black Mothers and Daughters: Traditional and New Perspectives." *Sage: A Scholarly Journal on Black Women* 1(2): 17–21.

Keller, Evelyn Fox. 1983. "Gender and Science." In *Discovering Reality*, edited by Sandra Harding and Merrill B. Hintikka, 187–206. Boston: D. Reidel.

———. 1985. *Reflections on Gender and Science*. New Haven, CT: Yale University Press.

King, Deborah K. 1988. "Multiple Jeopardy, Multiple Consciousness: The Context of a Black Feminist Ideology." *Signs* 14(1): 42–72.

King, Mae. 1973. "The Politics of Sexual Stereotypes." *Black Scholar* 4(6–7): 12–23.

Kochman, Thomas. 1981. *Black and White Styles in Conflict*. Chicago: University of Chicago Press.

Kuhn, Thomas. 1962. *The Structure of Scientific Revolutions*. 2d ed. Chicago: University of Chicago Press.

Kuykendall, Eleanor H. 1983. "Toward an Ethic of Nurturance: Luce Irigaray on Mothering and Power." In *Motherhood: Essays in Feminist Theory*, edited by Joyce Treblicot, 263–74. Totowa, NJ: Rowman & Allanheld.

Ladner, Joyce. 1972. *Tomorrow's Tomorrow*. Garden City, NY: Doubleday.

———. 1986. "Black Women Face the 21st Century: Major Issues and Problems." *Black Scholar* 17(5): 12–19.

———, and Ruby Morton Gourdine. 1984. "Intergenerational Teenage Motherhood: Some Preliminary Findings." *Sage: A Scholarly Journal on Black Women* 1(2): 22–24.

Lee, Andrea. 1984. *Sarah Phillips*. New York: Penguin.

Lerner, Gerda, ed. 1972. *Black Women in White America: A Documentary History*. New York: Vintage.

Lewis, Diane K. 1975. "The Black Family: Socialization and Sex Roles." *Phylon* 36(3): 221–37.

Lewis, Jerry M., and John G. Looney. 1983. *The Long Struggle: Well-Functioning Working-Class Black Families*. New York: Brunner/Mazel.

Lieb, Sandra. 1981. *Mother of the Blues: A Study of Ma Rainey*. Amherst: University of Massachusetts Press.

Lincoln, C. Eric. 1984. *Race, Religion and the Continuing American Dilemma*. New York: Hill and Wang.

Lindsay, Beverly, ed. 1980. *Comparative Perspectives of Third World Women: The Impact of Race, Sex, and Class*. New York: Praeger.

Loewenberg, Bert J., and Ruth Bogin, eds. 1976. *Black Women in Nineteenth-Century American Life*. University Park: Pennsylvania State University Press.

Lorde, Audre. 1982. *Zami, A New Spelling of My Name*. Trumansberg, NY: The Crossing Press.

———. 1984. *Sister Outsider*. Trumansberg, NY: The Crossing Press.

Lukes, Steven, ed. 1986. *Power*. New York: New York University Press.

Luttrell, Wendy. 1989. "Working-Class Women's Ways of Knowing: Effects of Gender, Race, and Class." *Sociology of Education* 62(1): 33–46.

Lyman, Stanford M. 1972. *The Black American in Sociological Thought: A Failure of Perspective*. New York: Capricorn.

Mannheim, Karl. 1936. *Ideology and Utopia*. New York: Harcourt, Brace & World.

Mapp, Edward. 1973. "Black Women in Films." *Black Scholar* 4(6–7): 42–46.

Marable, Manning. 1983. "Grounding with My Sisters: Patriarchy and the Exploitation of Black Women." In *How Capitalism Underdeveloped Black America*, 69–104. Boston: South End Press.

Marshall, Paule. 1959. *Brown Girl, Brownstones*. New York: Avon.

———. 1969. *The Chosen Place, the Timeless People*. New York: Vintage.

Martin, Elmer, and Joanne Mitchell Martin. 1978. *The Black Extended Family*. Chicago: University of Chicago Press.

Mayfield, Lorraine P. 1986. "Early Parenthood among Low-Income Adolescent Girls." In *The Black Family: Essays and Studies*. 3d ed., edited by Robert Staples, 211–31. Belmont, CA: Wadsworth.

Mbiti, John S. 1969. *African Religions and Philosophy*. London: Heinemann.

McAdoo, Harriette Pipes. 1985. "Strategies Used by Black Single Mothers against Stress." *Review of Black Political Economy* 14(2–3): 153–66.

McClaurin-Allen, Irma. 1989. "Incongruities: Dissonance and Contradiction in the Life of a Black Middle-Class Woman." Amherst: University of Massachusetts, Department of Anthropology.

McCray, Carrie Allen. 1980. "The Black Woman and Family Roles." In *The Black Woman*, edited by La Frances Rodgers-Rose, 67–78. Beverly Hills, CA: Sage.

McDowell, Deborah E. 1985. "New Directions for Black Feminist Criticism." In *The New Feminist Criticism*, edited by Elaine Showalter, 186–99. New York: Pantheon.

McGhee, James. 1984. "A Profile of the Black Single Female-Headed Household." In *The*

State of Black America, 43–54. New York: National Urban League.

McIntosh, Peggy. 1988. *White Privilege and Male Privilege: A Personal Account of Coming to See Correspondences through Work in Women's Studies*. Working Paper No. 189. Wellesley, MA: Center for Research on Women, Wellesley College.

McNall, Scott G. 1983. "Pornography: The Structure of Domination and the Mode of Reproduction." In *Current Perspectives in Social Theory, Volume 4*, edited by Scott McNall, 181–203. Greenwich, CT: JAI Press.

Millman, Marcia, and Rosabeth Moss Kanter, eds. 1975. *Another Voice: Feminist Perspectives on Social Life and Social Science*. New York: Anchor.

Mills, C. Wright. 1959. *The Sociological Imagination*. New York: Oxford University Press.

Mitchell, Henry H., and Nicholas Cooper Lewter. 1986. *Soul Theology: The Heart of American Black Culture*. San Francisco: Harper & Row.

Moody, Ann. 1968. *Coming of Age in Mississippi*. New York: Dell.

Moraga, Cherrie, and Gloria Anzaldua, eds. 1981. *This Bridge Called My Back: Writings by Radical Women of Color*. Watertown, MA: Persephone Press.

Morrison, Toni. 1970. *The Bluest Eye*. New York: Pocket Books.

———. 1974. *Sula*. New York: Random House.

———. 1987. *Beloved*. New York: Random House.

Mosse, George L. 1985. *Nationalism and Sexuality: Respectability and Abnormal Sexuality in Modern Europe*. New York: H. Fertig.

Moulton, Janice. 1983. "A Paradigm of Philosophy: The Adversary Method." In *Discovering Reality*, edited by Sandra Harding and Merrill B. Hintikka, 149–64. Boston: D. Reidel.

Moynihan, Daniel Patrick. 1965. *The Negro Family: The Case for National Action*. Washington, DC: GPO.

Mulkay, Michael. 1979. *Science and the Sociology of Knowledge*. Boston: Unwin Hyman.

Mullings, Leith. 1986a. "Anthropological Perspectives on the Afro-American Family." *American Journal of Social Psychiatry* 6(1): 11–16.

———. 1986b. "Uneven Development: Class, Race and Gender in the United States before 1900." In *Women's Work: Development and the Division of Labor by Gender*, edited by Eleanor Leacock and Helen Safa, 41–57. South Hadley, MA: Bergin & Garvey.

Murray, Pauli. 1970. "The Liberation of Black Women." In *Voices of the New Feminism*, edited by Mary Lou Thompson, 87–102. Boston: Beacon.

———. 1987. *Song in a Weary Throat: An American Pilgrimage*. New York: Harper & Row.

Myers, Lena Wright. 1980. *Black Women: Do They Cope Better?* Englewood Cliffs, NJ: Prentice-Hall.

Myers, Linda James. 1988. *Understanding an Afrocentric World View: Introduction to an Optimal Psychology*. Dubuque, IA: Kendall/Hunt.

Narayan, Uma. 1989. "The Project of Feminist Epistemology: Perspectives from a Nonwestern Feminist." In *Gender/Body/Knowledge: Feminist Reconstructions of Being and Knowing*, edited by Alison M. Jaggar and Susan R. Bordo, 256–69. New Brunswick, NJ: Rutgers University Press.

Nash, June, and Maria Patricia Fernandez-Kelly, eds. 1983. *Women, Men and the International Division of Labor*. Albany: State University of New York.

Naylor, Gloria. 1980. *The Women of Brewster Place*. New York: Penguin.

———. 1988. *Mama Day*. New York: Vintage.

Neverdon-Morton, Cynthia. 1989. *Afro-American Women of the South and the Advancement of the Race, 1895–1925*. Knoxville: University of Tennessee Press.

Nicola-McLaughlin, Andree, and Zula Chandler. 1988. "Urban Politics in the Higher Education of Black Women: A Case Study." In *Women and the Politics of Empowerment*, edited by Ann Bookman and Sandra Morgen, 180–201. Philadelphia: Temple University Press.

Noble, Jeanne. 1978. *Beautiful, Also, Are the Souls of My Black Sisters: A History of the Black Woman in America*. Englewood Cliffs, NJ: Prentice-Hall.

Noddings, Nel. 1984. *Caring: A Feminine Approach to Ethics and Moral Education*. Berkeley: University of California Press.

Okanlawon, Alexander. 1972. "Africanism—A Synthesis of the African World-View." *Black World* 21(9): 40–44, 92–97.

Omi, Michael, and Howard Winant. 1986. *Racial Formation in the United States: From the 1960s to the 1980s*. New York: Routledge & Kegan Paul.

O'Neale, Sondra. 1986. "Inhibiting Midwives, Usurping Creators: The Struggling Emergence of Black Women in American Fiction." In *Feminist Studies/Critical Studies*, edited by Teresa de Lauretis, 139–56. Bloomington: Indiana University Press.

Oppong, Christine. 1982. "Family Structure and Women's Reproductive and Productive Roles: Some Conceptual and Methodological Issues." In *Women's Roles and Population Trends in the Third World*, edited by Richard Anker, Mayra Buvinic, and Nadia H. Youssef, 133–50. London: Croom Helm.

Page, Clarence, ed. 1986. *A Foot in Each World: Essays and Articles by Leanita McClain*. Evanston, IL: Northwestern University Press.

Parker, Bettye J. 1979. "Mississippi Mothers: Roots." In *Sturdy Black Bridges*, edited by Rosann Bell, Bettye Parker, and Beverly Guy-Sheftall, 263–81. Garden City, NY: Anchor.

Patterson, Orlando. 1982. *Slavery and Social Death*. Cambridge, MA: Harvard University Press.

Pearce, Diana. 1983. "The Feminization of Ghetto Poverty." *Society* 21(1): 70–74.

Perkins, Linda M. 1982. "Heed Life's Demands: The Educational Philosophy of Fanny Jackson Coppin." *Journal of Negro Education* 51(3): 181–90.

———. 1983. "The Impact of the 'Cult of True Womanhood' on the Education of Black Women." *Journal of Social Issues* 39(3): 17–28.

Petry, Ann. 1946. *The Street*. Boston: Beacon.

Pinkney, Alphonso. 1984. *The Myth of Black Progress*. New York: Cambridge University Press.

Prestage, Jewell L. 1980. "Political Behavior of American Black Women: An Overview." In *The Black Woman*, edited by La Frances Rodgers-Rose, 233–50. Beverly Hills, CA: Sage.

Pryse, Marjorie, and Hortense J. Spillers, eds. 1985. *Conjuring: Black Women, Fiction, and Literary Tradition*. Bloomington: Indiana University Press.

Radford–Hill, Sheila. 1986. "Considering Feminism as a Model for Social Change." In *Feminist Studies/Critical Studies*, edited by Teresa de Lauretis, 157–72. Bloomington: Indiana University Press.

Rapp, Rayna. 1982. "Family and Class in Contemporary America: Notes toward an Understanding of Ideology." In *Rethinking the Family*, edited by Barrie Thorne and Marilyn Yalom 168–87. New York: Longmann.

Reagon, Bernice Johnson. 1983. "Coalition Politics: Turning the Century." In *Home Girls—A Black Feminist Anthology*, edited by Barbara Smith, 356–68. New York: Kitchen Table Press.

———. 1978. "African Diaspora Women: The Making of Cultural Workers." In *Women in Africa and the African Diaspora*, edited by Rosalyn Terborg-Penn, Sharon Harley, and

Andrea Benton Rushing, 167–80. Washington, DC: Howard University Press.

Reid, Inez. 1975. "Science, Politics and Race." *Signs* 1(2): 397–422.

Richards, Dona. 1980. "European Mythology: The Ideology of 'Progress.'" In *Contemporary Black Thought*, edited by Molefi Kete Asante and Abdulai Sa. Vandi, 59–79. Beverly Hills, CA: Sage.

———. 1990. "The Implications of African-American Spirituality." In *African Culture: The Rhythms of Unity*, edited by Molefi Kete Asante and Kariamu Welsh Asante, 207–31. Trenton, NJ: Africa World Press.

Richardson, Marilyn, ed. 1987. *Maria W. Stewart, America's First Black Woman Political Writer*. Bloomington: Indiana University Press.

Richie, Beth. 1985. "Battered Black Women: A Challenge for the Black Community." *Black Scholar* 16: 40–44.

Rollins, Judith. 1985. *Between Women, Domestics and Their Employers*. Philadelphia: Temple University Press.

Rosaldo, Michelle Z. 1974. "Women, Culture and Society: A Theoretical Overview." In *Woman, Culture and Society*, edited by Michelle Rosaldo and Louise Lamphere, 17–42. Stanford: Stanford University Press.

Rowell, Charles H. 1975. "An Interview with Margaret Walker." *Black World* 25(2): 4–17.

Russell, Karen K. 1987. "Growing up with Privilege and Prejudice." *New York Times Magazine*, June 14: 22–28.

Russell, Michele. 1982. "Slave Codes and Liner Notes." In *But Some of Us Are Brave*, edited by Gloria T. Hull, Patricia Bell Scott, and Barbara Smith, 129–40. Old Westbury, NY: Feminist Press.

Sacks, Karen Brodkin. 1984. "Computers, Ward Secretaries, and a Walkout in a Southern Hospital." In *My Troubles are Going to Have Trouble with Me*, edited by Karen Sacks and Dorothy Remy, 173–90. New Brunswick, NJ: Rutgers University Press.

———. 1988. "Gender and Grassroots Leadership." In *Women and the Politics of Empowerment*, edited by Ann Bookman and Sandra Morgen, 77–94. Philadelphia: Temple University Press.

———. 1989. "Toward a Unified Theory of Class, Race, and Gender." *American Ethnologist* 16(3): 534–50.

Sage: A Scholarly Journal on Black Women. 1984. "Mothers and Daughters I." Special Issue, 1(2).

———. 1987. "Mothers and Daughters II." Special Issue, 4(2).

Scarborough, Cathy. 1989, "Conceptualizing Black Women's Employment Experiences." *Yale Law Journal* 98: 1457–78.

Schildkrout, Enid. 1983. "Dependence and Autonomy: The Economic Activities of Secluded Hausa Women in Kano." In *Female and Male In West Africa*, edited by Christine Oppong, 107–26. London: Unwin Hyman.

Schroedel, Jean Reith. 1985. *Alone in a Crowd: Women in the Trades Tell Their Stories*. Philadelphia: Temple University Press.

Scott, James C. 1985. *Weapons of the Weak: Everyday Forms of Peasant Resistance*. New Haven, CT: Yale University Press.

Scott, Patricia Bell. 1982a. "Debunking Sapphire: Toward a Non-Racist and Non-Sexist Social Science." In *But Some of Us Are Brave*, edited by Gloria T. Hull, Patricia Bell Scott, and Barbara Smith, 85–92. Old Westbury, NY: Feminist Press.

———. 1982b. "Selected Bibliography on Black Feminism." In *But Some of Us Are Brave*, edited by Gloria T. Hull, Patricia Bell Scott, and Barbara Smith, 23–36. Old Westbury, NY: Feminist Press.

Shange, Ntozake. 1975. *For Colored Girls Who Have Considered Suicide/When the Rainbow Is Enuf.* New York: Macmillan.

———. 1982. *Sassafrass, Cypress and Indigo.* New York: St. Martin's Press.

Shimkin, Demitri B., Edith M. Shimkin, and Dennis A. Frate, eds. 1978. *The Extended Family in Black Societies.* Chicago: Aldine.

Shockley, Ann Allen. 1974. *Loving Her.* Tallahassee, FL: Naiad Press.

———. 1983. "The Black Lesbian in American Literature: An Overview." In *Home Girls: A Black Feminist Anthology*, edited by Barbara Smith, 83–93. New York: Kitchen Table Press.

Sidran, Ben. 1971. *Black Talk.* New York: Da Capo Press.

Simms, Margaret C. 1988. *The Choices that Young Black Women Make: Education, Employment, and Family Formation.* Working Paper No. 190, Wellesley, MA: Center for Research on Women, Wellesley College.

———, and Julianne Malveaux, eds. 1986. *Slipping through the Cracks: The Status of Black Women.* New Brunswick, NJ: Transaction.

Simone, Nina. 1985. *Backlash.* Portugal: Movieplay Portuguesa Recording.

Simonsen, Thordis, ed. 1986. *You May Plow Here: The Narrative of Sara Brooks.* New York: Touchstone.

Sizemore, Barbara A. 1973. "Sexism and the Black Male." *Black Scholar* 4(6–7): 2–11.

Smith, Barbara. 1982a. "Racism and Women's Studies." In *But Some of Us Are Brave*, edited by Gloria T. Hull, Patricia Bell Scott, and Barbara Smith, 48–51. Old Westbury, NY: Feminist Press.

———. 1982b. "Toward a Black Feminist Criticism." In *But Some of Us Are Brave*, edited by Gloria T. Hull, Patricia Bell Scott, and Barbara Smith, 157–175. Old Westbury, NY: Feminist Press.

———. 1983. "Introduction." In *Home Girls: A Black Feminist Anthology*, edited by Barbara Smith, xix–lvi. New York: Kitchen Table Press.

———, and Beverly Smith. 1981. "Across the Kitchen Table: A Sister-to-Sister Dialogue." In *This Bridge Called My Back: Writings by Radical Women of Color*, edited by Cherríe Moraga and Gloria Anzaldua, 113–27. Watertown, MA: Persephone Press.

Smith, Beverly. 1983. "The Wedding." In *Home Girls: A Black Feminist Anthology*, edited by Barbara Smith, 171–76. New York: Kitchen Table Press.

Smith, Dorothy. 1987. *The Everyday World as Problematic.* Boston: Northeastern University Press.

Smith, Janet Farrell. 1983. "Parenting as Property." In *Mothering: Essays in Feminist Theory*, edited by Joyce Trebilcot, 199–212. Totawa, NJ: Rowman & Allanheld.

Smitherman, Geneva. 1977. *Talkin and Testifyin: The Language of Black America.* Boston: Houghton Mifflin.

Sobel, Mechal. 1979. *Trabelin' On: The Slave Journey to an Afro-Baptist Faith.* Princeton: Princeton University Press.

Spelman, Elizabeth V. 1982. "Theories of Race and Gender: The Erasure of Black Women." *Quest* 5(4): 36–62.

Stack, Carol D. 1974. *All Our Kin: Strategies for Survival in a Black Community.* New York: Harper & Row.

———. 1986. "The Culture of Gender: Women and Men of Color." *Signs* 11(2): 321–24.

Stanback, Marsha Houston. 1985. "Language and Black Women's Place: Evidence from the Black Middle Class." In *For Alma Mater: Theory and Practice of Feminist Scholarship*, edited by P. A. Trechler, Cheris Kramarae, and R. Shafford, 177–93. Urbana: University of Illinois Press.

Staples, Robert. 1973. *The Black Woman in America.* Chicago: Nelson-Hall.

————. 1979. "The Myth of Black Macho: A Response to Angry Black Feminists." *Black Scholar* 10(6): 24–33.

Steady, Filomina Chioma. 1981. "The Black Woman Cross-Culturally: An Overview." In *The Black Woman Cross-Culturally*, edited by Filomina Chioma Steady, 7–42. Cambridge, MA: Schenkman.

————. 1987. "African Feminism: A Worldwide Perspective." In *Women in Africa and the African Diaspora*, edited by Rosalyn Terborg-Penn, Sharon Harley, and Andrea Benton Rushing, 3–24. Washington, DC: Howard University Press.

Sterling, Dorothy, ed. 1984. *We are Your Sisters: Black Women in the Nineteenth Century*. New York: W. W. Norton.

Stetson, Erlene, ed. 1981. *Black Sister: Poetry by Black American Women, 1746–1980*. Bloomington: Indiana University Press.

Sudarkasa, Niara. 1981a. "Female Employment and Family Organization in West Africa." In *The Black Woman Cross-Culturally*, edited by Filomina Chioma Steady, 49–64. Cambridge, MA: Schenkman.

————. 1981b. "Interpreting the African Heritage in Afro-American Family Organization." In *Black Families*, edited by Harriette Pipes McAdoo, 37–53. Beverly Hills, CA: Sage.

Sweet Honey in the Rock. 1985. *Feel Something Drawing Me On*. Chicago: Flying Fish Records.

Tabb, William. 1970. *The Political Economy of the Black Ghetto*. New York: W. W. Norton.

Tanner, Nancy. 1974. "Matrifocality in Indonesia and Africa and among Black Americans." In *Woman, Culture, and Society*, edited by Michelle Z. Rosaldo and Louise Lamphere, 129–56. Stanford: Stanford University Press.

Tate, Claudia, ed. 1983. *Black Women Writers at Work*. New York: Continuum Publishing.

Terborg-Penn, Rosalyn. 1978. "Discrimination against Afro-American Women in the Woman's Movement, 1830–1920." In *The Afro-American Woman: Struggles and Images*, edited by Sharon Harley and Rosalyn Terborg-Penn, 17–27. Port Washington, NY: Kennikat Press.

————. 1985. "Survival Strategies among African-American Women Workers: Continuing Process." In *Women, Work and Protest: A Century of U.S. Women's Labor History*, edited by Ruth Milkman, 139–55. Boston: Routledge & Kegan Paul.

————. 1986. "Black Women in Resistance: A Cross-Cultural Perspective." In *In Resistance: Studies in African, Caribbean and Afro-American History*, edited by Gary Y. Okihiro, 188–209. Amherst: University of Massachusetts Press.

Terrelonge, Pauline. 1984. "Feminist Consciousness and Black Women." In *Women: A Feminist Perspective*. 3d ed., edited by Jo Freeman, 557–67. Palo Alto, CA: Mayfield.

Thiam, Awa. 1978. *Black Sisters, Speak Out. Feminism and Oppression in Black Africa*. London: Pluto Press.

Thompson, Robert Farris. 1983. *Flash of the Spirit: African and Afro-American Art and Philosophy*. New York: Vintage.

Thompson-Cager, Chezia. 1989. "Ntozake Shange's *Sassafras, Cypress and Indigo*: Resistance and Mythical Women of Power." *NWSA Journal* 1(4): 589–601.

Troester, Rosalie Riegle. 1984. "Turbulence and Tenderness: Mothers, Daughters, and 'Othermothers' in Paule Marshall's *Brown Girl, Brownstones*." *Sage: A Scholarly Journal on Black Women* 1(2): 13–16.

Tuan, Yi-Fu. 1984. *Dominance and Affection: The Making of Pets*. New Haven, CT: Yale University Press.

Turner, James E. 1984. "Foreword: Africana Studies and Epistemology: A Discourse in the Sociology of Knowledge." In *The Next Decade: Theoretical and Research Issues in Africana Studies*, edited by James E. Turner, v–xxv. Ithaca, NY: Cornell University Africana Studies and Research Center.

U.S. Department of Commerce, Bureau of the Census. 1986. *Money Income and Poverty Status of Families and Persons in the United States: 1985*. Series P-60, No. 154. Washington, DC: GPO.

———. 1989. *Money Income of Households, Families, and Persons in the United States: 1987*. Series P-60, No. 162. Washington, DC: GPO.

Valentine, Bettylou. 1981. "Women on Welfare: Public Policy and Institutional Racism." In *Class, Race, and Sex: The Dynamics of Control*, edited by Amy Swerdlow and Hanna Lessinger, 276–87. Boston: G. K. Hall.

Vance, Carole S. 1984. "Pleasure and Danger: Toward a Politics of Sexuality." In *Pleasure and Danger: Exploring Female Sexuality*, edited by Carole S. Vance, 1–27. Boston: Routledge & Kegan Paul.

Vanneman, Reeve, and Lynn Weber Cannon. 1987. *The American Perception of Class*. Philadelphia: Temple University Press.

Wade-Gayles, Gloria. 1980. "She Who Is Black and Mother: In Sociology and Fiction, 1940–1970." In *The Black Woman*, edited by La Frances Rodgers-Rose, 89–106. Beverly Hills, CA: Sage.

———. 1984. "The Truths of Our Mothers' Lives: Mother-Daughter Relationships in Black Women's Fiction." *Sage: A Scholarly Journal on Black Women* 1(2): 8–12.

Wahlman, Maude Southwell, and John Scully. 1983. "Aesthetic Principles of Afro-American Quilts." In *Afro-American Folk Arts and Crafts*, edited by William Ferris, 79–97. Boston: G. K. Hall.

Walker, Alice. 1970. *The Third Life of Grange Copeland*. New York: Harcourt Brace Jovanovich.

———. 1976. *Meridian*. New York: Pocket Books.

———. 1977. "Zora Neale Hurston: A Cautionary Tale and a Partisan View." Foreword to *Zora Neale Hurston: A Literary Biography*, by Robert Hemenway, xi–xviii. Urbana: University of Illinois Press.

———, ed.1979a. *I Love Myself When I Am Laughing, And Then Again When I Am Looking Mean and Impressive: A Zora Neale Hurston Reader*. Old Westbury, NY: Feminist Press.

———. 1979b. "One Child of One's Own: A Meaningful Digression Within the Work(s)." *Ms* 8(2), August: 47–50, 72–75.

———. 1981. "Coming Apart." In *You Can't Keep a Good Woman Down*, 41–53. New York: Harcourt Brace Jovanovich.

———. 1982. *The Color Purple*. New York: Washington Square Press.

———. 1983. *In Search of Our Mothers' Gardens*. New York: Harcourt Brace Jovanovich.

———. 1988. *Living by the Word*. New York: Harcourt Brace Jovanovich.

Walker, Margaret. 1966. *Jubilee*. New York: Bantam.

Walker, Sheila S. 1980. "African Gods in the Americas: The Black Religious Continuum." *Black Scholar* 11(8): 25–36.

Wallace, Michele. 1978. *Black Macho and the Myth of the Superwoman*. New York: Dial Press.

Wallace, Phyllis A., ed. 1980. *Black Women in the Labor Force*. Cambridge: MIT Press.

Walton, Ortiz M. 1971. "Comparative Analysis of the African and Western Aesthetics." In *The Black Aesthetic*, edited by Addison Gayle, 154–64. Garden City, NY: Doubleday.

Ware, Helen. 1983. "Female and Male Life Cycles." In *Female and Male in West Africa*, edited by Christine Oppong, 6–31. London: Unwin Hyman.

Washington, Mary Helen, ed. 1975. *Black-Eyed Susans: Classic Stories by and about Black Women*. Garden City, NY: Anchor.

———, ed. 1980. *Midnight Birds*. Garden City, NY: Anchor.

———. 1982. "Teaching *Black-Eyed Susans*: An Approach to the Study of Black Women Writers." In *But Some of Us Are Brave*, edited by Gloria T. Hull, Patricia Bell Scott, and Barbara Smith, 208–17. Old Westbury, NY: Feminist Press.

———. 1984. "I Sign My Mother's Name: Alice Walker, Dorothy West and Paule Marshall." In *Mothering the Mind: Twelve Studies of Writers and Their Silent Partners*, edited by Ruth Perry and Martine Watson Broronley, 143–63. New York: Holmes & Meier.

———, ed. 1987. *Invented Lives: Narratives of Black Women 1860–1960*. Garden City, NY: Anchor.

Webber, Thomas L. 1978. *Deep Like the Rivers*. New York: W. W. Norton.

Weems, Renita. 1984. "'Hush. Mama's Gotta Go Bye Bye': A Personal Narrative." *Sage: A Scholarly Journal on Black Women* 1(2): 25–28.

Weisbord, Robert G. 1975. *Genocide?: Birth Control and the Black American*. Westport, CT: Greenwood Press.

West, Cheryl. 1987. "Lesbian Daughter." *Sage: A Scholarly Journal on Black Women* 4(2): 42–44.

West, Cornel. 1977–78. "Philosophy and the Afro-American Experience." *Philosophical Forum* 9(2–3): 117–48.

West, Dorothy. 1948. *The Living Is Easy*. New York: Arno Press/*New York Times*.

Westkott, Marcia. 1979. "Feminist Criticism of the Social Sciences." *Harvard Educational Review* 49(4): 422–30.

White, Deborah Gray. 1985. *Ar'n't I a Woman? Female Slaves in the Plantation South*. New York: W. W. Norton.

White, E. Frances. 1984. "Listening to the Voices of Black Feminism." *Radical America* 18(2–3): 7–25.

White, Evelyn. 1985. *Chain Chain Change. For Black Women Dealing with Physical and Emotional Abuse*. Seattle: The Seal Press.

Williams, Fannie Barrier. 1987. "The Colored Girl." In *Invented Lives: Narratives of Black Women 1860–1960*, edited by Mary Helen Washington, 150–59. Garden City, NY: Anchor.

Williams, Sherley A. 1979. "The Blues Roots of Afro-American Poetry." In *Chant of Saints: A Gathering of Afro-American Literature, Art and Scholarship*, edited by Michael S. Harper and Robert B. Steptoe, 123–35. Urbana: University of Illinois Press.

———. 1986. *Dessa Rose*. New York: William Morrow.

Wilson, William Julius. 1987. *The Truly Disadvantaged: The Inner City, the Underclass, and Public Policy*. Chicago: University of Chicago Press.

Woodson, Carter G. 1933. *The Miseducation of the Negro*. Washington, DC: Associated Publishers.

Young, Virginia Heyer. 1970. "Family and Childhood in a Southern Negro Community." *American Anthropologist* 72(32): 269–88.

Zahan, Dominique. 1979. *The Religion, Spirituality, and Thought of Traditional Africa*. Chicago: University of Chicago Press.

Zinn, Maxine Baca. 1989. "Family, Race, and Poverty in the Eighties." *Signs* 14(4): 856–74.

———, Lynn Weber Cannon, Elizabeth Higginbotham, and Bonnie Thornton Dill. 1986. "The Costs of Exclusionary Practices in Women's Studies." *Signs* 11(2): 290–303.

ABOUT THE AUTHOR

Patricia Hill Collins is associate professor of African-American studies at the University of Cincinnati and is the author of numerous articles on Black feminist thought. She was formerly the director of the African-American Center at Tufts University and was involved for many years in the community schools movement in Boston.

INDEX